BATTLES ON

THE BENCH

BATTLES ON
THE BENCH

CONFLICT INSIDE
THE SUPREME COURT

Phillip J. Cooper

 University Press of Kansas

Published by the University Press of Kansas (Lawrence,
Kansas 66049), which was organized by the Kansas Board of
Regents and is operated and funded by Emporia State
University, Fort Hays State University, Kansas State
University, Pittsburg State University, the University of
Kansas, and Wichita State University

Library of Congress Cataloging-in-Publication Data

Cooper, Phillip J.
Battles on the bench : conflict inside the Supreme
Court / Phillip J. Cooper.
p. cm.
Includes bibliographical references and index.
ISBN 0-7006-0737-4 (hardcover)
1. United States. Supreme Court. 2. United
States. Supreme Court—Officials and
employees—Biography. 3. Judicial process—United
States—Psychological aspects. 4. Interpersonal
conflict—United States. I. Title.
KF8742.C66 1995
347.73 '26—dc20
[347.30735]   95-31618

British Library Cataloguing in Publication Data is available.

Printed in the United States of America

10 9 8 7 6 5 4 3 2

The paper used in this publication meets the minimum
requirements of the American National Standard for
Permanence of Paper for Printed Library Materials
Z39.48–1984.

To Justice William J. Brennan, Jr.,
with appreciation from a grateful citizen of the republic
your skill and dedication have helped to preserve

CONTENTS

PREFACE

This is a book about conflict in the United States Supreme Court. It is also, however, about how the members of the Court manage to avoid conflict as much as they do and find ways to work together in what could be one of the most conflict-ridden work environments imaginable. When a small group of strong and independent people works together for as long as the justices do on issues that engender conflict throughout the nation and in a setting in which all members of the Court are equal with each needing the votes of the others to prevail, the seeds of potentially damaging conflict are apparent.

A degree of conflict is inevitable in the Supreme Court, just as it is in virtually all organizations. There are, however, a number of unique institutional aspects of the Court that encourage the justices to channel inevitable and even constructive disagreements into useful directions while discouraging disputes that are potentially destructive both for relationships within the Court and for the Court's external image. Of course, there are periods when conflict heats up and the control mechanisms appear to break down—witness some of the event of recent years.

However, this volume is no exposé, far from it. It is an exploration of an institution that seems to work reasonably well even though all the elements are present to make it fly apart. Although it is, I hope, interesting, useful, and informative to examine why and how the justices fight and what difference their disagreements make, it is perhaps even more interesting to contemplate why they do not fight more often.

This book is also about judicial biography. David Danelski[1] and Walter Murphy[2] demonstrated long ago that judicial biographical techniques can provide useful insights into the operations of courts, including the United States Supreme Court. Their work goes well beyond individual biography. But when they wrote their classic works, they had far fewer materials available than exist today. David O'Brien has taken us even further into the use of biographical materials, particularly documentary evidence and interviews.[3]

In addition to all of the papers and interviews, a large body of individual and dual judicial biographies is available that should not be ignored.

Most of these biographies describe themselves as data sources for more general research, but few scholars have taken the opportunity seriously. It is time to treat this wonderful collection of material as a body of data that is readily accessible and very much ignored. This study attempts to do just that.

This book has been brewing for a long time, and I therefore owe a great deal for its inspiration and support to many colleagues in many places. In a large sense, this book owes its entire existence to the many wonderful biographies that have been written about members of the Supreme Court over the years, extending at least as far back as Albert Beveridge's classic four-volume work on Chief Justice John Marshall. It is sad that so many of the older biographies are so seldom read these days, and even some of the newer ones that have much to offer, like Danelski's *A Supreme Court Justice Is Appointed*, are too rarely read by younger scholars of the Court. The good news is that the genre has enjoyed renewed interest in recent years with the publication of many excellent biographies almost too numerous to mention, though most are represented somewhere in the pages that follow.

The field of Supreme Court biography has benefited as well from the exploration of biographical tools for wider use by such scholars as Walter Murphy, whose pathbreaking *Elements of Judicial Strategy* remains in many ways as fresh today as when it was published in 1964. More recently, David O'Brien's award-winning *Storm Center* has demonstrated that the historical can very directly engage the contemporary, and Bernard Schwartz's carefully detailed analyses, such as *Super Chief,* have added greatly to our knowledge of how to use the tools of biography. This book owes a debt to the intellectual leadership of all of these authors.

I must also acknowledge my debt to colleagues who have particularly encouraged the writing of this book over the years, including William Richardson of Georgia State University, David O'Brien of the University of Virginia, and Howard Ball of the University of Vermont. Howard is as fine a colleague and friend as anyone could hope for, and he spent many hours in the Library of Congress struggling with copies of documents as we worked together on our comparative biography of Justices Black and Douglas and compared notes on other justices each of us was studying.

I am grateful, too, to the staffs of a number of presidential libraries and particularly to David Wigdor of the Library of Congress, without whose help most contemporary judicial biographers would be both less informed and less productive. Certainly I would be.

The people at University Press of Kansas have been delightful throughout, and I am particularly grateful to Michael Briggs who encouraged me to stop thinking about this book and write it! There were times when I thought he was even more enthusiastic about this project than I was, a kind of support too rare among editors these days.

Of course, I cannot let the opportunity pass to acknowledge Claudia who was at my side throughout the writing of this book, as she is in everything else.

ONE

THE SYMBOLIC HANDSHAKE

Before they move to the bench to hear oral arguments and before they begin conference discussions, each of the justices of the United States Supreme Court shakes hands with every other justice, a practice begun by Chief Justice Melville Weston Fuller in the 1880s as a reminder that "differences of opinion did not preclude overall harmony of purpose."[1] Of course, it was said of the Court shortly after Fuller's death: "It was a brutal Court in its personal relations. I heard that they actually shook fists at one another."[2]

The justices continue the ritual of the handshake to this day, but they have also been known, symbolically at least, to shake fists as well. Supreme Court observers have made much of increasing conflict in the Court in terms of the number of disagreements that have become public and the apparent intensity of the disputes, judged according to the level of rhetoric in opinions and in public statements. A *Wall Street Journal* story about "Low Roading on the High Court" began with the observation that "the Supreme Court is losing its cool. Opinions by justices during the 1980s and 1990s have shown unusual signs of acrimony that surprise some lawyers and law professors who monitor the Court's work. Comments by the justices, on and off the bench, have become more pointed."[3] Justice Sandra Day O'Connor has referred to these clashes as "the battle of the footnotes" because many of the public confrontations have taken the form of sharp exchanges in footnotes to opinions in which the justices challenge each other by name.[4] Some justices have even felt the need to publicly deny the rumors of hard feelings within the Court—Justice Clarence Thomas went out of his way during a 1994 speech to the Second Circuit Judicial Conference to dispute the public image, though his denial seems to have had little effect.

Yet it is hard to think about conflict in the Supreme Court. We have no difficulty discussing clashes between the Court and other levels or branches of government, but within the Court itself? Many Americans would consider the notion tantamount to contemplating fist fights in the College of Cardinals.[5] Instead, people writing about the Court tend to emphasize persuasion, or, if they are particularly adventurous observers of the institution, bargaining among the justices—and they hasten to add, quite appropriately, that it is a different kind of bargaining than one sees, for example, in Congress or a state legislature. Supreme Court bargaining is not about the trading of votes on bills, but accommodations over the content of legal opinions where the outcome of a case may not change but the explanation of the meaning of the law that will guide future actions certainly does.

Walter Murphy has discussed the sense that the critical study of the Court is to be approached directly but with care. Murphy cautioned:

> The role of that scholar, insofar as it is critical, is to hold decisions and opinions of judges up to the highest criteria of craftsmanship and statesmanship—to determine not whether judges have exercised discretion but whether they have done so to an extent and in a manner permitted by relevant standards; to determine not whether judges have influenced policy but whether that influence is to the benefit, both in the long and the short run, of society.[6]

Statesmanship embraces both the ends one seeks to attain and the manner in which one behaves in office.[7] Therefore, statesmanship also concerns how well or badly a justice works toward achieving support for a decision within the Court. To be a statesperson, a justice must be concerned with more than eliciting votes in support of a draft opinion. Statesmanship requires a sense of one's office and of the institution of which that office is a part. It also requires a sense of the position of that office in the polity. As Justice Black's former clerk, John Frank, put it, when we ask whether a justice was great, "the answer is partly a matter of results and partly a matter of method."[8] An examination of conflict within the Court, however, seems to suggest a clash with the idea of statesmanship, notwithstanding that conflict is a normal aspect of life in any organization.

Not only do our political socialization and the Court's unique institutional characteristics tend to encourage discussion of consensus and discourage thoughts of disharmony, but we tend to want to carry over our pluralistic and incremental view of the political world to the Court. We try to understand politics as a non–zero sum game in which everyone can gain something and the losers can lose less if they seek accommodation and avoid conflict. We still use the pluralist and exchange theory language of making demands and trading political bads as well as goods, but we assume that the object of the interaction among justices is negotiation, not confrontation—agreement, rather than pitched battle to achieve the "right" outcome.

Much can be said for such a view of the Court and for politics generally, but it does not describe all of political behavior, either in the polity at large or in the Supreme Court. In his classic *Semi-Sovereign People,* Schattschneider argued that often, where it matters most, politics is about conflict, not consensus, and has more to do with the shape, scope, and nature of the fight than it does with efforts of counterbalanced groups to reach agreement.[9] Pushed too far, the consensus argument would explain very few of the political issues we find most interesting. Similarly, if we stretched Schattschneider's argument too far, every political debate would turn into a civil war.

The point is, of course, that it is useful to try to understand the character of American political institutions and the behavior of their inhabitants from both perspectives. This book examines conflict in the Supreme Court. More specifically, it attempts to address four relatively simple but important questions: Why do the justices fight? How do they fight? What difference does it make? Why do they not fight more often?

Given the importance of conflict in the history of the Court, it is surprising that so little has been written about the subject and that what has been written centers largely on voting alignments in particular cases with a bias by commentators toward reducing fragmentation in opinions.[10]

The method here is judicial biography. The analysis is based upon the use of papers, biographical studies, and interviews with members of the Court. We frequently speak of judicial biographies as rich sources of data for wider analyses, but few works actually mine the numerous important volumes that make up the literature. This book takes seriously the admonition to do something more with judicial biography.

This study suggests that conflict is a significant and normal dynamic force within the Court. It can have important consequences that may or may not be manifested in particular decisions. We can begin to understand this conflict by categorizing it into professional versus personal disagreements and by assessing the locus of the conflict according to whether it was pursued internally or was taken into the public arena.

What is perhaps most important and surprising upon reflection is that justices do not fight even more often. At critical periods in its history, the

Court's significance as an institution and the presence of particular justices who saw the importance of maintaining good working relationships have averted what could have been even more serious clashes. It is useful to consider first the forces that move a justice to engage in conflict or avoid it.

THE PRESUMPTION AGAINST CONFLICT AS A MODE OF BEHAVIOR

Most studies of the Court quickly point to the several factors that counsel a justice to accommodate his or her colleagues. The Court is a small and, in many respects, isolated community, as Earl Warren suggested in his famous admonition that membership on the Court is like a marriage, pure misery if the justice is going to fight over every disagreement.[11] Although it is true that the Court has its "nine separate law firms" and is not a place where justices spend hours visiting in chambers, the nine justices must face one another day after day. Charles Evans Hughes warned: "Independence does not mean cantankerousness and a judge may be a strong judge without being an impossible person. Nothing is more distressing on any bench than the exhibition of a captious, impatient, querulous spirit."[12]

On a more pragmatic note, it is quite difficult in fact to win a conflict within the Court, for all justices are equal (if not in ability, certainly in voting power) and, for almost any victory, the fighting jurist needs four allies to carry the day. But issues change, and so do voting alignments. To alienate a justice who is an adversary on one issue today may very well mean losing that person's support in another battle tomorrow. Since the members of the Court serve on average for more than a decade, today's victory could mean serious long-term difficulties.

There is also the more abstract but nevertheless real fact that the justices want to protect the image of the Court as a calm, deliberative body above the political fray. There is common assumption in American political science that the legitimacy of the Court is fragile and always, or at least potentially always, up for reexamination by the public and other officials. After all, the argument runs, the Court is antidemocratic. It is historically a place where appointees from the social, economic, and political elite[13] pass judgments on decisions made by the elected representatives of the people in Congress, their states, or even their local governments. Often, these debates concern issues, such as abortion[14] or the right to die,[15] that elected officials have been unwilling or unable to address to anyone's satisfaction. One of the justices' assigned tasks is to say no to elected officials when their answers to issues are in violation of the Constitution. All of these factors could easily justify doubts about the Court's legitimacy in the body politic (though our knowledge of the exact nature and extent of the legitimacy question is surprisingly limited).[16] That sense of legitimacy is considered important because, in the oft-quoted words of Alexander Hamilton, the Court has neither the power of the purse nor that of the sword. If the justices would like others to obey their rulings, then they had better be aware of the reservoir of legitimacy on which the Court can draw when it renders difficult judgments.

Whether the concern about legitimacy is valid or not, the fact is that many members of the Court have regarded it as a fragile institution and have adopted its preservation as a central part of their obligation. Hugo Black's widow recalled his warning to her when he proposed.

I have had a prior love affair for almost twenty years now with an institution. It is with the Supreme Court. I have a tremendous respect for the prestige of the Court. We have to act on so many controversial matters, and we are bound to make some people mad at every decision we make. Therefore, in my personal life I have to be like Caesar's wife: above reproach. I have to know that the woman I marry is a one-man woman. . . . I am seventy-one years old. You are twenty-two years younger than I. In another five or ten years you may not find me as attractive as you do now. If that were to happen and you wanted a divorce, I would give you one. But I think it would finish me and hurt the prestige of the Court.[17]

So intent was Black on addressing this issue that he forgot something. Thirty minutes after he left Elizabeth he called and said: "I forgot something. I forgot to tell you I love you, darling—and good night."[18]

The risk that internal conflicts will reach the public ear is not a pleasant prospect for people who have great respect for the Court, nor for the justices themselves. Historically, members of the Court have been able to maintain strong personal relationships with colleagues whose views on the cases before the Court have diverged wildly. When a difference of opinion becomes an open battle, however, the desirable mix of personal and professional relationships is difficult to maintain.

THE PROCLIVITY TO FIGHT

The wisdom of accommodation notwithstanding, there are natural tendencies within the Court toward conflict as well as consensus. Conflict erupts sporadically with varying degrees of intensity and will likely continue to do so. Just as certain institutional forces tend to suppress conflict, other characteristics encourage or at least admit the likelihood of conflict.

The fact that a justice is appointed for life means that, unlike members of Congress, one need not use political bargaining to win concessions for constituents to ensure a happy outcome at the next election. As numerous presidents have bitterly complained, it is not even possible to expect loyalty to the person who put the justice on the Court in the first place. Moreover, different members are appointed by different presidents, occasionally with dramatically different ideologies and agendas. This historical dynamic suggests a natural tendency toward adamant disagreement across a wide range of issues.

The effort to suppress the proclivity for conflict in the interest of harmony over a long period can lead to intense grudges that sooner or later surface in bitter words and behavior among the justices. In one sense, the elected official has an advantage over a justice. It is sometimes possible to win clearer victories. Legislators can battle a political foe, explain their fight for truth and justice to constituents, and emerge from the conflict even stronger than before. On the Court, however, clashes often produce unclear outcomes that leave lingering bad feelings.[19]

The fact that a justice cannot fight in quite the same ways as a member of Congress, does not, however, mean that a justice cannot fight. There are direct and indirect modes of conflict, professional and personal possibilities for a clash, and the ever present availability of battle by surrogates outside the court in a variety of arenas. Furthermore, many members of the Court are strong-willed, tough-minded veterans of years of political or professional infighting, well-schooled in the fine art of political combat. They are very much aware of their position and their independence. As one justice said of another "Justice _____ asks no quarter, and gives none."[20] Or, as Justice Blackmun put it in a televised interview, "If someone wants to play hardball with me, I'll play hardball back."

It would be dangerously wrong, however, to assume that disagreements on the Court are merely the self-indulgent misbehaviors of prima donnas. Far from it. Conflict arises in the Court for many of the same reasons that it does elsewhere in politics. Judicial conflicts often stem from honestly and fervently held positions on the many critical and difficult issues before the Court. They stem from alliances made and broken. And they do, at times, arise from personal misunderstandings and dislikes.

MAJOR CONFLICTS IN THE COURT'S HISTORY

What, then, are the modes of conflict that we find in the Court and how can we conceptualize them? Judicial biographies, opinions, and interviews indicate that the justices themselves perceive differences between conflicts that are principally personal and those that are professional. The justices and scholars of the Court expect the latter, but the former elicit their great concern. Disagreement is normal, and even serious disagreement—or conflict—is not considered particularly problematic as long as it stops short of personal attacks.

The more personal the conflict, the less comfortable we are with it; hence the alarm over the recent strident and seemingly personal exchanges among justices. Majority and dissenting opinions generally focus on arguments and rebuttals, but the debate has shifted to sharp, direct exchanges between specific justices in footnotes, and tension has increased correspondingly. When those battles move from the footnotes into the body of the text and are presented in terms that seem to move beyond professional disagreement, concern intensifies. When conflicts reach the stage where justices cannot communicate comfortably or are too ready to assume that some of their colleagues are reliable anti-authorities, justices and observers alike begin to worry about the well-being of the institution.

A final issue that appears to concern the justices is the locus of conflict. Historically, conflict kept largely within the Court has not been perceived as nearly as serious as conflicts that go public. Indeed, a number of justices have used the threat of going public to convince their colleagues to yield or moderate their views.[21] In theory at least, a publicly conflict-laden Court would encourage noncompliance because it suggests that a ruling is but a temporary victory in a particular case and does not announce a carefully considered principle that the Court is likely to apply uniformly in the future. Another assumption is that public battle undermines public respect for the institution because open conflict appears to mimic the behavior of other political bodies rather than remaining above the fray.

These premises suggest four categories of Supreme Court conflict: (1) internal personal clashes; (2) internal professional conflicts; (3) external personal disputes; and (4) external professional challenges. This conceptualization accommodates some of the more common modes of conflict that we find in the history of the Court. Although partial and limited, this conceptual map helps to relate different kinds of conflict to the perceptions that justices themselves seem to hold about them. Clearly, these categories have porous boundaries in any given controversy. That is, a dispute that begins as a disagreement within the Court can grow into a serious dispute between particular justices that can later spill over into the public arena. Yet each stage has its own character, and each suggests different consequences in the short and the long term.

CONCLUSION

In sum, it is useful to study conflict within the Court and also the ways in which the justices are able to cope with it. As this study has progressed, it has become increasingly interesting to think about what a complex task it is to live and work cooperatively in such a small organization over a long period of time with strong-willed independent colleagues. In order to address that question, however, it is essential to begin with an understanding of the sources of conflict.

TWO
WHY DO THEY FIGHT?

Felix Frankfurter once sought to impress a law clerk with just how opposed he was to his colleagues Hugo Black and William O. Douglas. Commenting on notes the clerk had prepared for an upcoming conference argument, Frankfurter raged, "This is a war we're fighting! Don't you understand? A War!"[1] For his part, Douglas once said of Frankfurter:

> The continuous violent outbursts against me in Conference by my brother Frankfurter give me great concern. They do not bother me. For I have been on the hustings too long.
>
> But he's an ill man; and these violent outbursts create a fear in my heart that one of them may be his end. . . .
>
> I have reluctantly concluded to participate in no more conferences while he is on the Court.[2]

Justice Robert Jackson wrote President Truman to warn him of his attitude toward Justice Black, whom Jackson assumed was out to get him: "If war is declared on me, I propose to wage it with the weapons of the open warrior, not those of the stealthy assassin."[3]

What would possess bright, politically sophisticated people to say such things in the context of an institution in which they must live and work closely for years? In truth, many forces override the traditional norms of the Court and cause its members to become more than customarily aggressive. The foundations of conflict include battles set up by events in the lives of justices before they came to the Court, ideological disputes, ego clashes, behavior on the bench, leadership contests, the instability of transitions in the Court, arguments over the proper role and nature of the institution, disputes over off-the-bench activities, conflicts over internal court processes, and issues of style.

BATTLES BROUGHT TO THE BENCH

Occasionally, tensions within the Court have their source in an earlier time, before the aggrieved parties had even been appointed justices. These tensions are sometimes specific, whether personal or professional; in other cases they revolve around more general issues of reputation or attitude.

Robert Jackson was ready for a clash with Frank Murphy from the very beginning. Jackson had followed Murphy as attorney general and had not been pleased with his predecessor's performance in that office. In fact, Jackson thought he had been left to pick up the pieces of problems left unresolved by Murphy. Nor was Jackson pleased by Murphy's elevation to the Court. He did not regard the former Michigan governor as particularly well qualified, except in a crass political sense. He recognized that one of the crucial factors in Roosevelt's decision to appoint Murphy was his Catholicism, but Jackson concluded that Roosevelt had chosen the wrong Catholic.[4]

Once the two were on the Court, the stage was already set for a clash, and it came, not surprisingly, in a case that pitted one former attorney general against another over actions each had taken while at the Justice Department. Murphy took a strong position against the surveillance of a suspect that had taken place during Jackson's term as attorney general.[5] Jackson took Murphy's position as a personal attack and responded that if Murphy did not change his rhetoric and approach, he, Jackson, would make the facts clear:[6] that is, that although the actual surveillance operation was conducted during Jackson's tenure, it had been originally ordered by Murphy! Murphy backed off.

For most of the first century of the Court's history, there was a more obvious cause for this sort of preexisting conflict. Back then, the justices rode circuit and sat as members of panels around the nation. Many of the cases in which justices had participated reached the Supreme Court on appeal (there was of course no certiorari control over the docket until the Judiciary Act of 1925). It was not at all uncommon for the whole Court to overturn the decision of a circuit court on which one of the justices had served. Justice Story found himself at odds even with his close colleague John Marshall in such matters.

The chief justice himself took on Story in [one such] case, arguing that when fraud is imputed, both parties have full liberty "to adduce further proof on every point in the case." Upon reargument on the basis of the additional evidence, Justice Johnson and the majority reversed Story's circuit decree, which had put the burden of proof on the defendant, by holding that in the absence of conclusive evidence of fraud, the Court "must pronounce in favor of innocence."[7]

Another set of battles on the early Court was more or less preordained. Justice William Johnson was appointed by Thomas Jefferson with instructions to battle as vigorously as possible against John Marshall and the other incumbent justices. Jefferson called upon Johnson to " 'throw himself in every case on God and his country' and write his own separate opinions, dissents if necessary, so that Marshall's hold on the Court might be broken."[8] Johnson did just that.[9]

Justice Brandeis faced a problem with Justice McReynolds, not for anything he had done before coming to the Court but merely for who he was. A rabid anti-Semite, McReynolds took every opportunity to deliberately snub his younger Jewish colleague. Alpheus T. Mason explained that "for McReynolds the Court's bête noire was . . . Justice Brandeis."[10] There is the now well-known story that McReynolds once refused Chief Justice Taft's invitation to join the Court on a train ride to a ceremonial occasion because Brandeis would be aboard.[11] In fact, McReynolds also refused to sit for an annual Court picture for the same reason.[12]

More recently, Justice Thurgood Marshall had considerable difficulty with Lewis Powell. Powell had formerly served as a member of the Richmond, Virginia, Board of Education during the period when Marshall had led the NAACP's efforts to force an end to "separate but equal" education in the South. Well after *Brown v. Board of Education*[13] had been delivered by a unanimous Supreme Court, Virginia, along with other southern states, engaged in what was termed a campaign of "massive resistance" to court-ordered desegregation.[14] Powell was a continuing reminder of that battle. Moreover, Powell's heritage, status, and demeanor made him an ever-present symbol of everything Marshall had fought against throughout his professional and personal life. "Powell's courtly ways and soft Virginia accent reminded Marshall of the educated and impeccably well mannered Southerners who for so long had maintained the subjugation of blacks."[15] Powell's biographer, John Jeffries, recalled a number of situations in which the tension was apparent.

Powell once made the mistake of saying in Conference that only he and Thurgood would understand a certain point because they were the only Southerners. Marshall's head snapped up in dismay. He came from the border state of Maryland, but in a more fundamental way than geography, he and Powell came from different worlds.[16]

IDEOLOGICAL TENSIONS: THE CLASH OF BASIC PRINCIPLES

Beyond mere symbolism, Justice Lewis Powell brought to the Court constitutional positions that were both very strongly felt and very clearly opposed to those championed by Thurgood Marshall. Thus the tension between the two men exemplified another set of causes of conflict among members of the Court.

It was no small matter for Marshall that the first major ruling for the Court prepared by Powell, *San Antonio Independent School District v. Rodriguez,*[17] was widely considered as a direct attack on *Brown v. Board of Education* and its legacy. In the *San Antonio* case, the Court rejected a challenge to a Texas state education funding system brought on equal protection grounds. Marshall was upset as much by the language and argument of the opinion as by the holding itself.

The Court had held in *Brown* that education, "where a state has undertaken to provide it, is a right which must be made available to all on equal terms." Writing for the Court in *San Antonio,* Powell said: "Education, of course, is not among the rights afforded explicit protection under our Federal Constitution. Nor do we find any basis for saying it is implicitly so protected."[18] Marshall answered in one of his most powerful dissents, "The majority's holding can only be seen as a retreat from our historic commitment to equality of educational opportunity and as unsupportable acquiescence in a system which deprives children in their earliest years of the chance to reach their full potential as citizens."[19]

The frustration that Marshall felt with Powell's ideology (sometimes described as moderate conservatism or southern progressivism) did not surface in only one ruling. Powell's strong commitment to local control of schools and deference to the states in questions of federal intervention seemed to Marshall nothing less than polite justifications for a segregated status quo: "For the record, it is apparent that the State's purported concern with local control is offered primarily as an excuse rather than as a justification for interdistrict inequality."[20] The states had for many years displaced local governments to dominate significant aspects of education, such as the design of systems of school finance, rarely leaving the matter to "local control." Besides, when local districts were challenged, their reaction was too often an argument that they had to accommodate state standards. Marshall had seen this Catch-22 many times. As far as he was concerned, the Texas system under review amounted to little more than a "mere sham" version of equality.[21]

While the battle raged over the *San Antonio* case, two other critical cases that were to be every bit as difficult for Marshall were in various stages of litigation. His frustration and anxiety were exacerbated by what he saw happening in the Richmond, Virginia, and Detroit, Michigan, cases. These cases posed the question of the authority of federal district judges, who had found discrimination in the schools, to require remedial plans that included more than one (and usually several) districts. The fact was that states had engaged in deliberate segregation in housing and education, creating community residence patterns that virtually assured continued segregation even after the formal legal bans on integration had been removed. In most instances, judges found themselves with largely black, often urban, districts surrounded by mostly white suburban districts. Remedies for segregated schools that involved only the city district would mean little more than moving black children around and perhaps providing the remaining white families with an impetus to flee the cities. The result would be a continuation of the dual school systems that the Court had worked for so long to eliminate.

Judge Mehrige had faced just such a case in Richmond and had contemplated a remedy that would have involved three districts. The Court of Appeals rejected the proposal and the case went to the Supreme Court. Justices Marshall, White, Brennan, and Douglas voted to hear it.[22] The Court had discussed holding the Richmond matter to be decided with the Detroit case, but decided that the Richmond case could not be delayed.[23] Justice Powell could not participate because of his Virginia school board involvement, leaving the Court with eight voting members. Initially, it appeared that Justice White had produced a compromise that would command five votes. It concluded that district courts were authorized to look at the larger picture to determine whether plans for neighboring districts would be independently adequate. If not, the judge would be free to determine "whether the shortcomings of the individual county plans provided a sufficient federal foundation for merging the three districts or in any other way crossing district lines so as to eliminate, to the extent reasonable and practicable, racially identifiable schools and hence disestablishing what had been dual school systems in each of the three Counties."[24] Rehnquist took up the challenge and urged a more severe limit on district court remedial plans.[25]

Marshall opposed the idea of setting significant limits on district courts in cases where there plainly had been legal segregation and massive resistance to desegregation after repeal of the legal bars. He wrote White; "After worrying with the law, the precedents and my conscience, I now find myself willing to agree with your memorandum in the case."[26] The Court's deliberations ended with a 4–4 split, which meant that Mehrige's plan was rejected.

Marshall quickly realized that with Powell free to participate in the *Milliken v. Bradley*[27] case, which concerned a multidistrict remedy in Detroit, there would be a clear majority against metropolitan remedies even when they seemed necessary to achieve any meaningful response to historic discrimination. The opinion striking down the multidistrict remedy in the Detroit case came the day after the announcement of the ruling in the Watergate tapes litigation.

Marshall was frustrated on several counts. On the merits, *Milliken* meant that the Court would permit structural barriers to block the ultimate realization of the promise of *Brown*. The Court had not disturbed the findings of the lower courts that it would be impossible to achieve any meaningful desegregation with a city-only remedy in Detroit, but it refused, nevertheless, to permit the district judge to go beyond the city district without evidence that the suburban districts were guilty of purposeful discrimination that implicated the city. And there was more. Justices Marshall and White, in dissent, challenged the Court's opinion on grounds that it obviously showed little concern for accuracy or careful analysis of the facts in the *Milliken* case.[28] The press of the Watergate case and the fact that the real argument in the Court over the issues in *Milliken* had occurred during the debate over the Richmond case, meant that the Detroit case did not receive the attention it deserved. To add insult to injury, Marshall was told that the opinion would be announced even though he had insisted that he needed more time to work on his dissent.

It was not surprising, then, that Marshall's dissent in the Detroit case was even stronger than his *San Antonio* rendering. He made it absolutely clear that he saw these rulings as "making a solemn mockery of *Brown*,"[29] warning that

Today's holding, I fear, is more a reflection of a perceived public mood that we have gone far enough in enforcing the Constitution's guarantee of equal justice than it is the product of neutral principles of law. In the short run, it may seem to be the easier course to allow our great metropolitan areas to be divided up each into two cities— one white, the other black—but it is a course, I predict, our people will ultimately regret.[30]

The ideological premises that motivated Marshall and Powell were simply too deeply held to be reconciled. The tension was particularly strong at the time of the Court's ruling in its first major affirmative action case, *Regents v. Bakke.*[31] The Court struck down an affirmative action admission program at the medical school of the University of California, although it permitted consideration of racial diversity as one element in admissions. The badly fragmented Court spoke through a plurality opinion authored by Powell.

In conference, John Paul Stevens observed that African Americans might not need the assistance of affirmative action for a long period. "At this point Marshall broke in to say that it would be another hundred years. This remark left Powell speechless."[32] Powell came away from the discussion unwilling to accept Marshall's judgment and aware of the distance between himself and his colleague on this critical issue.

Powell's biographer noted that "one inside source reported that Marshall was 'livid' over Powell's opinion and regarded it as 'racist.'" Jeffries pointed particularly to the line in Powell's opinion that held "it is far too late to argue that the guarantee of equal protection to all persons permits the recognition of special wards entitled to a degree of protection greater than that accorded others."[33]

There is no question that Powell's opinion outraged Marshall. He wrote in dissent:

I do not agree that petitioner's admissions program violates the Constitution. For it must be remembered that, during most of the past 200 years, the Constitution as interpreted by this Court did not prohibit the most ingenious and pervasive forms of discrimination against the Negro. Now, when a State acts to remedy the effects of that legacy of discrimination, I cannot believe that this same Constitution stands as a barrier.[34]

As powerful as these words were, they were tame by comparison with what he said within the Court. He was outraged by the idea that given the sordid history of Jim Crow the problems of segregation should now be dismissed with vague references to color blindness. In a memorandum to the Court, Marshall rejected the effort to evade the consequences of history.

> If only the principle of color-blindness had been accepted by the majority in *Plessy* in 1896, we would not be faced with this problem in 1978. We must remember, however, that this principle appeared only in the dissent. In the 60 years from *Plessy* to *Brown,* ours was a Nation where, by law, individuals could be given "special" treatment based on race. For us now to say that the principle of color-blindness prevents the University from giving "special" consideration to race when this Court, in 1896 licensed the states to continue to consider race, is to make a mockery of the principle of "equal justice under law."[35]

He could not shake his anger at the way that idea had been addressed in conference. His memorandum concluded:

> As a result of our last discussion on this case, I wish also to address the question of whether Negroes have "arrived." Just a few examples illustrate that Negroes most certainly have not. In our own Court, we have had only three Negro law clerks, and not so far have we had a Negro Officer of the Court. On a broader scale, this week's *U.S. News and World Report* has a story about "Who Runs America." They list some 83 persons—not one Negro, even as a would-be runnerup. And the economic disparity between the races is increasing. . . .
>
> The dream of America as the melting pot has not been realized by Negroes—either the Negro did not get into the pot, or he did not get melted down. The statistics on unemployment and the other statistics quoted in the briefs . . . document the vast gulf between White and Black America. That gulf was brought about by centuries of slavery and then by another century in which, with the approval of this Court, states were permitted to treat Negroes "specially."
>
> This case is here now because of that sordid history. So despite the

lousy record, the poorly reasoned lower court opinion, and the absence as parties of those who will be most affected by the decision (the Negro applicants), we are stuck with this case. We are not yet all equals, in large part because of the refusal of the Plessy Court to adopt the principle of color-blindness. It would be cruelest irony for this Court to adopt the dissent in Plessy now and hold that the University must use color-blind admissions.[36]

Powell's approach to issues of discrimination grated on Marshall even when the two men were on the same side. Justice Powell wrote for the majority in *Batson v. Kentucky*,[37] striking down efforts by prosecutors to use race as a basis for rejecting potential black jurors. When Justice Brennan tried to get Marshall to soften the language in his concurrence, Marshall replied: "I continue to believe that the majority's approach will by its nature be ineffective in ending racial discrimination in the use of peremptories. I see no reason to be gentle in pointing that out, and I doubt that pulling my punches would make the situation any better."[38]

The tension between Marshall and Powell is a relatively contemporary example of a phenomenon that has been very common over the years. Clashes occurred between the so-called four horsemen (Sutherland, Butler, McReynolds, and Van Devanter) and Justices Holmes and Brandeis, between Black and Frankfurter, between Douglas and Frankfurter, Black and Fortas, Douglas and Burger, and Brennan and Rehnquist. It is important to note, however, that the level of conflict has not always been felt equally by both sides, nor have these internal, professional differences prevented some of the harshest of adversaries from maintaining warm personal associations. Justice Brennan, for example, who lost his first wife to cancer, was quick to come to the support of Justice Rehnquist as his wife suffered the same fate.

It is also important to understand that differences that arise over strongly held issue positions are not quite the same thing as ideological clashes. Members of the Court react relatively sharply when they are too easily labeled liberal or conservative because of one or two strongly held views.

It is true that the Justices Brennan and Marshall, who were identified from the decade of the 1970s through the 1980s as the Court's liberals, were adamantly opposed to the death penalty, and the two men dissented in literally hundreds of cases in which the Court upheld the penalty or refused to grant stays of execution.[39] Brennan described electrocution as "nothing less than the contemporary technological equivalent of burning people at the stake."[40] He and Marshall maintained their vocal opposition despite the fact that they were clearly on the losing side. In his Holmes lecture at Harvard Brennan insisted, "The calculated killing of a human being by the state involves, by its very nature, an absolute denial of the executed person's humanity and thus violates the command of the eighth amendment."[41] Their positions were no surprise, given their ideology. Significantly, however, Justices Blackmun and Powell, who came to the Court favoring the death penalty and who voted for it in many cases, ultimately repudiated their position.[42] Blackmun came to be labeled a liberal largely because of his abortion position, but it would be far too simplistic to attribute his change on the death penalty to ideology.

By contrast, Blackmun was adamant with respect to the erosion of the right to abortion announced in his 1973 *Roe v. Wade* opinion.[43] When he first joined the Court and promptly received the assignment from Chief Justice Burger, Blackmun came to a resolution of the question of abortion slowly and even attempted to dodge the basic question in *Roe*. In his first memorandum to the Court concerning the *Roe* opinion, Blackmun suggested resolving the Texas case on the claim that the state law was unacceptably vague, but his colleagues would have none of it.[44]

After all of the difficulty of producing the 1973 opinions, and the anguish he suffered at being called names he never before would have imagined, Blackmun was convinced that *Roe* was correct and feared that the Court would undermine it. His frustration and anger surface in his concurring opinion in a 1989 Missouri case as he wrote:

> Nor in my memory has a plurality gone about its business in such a deceptive fashion. At every level of its review, from its effort to read the real meaning out of the Missouri statute, to its intended evisceration of precedents and its deafening silence about the constitutional protections that it would jettison, the plurality obscures the portent of its analysis. With feigned restraint, the plurality announces that its analysis leaves Roe "undisturbed," albeit "modif[ied] and narrow[ed]." . . . But this disclaimer is totally meaningless. The plurality opinion is filled with winks, and nods, and knowing glances to those who would do away with Roe explicitly, but turns a stone face to anyone in search of what the plurality conceives as the scope of a

woman's right under the Due Process Clause to terminate a preg-
nancy from the coercive and brooding influence of the State. . . . I
fear for the future. I fear for the liberty and equality of the millions
of women who have lived and come of age in the 16 years since Roe
was decided. I fear for the integrity of, and public esteem for, this
Court.[45]

Blackmun concurred in part and dissented in part in a 1992 Pennsylvania case that was argued with the idea of overturning *Roe*. Blackmun
wrote:

Three years ago, in *Webster v. Reproductive Health Services,* 492
U.S. 490 (1989), four members of this Court appeared poised to
"cas[t] into darkness the hopes and visions of every woman in this
country" who had come to believe that the Constitution guaranteed
her the right to reproductive choice. . . . All that remained between
the promise of *Roe* and the darkness of the plurality was a single
flickering flame. Decisions since *Webster* gave little reason to hope
that this flame would cast much light. . . . But now, just when so
many expected the darkness to fall, the flame has grown bright.
   I do not underestimate the significance of today's joint opinion.
Yet I remain steadfast in my belief that the right to reproductive
choice is entitled to the full protection afforded by this Court before
Webster. And I fear for the darkness as four Justices anxiously await
the single vote necessary to extinguish the light.[46]

Hugo Black was another justice who often came slowly to his ultimate
view, but, once having developed it, hung on with bulldog tenacity. During the battle between Black, for the majority, and Rutledge, for the dissenters, in the New Jersey religious school support case *Everson v. Board
of Education,*[47] Black expanded and developed his own understanding of
the meaning of the "no establishment" clause of the First Amendment.
After that case, Black was iron-willed. He had stated his position in *Everson* and would not move.
   Following the 1947 *Everson* ruling, Felix Frankfurter led a group he
termed "the anti-Everson lads" in an effort to continue the battle in the
first of the released-time cases (so-called because they involved programs
that permitted children to be released from the public schools to attend

various kinds of religious instruction).[48] They caucused on the matter beginning on January 6, 1948, and worked together on revisions of the draft concurrence among themselves.[49]

Black was writing the majority opinion and very much needed Justice Burton's vote. For his part, Burton was attempting to pull Black and the Frankfurter's "anti-Everson lads" closer together. He sent a memorandum to "Hugo and Felix" on February 7, 1948, suggesting a formula for a possible opinion that should command seven votes. He suggested changes in Black's opinion that essentially removed references to *Everson,* and he proposed modifications in Frankfurter's concurrence that called for a narrowing to this particular program only as opposed to a more global critique of Black's opinion. However, Frankfurter's concurrence would still note disagreement with *Everson.* The critical paragraph from *Everson* defining Black's view of freedom of religion was simply not negotiable. Frankfurter, meanwhile, made some, but not all, of the suggested changes.

The irresistible force had met the immovable object. Black wrote to the conference on February 11. "I have just been handed a memorandum from Justice Frankfurter to the effect that he will not agree to any opinion in the *McCollum* case which makes reference to our decision in the *Everson* case. I will not agree to any opinion in the *McCollum* case which does not make reference to the *Everson* case."[50]

EGO CLASHES

As this discussion of one of the many pitched battles between Frankfurter and Black suggests, some of these disputes involve baggage from earlier disputes as well as a substantial measure of ego. Of course, ego clashes are difficult to resolve, since they are by definition personal. As is true in virtually all organizations, ego clashes are common, though some organizational citizens are more prone to that kind of contest than others. It is also common to find that those who protest the loudest about the egocentric behavior of others are often the most likely people to be guilty of it.

Probably the best known exemplar of the ego warrior, and the first one to accuse others of it, was Felix Frankfurter. His pattern of behavior was familiar to all members of the Court. When word of a new appointee to the Court came, Frankfurter was quick to send a welcoming letter prom-ising help and support. Indeed, new arrivals found Frankfurter regularly on hand with all manner of recommendations and good wishes. Assum-ing that one's first opinion agreed with Frankfurter's vote, the new justice could expect fulsome, even embarassing, praise. If one were then to take a position contrary to the "little Professor's," however, the apostate would receive not only a rebuke but also a general distribution of memoranda from Frankfurter declaring that his or her appointment had been a terri-ble error. Should the miscreant continue the errant behavior, the criticism could quickly turn to real conflict.

Justice William Brennan was appointed by President Eisenhower to re-place Justice Minton. It took very little time for Frankfurter to realize that Brennan, although once his student at Harvard law school, would vote his own mind. Brennan was no more pleased than many of his col-leagues with the Frankfurter treatment. Justice Harlan's biographer ex-plained Frankfurter's reaction.

> Brennan, Frankfurter decided, simply had an "ego" problem. "Af-ter sleeping on it," he wrote Harlan during the Court's debate over one 1958 case, "I have decided to curb my temperamental spontane-ity and not talk to Bill Brennan. 'Too much ego in his cosmos.' When [Harvard law professor] Paul Freund was here recently . . . he asked, 'Is my classmate Bill as cocksure as his opinions indicate?' Cocksuredness begets sensitiveness, and as his erstwhile teacher, I have to be particularly careful with Bill. He was plainly displeased at the thought of my writing anything before I saw what he will pro-duce, on the assumption that he will take care of all there is to be said. Therefore, I do not think I ought to tell him what I think should be the conception and temper of our opinion. All this had nothing to do with my personal relations with him, which are as pleasant as they can be."[51]

But Brennan and his colleagues had had quite enough of Justice Frank-furter's own displays of ego. The examples are too numerous to chronicle, but the one that particularly infuriated Brennan and the other justices was the famous Little Rock, Arkansas, High School desegregation case, *Cooper v. Aaron.*[52] Governor Orville Faubus and others bent on main-taining segregated schools had resisted the lower courts, concluding by sending the very obvious threat that the state would be unable to ensure the safety of the black children who came to integrate Little Rock Central High School. They sought postponement of the desegregation orders. The members of the Supreme Court were scattered at the time, with several justices attending events on the West Coast. Quick communications among the justices indicated that there was strong sentiment for issuing a vigorous, immediate response to what was obviously an attempt to threaten the federal courts. There was no time for the ordinary process and circulation of drafts. Instead, Justice Brennan crafted an opinion that, it was agreed, would be signed by all the justices—an unprecedented step. Although some justices, like Douglas, wondered aloud about the appropriateness and utility of having everyone sign, all ultimately agreed. Brennan explained what happened.

> Earl Warren, Tom Clark, and I were at the ABA convention in California when Charlie Whittaker got the petition. . . . We had a special session. Flying back, Earl Warren asked whether I would try to draft something. . . . We were unanimous. We used the memorandum as the basis of the opinion. The last day before the case was going to come down, Felix said that he was going to issue a concurrence. We almost cut his throat![53]

Frankfurter reasoned that since many of his former students were practicing law in the South, a special signal from him would enhance the likelihood that those southern lawyers would urge their colleagues to comply with the Court's orders. The unmistakable declaration of ego was more than the other justices could stomach, for the whole point of the exercise was to speak with one voice in the strongest possible way to make the Court's position unmistakably clear. The mere presence of a concurrence by anyone would undermine that effort, and the fact that Frankfurter's plan was based on unvarnished egotism was all the more frustrating.

There was nothing new or surprising in the fact that Frankfurter would pull such a stunt, but this time the stakes were too high, the situation too volatile, and the dangers of breaking the unified message too obvious to be tolerated. "Frankfurter's interjection into the opinion infuriated Brennan and Black. The Irishman was not without a temper, but his clerks had never seen him as angry as he was at Frankfurter's insistence on stepping on what was to have been unanimous."[54]

Brennan and Black threatened that if Frankfurter issued his concurrence, they would issue their own statement asserting that "Mr. Justice Black and Mr. Justice Brennan believe that the joint opinion of all the justices handed down on September 29, 1958, adequately expresses the view of the Court and they stand by that opinion as delivered. They desire that it be fully understood that the concurring opinion filed this day by Mr. Justice Frankfurter must not be accepted as any dilution or interpretation of the views expressed in the Court's joint opinion."[55] Recognizing that such a statement would publicly display the clash within the Court, Justice Harlan convinced Brennan and Black to drop their statement. "It is a mistake to make a mountain out of a molehill. *Requiescat in pace.*"[56]

Frankfurter's ego was a continuing problem. Professor Hirsch argues very effectively that "Frankfurter can only be understood politically if we understand him psychologically, and . . . we can understand him psychologically as representing a textbook case of a neurotic personality: someone whose self-image is overblown and yet, at the same time, essential to his sense of well-being."[57] He needed to lead, but his strong-willed colleagues were not about to be dominated by Felix.[58] That infuriated Frankfurter.

The key aspect of Frankfurter's personality as it affected his public behavior was his attitude toward political opposition. Because his self-image was inflated, and because his psychological peace rested upon that self-image, Frankfurter could not accept serious, sustained opposition in fields he considered his domain of expertise; he reacted to his opponents with vindictive hostility. Unconsciously, such hostility was a projection of his own self-doubt.[59]

Two factors made the situation much worse. First, it was becoming clear, inside and outside the Court, that Frankfurter was losing whatever initial force as a leader he had once exercised.[60] The turning point was the running debate over the mandatory flag salute cases, beginning with *Minersville v. Gobitis* in 1940.[61] Frankfurter had written for the Court, with only Stone dissenting, but there was great discomfort with the idea of mandating patriotic ceremonies in the face of Hitler's behavior in Europe. By the time *Jones v. Opelika*[62] was decided in 1942, things had changed. In the Jones case, Justices Black, Murphy, and Douglas dissented, proclaiming that they had made a mistake in *Minersville*. Following that decision, Justice Byrnes was replaced by Justice Rutledge, and with Justice Stone, there were now five votes to reverse Frankfurter's opinion. The opportunity to take that step came quickly, in the case of *West Virginia Board of Education v. Barnette*.[63]

Black and Douglas were often asked in later years just what had caused them to join Frankfurter's first flag salute opinion and then to make such a dramatic switch in so short a time. Douglas proposed several explanations, but there probably is no single reason. Douglas wrote of the *Minersville* decision, "In those days, Felix Frankfurter was our hero. He was indeed learned in constitutional law and we were inclined to take him at face value."[64] Douglas believed that Black and he "were probably naive in not catching the nuances of his position from the opinion he had been circulating for some time." Douglas also claimed that things might have been different had Stone's powerful dissent been presented earlier than the day preceding the last conference before the *Gobitis* opinion was released and had Stone sought to "campaign for it." At that late date, junior justices like Black and Douglas felt constrained to maintain the position they had taken in support of Frankfurter's opinion, though in later years neither would have hesitated to change his vote even at the last minute. However, Douglas said, "as the months passed and new cases were filed involving the same or a related problem, Black and I began to realize that we had erred."[65]

In fact, Douglas later admitted, "Hugo and I could never understand why we agreed to [Frankfurter's *Minersville* opinion] to begin with."[66] For his part, Frankfurter could never accept his colleagues' defection. Frankfurter's closest colleague, Robert Jackson, wrote the *Barnette* opinion, which made the defeat even more bitter. Worse yet, it was one of the most powerful pieces of constitutional rhetoric in the Court's history. Frankfurter's angry dissent began in a very personal tone, an approach Justice Murphy had urged Frankfurter to avoid.

Frankfurter's lashing out only underscored what was by then clear to readers of leading newspapers—that the justice had been on the losing side in a string of major cases during the previous two years. Not only did the newspapers publicize his declining influence, they also lauded the dissenters for changing their position in *Jones v. Opelika* and then supported the *Barnette* ruling. They thus depicted Frankfurter as supporting the same kind of dictatorial regimentation of citizens in violation of freedom of conscience as our enemies in World War II. Indeed, Hirsch argued, "The Barnette case marks a clear transition for Frankfurter and for the Court. The lines of battle have been sharply drawn; positions have been elaborated; sides have been chosen and stances taken. In a sense, Frankfurter will devote his remaining years on the Court to refighting the battle—and the opponents—of Barnette."[67]

Beyond the individual battles, Frankfurter's attitudes and tactics alienated other members of the Court in a very personal way. Frankfurter was well known for his flattery and his subsequent attacks on anyone who failed to measure up to the professor's expectations. As the miscreant listened to a sermon from Felix, his colleagues received memoranda that challenged the offender's competence as a judge and value as a person. They all knew that much of the criticism would describe flaws of which Frankfurter himself was the best exemplar. For instance, he wrote to Justice Roberts attacking Douglas:

> Except in cases where he knows it is useless or in cases where he knows or suspects that people are on to him, he is the most systematic exploiter of flattery I have ever encountered in my life. He tried it on me when he first came on the Court—every opinion of mine that he returned, he returned with the most extravagant praise, all of which ceased after I left him in no doubt that I did not come on the Court to play politics on the Court but to vote in each case as my poor lights guided me.[68]

That kind of hypocritical, back-stabbing behavior made Felix hard to endure for many of his colleagues, even though they respected the power of his mind.

Frankfurter found it extremely difficult to tolerate, much less to cooperate with, several of his colleagues. He wrote to Justice Jackson:

> Look at them. Hugo is a self-righteous, self-deluded part fanatic, part demagogue, who really disbelieves in law, thinks it is essentially manipulation of language. Intrinsically, the best brain in the lit, but undisciplined and "functional" in its employment, an instrument for supporting a predetermined result, not a means for responsible inquiry. Withal, he is quite devoid of play and humor. Reed is largely

vegetable—he has managed to give himself a nimbus of reasonableness but is as unjudicial-minded, as flagrantly moved, at times, by irrelevant considerations for adjudication, as any of them. He has a
reasonable voice in the service of a dogmatic, worldly, timid mind.
Bill is the most cynical, shamelessly immoral character I've ever
known. With him I have no more relation than the necessities of
court work require. He is too unscrupulous for any avoidable engagement.[69]

Frankfurter did not limit his attacks to his favorite targets, Hugo Black
and William O. Douglas. "By the late fifties and early sixties Frankfurter
was referring to Brennan as 'shoddy'; he referred to a liberal English
judge as 'the Black-Douglas-Brennan of the English judiciary.' Although
initially Frankfurter had high hopes for Earl Warren, the Chief Justice's
liberalism proved a major disappointment; by 1957, Frankfurter was referring to Warren's work as 'dishonest nonsense.' "[70] Indeed, the relationship between Frankfurter and Warren became extremely bitter, partly because Frankfurter had initially—and mistakenly—thought that he would
be able to win and control Warren.[71]

Frankfurter addressed wounds to his own ego and, according to
Hirsch, reacted to his own insecurities by finding and attacking flaws in
the character of others. One of the most vicious personal feuds on the
Court arose between Frankfurter and William O. Douglas, a man second
to none in his ability to turn to pure ice when he wanted to convey contempt or white heat when he became angry enough to cross swords with a
rival. Neither man could tolerate the other, neither was shy about saying
so, and both men identified character as the central issue.

Douglas found Frankfurter arrogant, pompous, cowardly, and dishonest.
He never missed an opportunity to needle Frankfurter in public or among
the justices; and if something went wrong at the Court, Douglas was more
than ready to assume that Frankfurter was behind it. When Justice Black
was not appointed to follow Charles Evans Hughes as chief justice, Douglas
wrote Hugo about having heard the news as he drove through Arkansas en
route to New Mexico. "I said to Mildred 'Felix had done it again!' and there
is no question in my mind that he was responsible."[72]

He was just as certain that Frankfurter had been conspiring to get
Roosevelt to appoint him to a defense-related job in order to get him off
the Court. He made the point to Black in a letter from his summer place

in Lostine, Oregon. "I am quite sure that F.F. has inspired this offer—at least that he has been influential. It has come to me 'straight' that he thinks I am the only man. If he could get me there and you back in the Senate I am sure he would be happier."[73]

Frankfurter gave as good as he got, blasting Douglas for using the Court as a political springboard to the White House. He wrote Learned Hand that Douglas "is the most cynical, shameless immoral character I've ever known."[74] He recorded in his diary a now famous conversation with Justice Murphy in January 1943 in which Frankfurter declared Douglas guilty of violating the sanctity of the monastery because of his assumed desire to run in 1944. Frankfurter insisted, "this Court has no excuse for being unless it's a monastery."[75]

In his final years, Douglas spoke more positively of Frankfurter, suggesting in his autobiography that he had actually always respected Frankfurter and had not really had the kind of conflictual relationship that Court watchers had discussed openly for years.[76] In an interview with Elizabeth Black, Justice Black's widow, Douglas said that every Court needs a Felix Frankfurter, even as he described how he and Black had been taken in by Frankfurter on the *Gobitis* case.[77] It is quite clear that Douglas's comments were an appeal to history and not the real picture of his relationship with Frankfurter.

LEADERSHIP CONTESTS

As the discussion of Frankfurter's machinations in the 1940s suggests, these ego clashes may be associated with rivalries for leadership within the Court. Clearly, Frankfurter saw himself in a clash with Black for stature, both among colleagues and in terms of external perceptions. Warren Burger appeared at times to have had a similar attitude toward Justice Brennan. Burger may have worn the mantle of chief justice, but he clearly was not regarded as either a strong jurist or a leader. In fact, at times his efforts to assert what he obviously regarded as his right to leadership got in the way of the Court's work.[78] Meanwhile, it was increasingly clear to the members of the Court that Brennan was a very effective leader. That he was on the other side in most cases from Burger and that, after 1975, he was most often the senior justice in opposition to the Nixon appointees only made the leadership issue more obvious.

At various points in history jealousy has arisen over the appointment of the chief justice. Justice Story saw himself as an obvious heir to Chief Justice John Marshall, though he knew full well that President Andrew Jackson would never appoint him to the job. Nevertheless, there was reportedly a degree of tension.

> The appearance of Roger Taney as chief justice made life in Washington even more untenable for Story, at least temporarily. He had nothing personal against him, and indeed they would develop a relationship based on mutual respect, if not affection. Yet in 1837 Story knew that what his friends said was true: that if justice prevailed, that is talents, service, and dedication counted, then he, Story, would have assumed Marshall's mantle as chief justice.[79]

Similarly, when Chief Justice Fuller died in 1910, Justice John Marshall Harlan was "obviously hungry for the honor" and thought "the President could reasonably reward him for long service rendered and then, after a comparatively brief period, make Hughes his successor."[80] Justice White thought he deserved the appointment. "With Harlan presiding as senior Associate Justice, White had little to say in conference and his usually amiable disposition seemed to have passed under a cloud. Throughout the fall he was offish and disgruntled."[81]

Of course, the harshest and most public battle over the center seat was the one waged by Justice Jackson against Hugo Black when Jackson concluded that he was not selected because Hugo Black had intimidated Truman by threatening to resign if Jackson were selected. Jackson was ready to explode anyway, because he believed he had been cheated out of his rightful chair when Stone was nominated to replace Charles Evans Hughes. Jackson had a promise from Roosevelt to name him to the center seat but, at the time, there were other considerations. The man who was closer to Jackson on the Court than anyone else urged the president to take another course. When Roosevelt asked Justice Frankfurter whether he would select Jackson or Harlan Fiske Stone, he chose Stone:

> For me the decisive consideration, considering the fact that Stone is qualified, is that Bob is of your political personal family, as it were, while Stone is a Republican.
> Now it doesn't require prophetic powers to be sure that we shall,

sooner or later, be in war—I think sooner. It is most important that when war does come, the country should feel that you are the Nation's, President, and not a partisan president. Few things would contribute as much to confidence in you as a national and not a partisan President than for you to name a Republican, who has the profession's confidence, as Chief Justice.[82]

Douglas had wanted Black to be selected. He wrote Hugo with more prescience than he could know.

Felix has done it again. And there is no question in my mind that he was responsible. You will recall that I expressed my fear that Felix would make that move. I am sorry that it did not go to you. I thought you *deserved it*. And I know it would strengthen the Court greatly if you were the Chief. The bar—being a conservative outfit— hails Stone's appointment. But unless the old boy changes, it will not be a particularly happy or congenial atmosphere in which to work.[83]

And indeed it was not a congenial atmosphere. Justice Murphy found personal clashes on the Court particularly troublesome. As Murphy's biographer observed, "The closing days of Stone's chief justiceship ranked as one of the bitterest, most schismatic periods in judicial history."[84] They contributed to Murphy's discomfort on the Court, and when he indicated to Felix Frankfurter that he would just as soon be offered a job elsewhere, Frankfurter tried to find him one.[85]

For his part, Jackson felt he had a commitment to succeed Stone if the opportunity presented itself, but, by that time, Franklin Roosevelt was dead and Harry Truman was president. Black did not go to Truman to block Jackson's appointment, but Jackson, then in Germany as America's prosecutor at the Nuremburg War Trials, believed that he had and acted on that assumption. His response is considered further in the next chapter, but he unquestionably regarded himself as engaged in a war. The real irony is that Truman later declared that he had intended to name Jackson to the center seat, but his behavior made that impossible.[86] Truman then nominated Fred Vinson.

That occasion was not the only time that suspicions about former Senator Hugo Black's alleged involvement in appointment politics led to trouble. There were tensions between Abe Fortas and Hugo Black over several professional issues, particularly disputes over interpretations of the First and Fourteenth Amendments. Their differences intensified when Fortas became convinced that Black had worked against his confirmation through Senator Lister Hill.[87]

COURT TRANSITIONS

Of course, the clash between Black and Fortas culminated when both men left the Court, albeit by very different means. Their departures were central to the transition from the Warren to the Burger Courts. Such periods of transition in the Court's history have sometimes been significant flash points.

The shift from the Marshall Court to the Taney Court marked the first major transition in the Court's history. As Justice Daniel's biographer, John P. Frank, noted, Daniel was one of the new members who came to the Court just as the transition was underway. "The death of the great Chief Justice Marshall in 1835 and his replacement by Taney marked the end of an era, and the mass of Jackson and Van Buren appointments within a six-year period radically changed the Court's goals and values."[88]

The Jacksonians had long awaited the opportunity not merely to get their president into office but also to clean out John Marshall and his colleagues on the Court. The Marshall Court was the antithesis of virtually everything for which the Jacksonians stood. It was no accident and no surprise that Jackson appointed the man who had been his principal warrior in the battle against the Second Bank of the United States, Roger Taney, to be chief justice. Nor was there any question as to his commitment, for he made the nomination to a Congress that had rejected Taney the first time he was nominated to the Court.

The intentions and expectations were not lost on the members of the Marshall Court who awaited the new justices. Story wrote to a colleague: "You will know that I have for a long time desponded as to the future fate of our country. I now believe that we are too corrupt, imbecile and slavish, in our dependence upon and under the auspices of demagogues, to maintain any free constitution, and we shall sink lower and lower in national degradation."[89] Justice McLean replied, suggesting that it might be time for the latter to move out of the boardinghouse where the members of the Court had traditionally lived together. "I do not believe you will enjoy yourself with our brother judges," McLean observed.[90]

The tensions in this case arose, by all accounts, primarily over doctrine and were not matters of personal conflict. The chief justice, as well as Justices Daniel, Catron, and Wayne, were intense but gentlemanly in their demeanor and relationships with others.

The Stone Court, by contrast, was wracked with personal strife. Stone presided over a little understood period of transition from the Roosevelt Court to the Truman Court. It is often overlooked that Harry Truman appointed Chief Justice Vinson and Justices Burton, Minton, and Clark. There is also a tendency to underappreciate the very significant differences in politics and ideology between the Truman and Roosevelt administrations,[91] forces that affected their nominees to the bench.

Although Truman appointed Vinson with the hope that he would bring peace to the Court, the effort failed. In fact, when Vinson died, Felix Frankfurter remarked, "This is the first indication that I have ever had that there is a God."[92] One of Frankfurter's former clerks, Solicitor General Philip Elman, wrote to Felix:

> What a mean little despot he is. Has there ever been a member of the Court who was deficient in so many respects as a man and as a judge. Even that s.o.b. McReynolds, despite his defects of character, stands by comparison as a towering figure and powerful intellect. . . . This man is a pygmy, morally and mentally. And so uncouth.[93]

Even Justice Reed, hardly regarded as an intellectual power himself, nevertheless felt that Vinson was inadequate to the task. Speaking of Vinson to Frankfurter, Reed said: "He's just like me, except that he is less well-educated and has not had as many opportunities."[94] What amazed Frankfurter about Vinson was that he could have so much experience in public life and yet know so little about human nature.[95]

Despite a multitude of warnings about the dangers of attempts by presidents to "pack the Court" with like-minded judges, some chief executives have been quite successful in molding the Court. President Nixon made the federal judiciary, and the Warren Court in particular, a target in his bid for the presidency. It worked, and in his first term, Nixon saw four of his appointees on the Court. In several doctrinal fields, Justices White and Stewart, though popularly known as swing voters, frequently joined the Burger Court group. Burger was himself a controversial choice as chief justice, within the Court as well as outside it.

Positions taken by Justices Rehnquist, Burger, and Powell, in particular, pushed Douglas, Brennan, and Marshall into stronger, more frequent, and more intense opposition. By 1974 and 1975, the emerging Burger Court was coming into its own. In the areas of due process, both criminal and civil, equal protection, and court access rules, there is no question that the Court was moving away from the path of the Warren Court and closer to positions favored by President Nixon. William O. Douglas was thoroughly frustrated by the time he left the bench in 1975, and Marshall was fast coming to the same point. Brennan was fighting the long battle, but even the good natured Justice Brennan was tested by harsh rhetoric from opposing justices.[96]

Ronald Reagan had been running against the Supreme Court since his work on the Goldwater campaign in 1964, and he carried the theme with him to the 1980 presidential contest that took him to the White House for eight years. During those years, and during the Bush presidency that followed, the conservative Republican presidents were able to replace several members of the Court. And although it is true that the Court did not overturn the earlier Warren era rulings on prayer in the schools or birth control, the Court did move toward the conservative agenda in many areas of the law.

More and more, Marshall and Brennan were in strong dissent. Increasingly, Harry Blackmun, himself a Nixon appointee, was identified in the media as a liberal and polarized further from his Republican colleagues. The question, however, was whether any of these justices had actually moved to the left—or was it simply the case, as Blackmun often said, that the Court had moved under them to the right? As the Court filled increasingly with conservatives, differences arose among justices appointed by presidents of similar ideological bent. The old political saw that the dominance of one party breeds fragmentation appeared to be true for the Supreme Court.

In sum, the dynamics of transition within the Court, whatever the origins of that change, can sometimes provide a context for conflict.

ROLE DEFINITION: THE UNDERSTANDING OF INSTITUTIONAL CHARACTER

Whether the differences are highlighted by periods of court transition or for other reasons, differences among the justices in their understanding of the proper character and role of the Court have been a source of frustration and tension. Three sets of disputes highlight this longstanding issue: the monastery metaphor, the new rights problem, and the court access rules debate.

One of the oldest sources of bickering about and within the Court is the sense that one or more of the justices might harbor ambitions for more active political involvement, whether overt involvement in electoral politics or less public, but often not completely secret, cooperation with others up to and including the president.

There has been no small amount of hypocrisy among some members of the Court in discussions of this point over the two centuries of the Court's existence. The most often cited statement was advanced by none other than Felix Frankfurter: "When a priest enters a monastery, he must leave—or ought to leave all sorts of worldly desires behind him. And this isn't idle, high flown talk. We are all poor human creatures and it's difficult enough to be wholly intellectually and morally disinterested when one has no other motive except that of being a judge according to one's full conscience."[97]

Justice Hugo Black did not put the matter in quite the same terms as Felix, but he often invoked the notion of a nearly sacred vow to service and protection of the Court.[98] As his second wife, Elizabeth, put it, the Court was so much a part of him that almost everything else had to be subordinated to the good of the institution. Justice Brennan's commitment to the institution was similarly intense, leading him to recuse himself in situations in which others might not have thought twice about participating. And until his last few years on the Court, when utter frustration compelled him to speak out, Justice Thurgood Marshall rejected virtually all requests for interviews and refused many invitations to publish articles or books.

High-minded assertions notwithstanding, nothing stopped Frankfurter

or Black from communicating with presidents. The history of justices lobbying the White House on judicial appointments is clear, from Chief Justice
Taft to Chief Justice Burger. Justice Douglas wrote his friend Lyndon Johnson to suggest people for various positions in the administration or the judiciary. Indeed, he had done such things from his earliest days on the Court,
when Black and he had together urged President Roosevelt to appoint
Jerome Frank to a seat on the Second Circuit, the promised reward for his
service on the Securities and Exchange Commission.[99] (Frank had really
wanted to return to private practice in order to bolster his failing financial
situation.) Felix Frankfurter was involved in the same kind of activity on a
continuing basis, at least during the Roosevelt administration.

In earlier times, members of the Court actively ran for office from the
bench or participated in the campaigns of others. Justice Davis, for instance, was nominated by the Labor Reform Party for president in 1872.[100]
Others participated in campaigns.

A number of justices accepted various official assignments more or less
voluntarily. John Jay had been ambassador to Great Britain while he was
Chief Justice.[101] Oliver Ellsworth had been a U.S. negotiator in talks with
the French over seizure of U.S. vessels.[102] These activities were sufficiently
controversial that Chief Justice Stone later refused Roosevelt's request
that he take an active role in war resources efforts, reminding the president:

> I cannot rightly yield to my desire to render for you a service which as a
> private citizen I should not only feel bound to do but one which I
> should undertake with zeal and enthusiasm. . . . We must not forget
> that it is the judgment of history that two of my predecessors, Jay and
> Ellsworth, failed in the obligation of their office and impaired their le-
> gitimate influence by participation in executive action in the negotia-
> tion of treaties. . . . True, they repaired their mistake in part by resign-
> ing their commissions before resuming their judicial duties, but it is not
> by mere chance that every Chief Justice since has confined his activities
> directly to the performance of his judicial duties.[103]

These concerns had not, however, stopped Stone from serving as a member of the informal advisory group known as "Medicine Ball Cabinet"
during the Hoover administration.[104]

Nor did Stone's warnings stop others from accepting active roles. Justice Murphy accepted a commission in the Army Reserve, and as Lieutenant Colonel Murphy even went so far as to wear his uniform under his robes. Justice Jackson's decision to accept the assignment as the Nuremburg War Trials prosecutor was more than a little controversial, both within the Court and outside it. More recently, Justice Abe Fortas engaged in an ongoing involvement with the Johnson administration. Laura Kalman, Fortas's biographer, observed: "During the Johnson years, Fortas was part of the judicial branch and, as well, an unofficial member of the executive branch."[105] The degree of his involvement and the amount of time he spent at the other end of the avenue excited the concern of some of his colleagues. "One clerk knew he could safely take naps in the justice's chambers because Fortas spent so much time [at the White House]."[106]

Douglas's well known off-the-bench activities ranged from controversial publications on international affairs to a nearly successful attempt to launch negotiations between Hanoi and the United States before the Tet offensive.[107] Those efforts had been sanctioned by the White House but were later scuttled by Johnson.

This off-the-bench activity has been common and has existed since the earliest days of the Court, but its frequency and longevity have not made it any the less controversial. Indeed, those kinds of activities have been the source of numerous tensions in the Court. Chief Justice Taft was convinced that Justice Brandeis was attempting to undermine his lobbying efforts in Congress.[108] Justice Murphy's commission forced Chief Justice Stone to respond to troublesome inquiries from Congress about a lieutenant colonel on the bench.[109] Justice Jackson's acceptance of the Nuremburg role created a host of difficulties, ranging from the simple fact that he was not available to do his judicial work to the attack on Justice Black.

William O. Douglas was irked by Frankfurter's sanctimonious pronouncements on the monastery, for he knew full well that Felix was up to his ears in all kinds of off-the-bench activities. Frankfurter campaigned against Douglas with his colleagues and others outside the Court, claiming that Douglas was a political opportunist using the Court to further his presidential ambitions. He recorded in his diary a now famous conversation with Justice Murphy in January 1943 in which Frankfurter declared Douglas guilty of violating the sanctity of the monastery because of his assumed desire to run in 1944. Frankfurter reminded Murphy, "This Court has no excuse for being unless it's a monastery."[110]

Hugo Black, a close friend of Douglas's, was nevertheless troubled by the criticism of the Court fueled by Douglas's off-the-bench activities and his highly publicized domestic problems. Douglas was married four times, three times to women under twenty-five when he was in his sixties and seventies. Although no one ever accused Douglas of not shouldering his share of the work, he frequently departed from the Court before its final conference of the year, leaving Justice Brennan or Black with a memorandum outlining his positions on remaining cases.

On occasion, Black and others suggested to Douglas that he might do well to remain in Washington. In June 1957, for example, Warren and Black both talked to Douglas about his decision to leave on a trip to Istanbul, Beirut, and Karachi.

> After talking with you yesterday, and after talking with Hugo, I considered seriously the possibility of revising my schedule so as to stay here through July 8 to sit on the Girard case. But I had made so many engagements and laid so many plans in the Middle East that involved so many people, it seemed that I could not readily change the schedule unless I called the whole trip off. I hated to call my trip off because I had shipped out a great amount of material for the long automobile journey from Karachi to Istanbul. Moreover, it seemed to me that with at least seven, and more probably eight, judges sitting, there would be no difficulty in reaching rather quickly a unanimous decision. It seemed to me in looking over the papers that the issue was a relatively simple one upon which the Court would in all probability reach a unanimous conclusion. Therefore it seemed to me that if I left it would not embarrass anyone at all or interfere to any degree with the functioning of the Court.[111]

The mere fact that a justification was required should have made obvious the problem his trip would pose. For Douglas, it did not.

Justice Douglas bristled when Chief Justice Burger issued a memorandum in May 1971 that would make it possible for those seeking stays or other actions by a circuit justice to go to another justice if the justice specifically assigned to their circuit happened to be out of town. Douglas took it as reference to his practice of leaving immediately at the end of term for his cabin in the mountains. He wrote:

> Your memorandum of May 18 to Bob Seaver respecting summer applications to a single Justice is susceptible of meaning that if the Justice is "out of the area," the application is passed on to another.
>
> Goose Prairie, Washington, gets six mail deliveries a week, and there is no more of a problem in reaching me there than there is of reaching John in Connecticut.
>
> Emergency cases can be imagined where instant action is needed. But on the basis of past experience there is in most cases no reason not to send application to those of us who are at our homes outside this metropolitan area.[112]

Actually, his summer habits did present some interesting challenges. The *Portland Oregonian* ran a story about attempts by the ACLU to get an injunction against Portland police in August 1970. Two lawyers went to Douglas's cabin, which did not have a telephone, only to find that he had gone on a ten-day pack trip into the mountains. U.S. forest rangers used aircraft to locate Douglas's camp, but the attorneys, clad in business suits, had to hike six miles into the mountains from the closest road to get there. When they found the justice's camp, he listened to their arguments and told them to return the next day at noon. He would "leave the decision on that tree stump over there." When the one attorney who was not too sore and bruised to make the return trip the next day arrived at the now abandoned camp, he found written on a small piece of paper a decision denying the petition![113]

Although Black and others did not care all that much about what Douglas was doing, they were bothered that it made Douglas, and by extension the Court, an easy target for the many Warren Court critics who needed no prompting to go after the justices.

Warren, notwithstanding his active political career before entering the Court, had relatively strong views about off-the-bench activities. He was very uncomfortable about the fact that President Johnson had been able to manipulate him (as only Johnson knew how) into heading what became known as the Warren Commission investigation into the assassination of President Kennedy.[114] One difficult aspect of the commission was simply the amount of Warren's time and energy that it consumed, and there was no escaping the fact that it placed the Court squarely in the middle of a politically sensitive and volatile matter.

Warren was not pleased by the negative attention Douglas's and Fortas's activities brought to the Court. When the full story of Fortas's activities became known to him, Warren convened a conference to disclose what he knew.[115] It was clear that Warren felt Fortas should step down and made no effort to achieve any other outcome in the matter. In fact, his biographer concludes that Warren would have taken steps to attempt to press Fortas if he had not stepped down on his own.[116]

In recent years, sparks have flown over speeches in which members of the Court have criticized their colleagues. More often, however, clashes have emerged over claims for protection of new rights and, by contrast, efforts to limit access to the Court through tightened interpretations of court access rules.

Hugo Black led the battle within the Court against what he saw as attempts to create new rights not authorized by the Constitution or statutes. Ironically, one of the first targets was his friend Bill Douglas. Black did not see this offensive only or even primarily as a battle over particular issues of law, but as an effort by some of his colleagues to redefine the role of the Court. He had opposed similar activities, albeit from the other end of the political spectrum, when he was in the Senate and the Nine Old Men were creating rights to block efforts by state and national legislatures to fashion solutions to pressing policy problems. Since Douglas always began with a presumption of liberty, he really did not see himself as defining new rights as much as explaining the longstanding limits to government power. He began from the premise that many of our freedoms are natural rights that are prior to man-made law, including the Constitution. This approach drove Black to distraction. He rejected the idea that it was the task of the Court to keep the Constitution current with the times or to solve the problems that the Congress had not addressed. He wrote: "I have known a different court from the one today. What has occurred may occur again. I would much prefer to put my faith in the people and their elected representatives to choose the proper policies for our government to follow, leaving to the courts questions of constitutional interpretation and enforcement."[117] Black concluded by the late 1960s that Douglas was "leaving him." Such cases as the right to privacy claims, due process arguments, protections for demonstrations, and the challenge to the poll tax furnished evidence of that apostasy. To Douglas's opinion creating a right to privacy, Black replied: "I like my privacy as well as the next one, but I am nevertheless compelled to admit that government has a right to invade it unless prohibited by some specific constitutional provision."[118]

Black rarely gave published lectures or wrote for publication. Yet on the most important occasion when he did so (the Carpentier lectures, later published as *A Constitutional Faith*) Black went after his long-time friend and colleague, William O. Douglas. Citing Douglas's poll tax opinion, Black warned that "there is creeping into Court opinions a willingness to hold laws unconstitutional on the same 'shock the conscience' basis [as the earlier due process opinions] by invoking equal protection or some other clause."[119] If Black was frustrated with Douglas, he was downright angry at Fortas. In the end, Black tried to hang on despite his advancing age and physical condition in large part because he felt the need to fight off the justices who seemed bent on the new rights mission.

For their part, Douglas, Brennan, and Marshall strongly resisted the attack on standing and other rules controlling access to the Court during the 1973 and 1974 terms. Douglas was particularly adamant, for he felt that the Court had long been too willing to entertain the claims of the haves and to avoid its duty with respect to the have-nots. He argued that the Court was too willing to simply write off disputes Douglas considered to be absolutely clear "cases and controversies" within the meaning of Article III of the Constitution.[120] One of his last opinions was a dissent in one of the very controversial standing cases of this period, *Warth v. Seldin:*

Standing has become a barrier to access to the federal courts, just as "the political question" was in earlier decades. The mounting caseload of federal courts is well known. But cases such as this one reflect festering sores in our society; and the American dream teaches that if one reaches high enough and persists there is a forum where justice is dispensed. I would lower the technical barriers and let the courts serve that ancient need. They can in time be curbed by legislative or constitutional restraints if an emergency arises.[121]

He regarded the decisions made, mostly with the support of the recent Burger Court appointees, as "monuments to the present Court's abdication of its constitutional responsibility to decide cases properly within its jurisdiction."[122]

CONFLICTS OVER INTERNAL COURT PROCESSES

One of the ways members of the Court define and redefine the nature of the institution is the way they define and participate in its processes. The debates that emerge over these questions are sometimes symptoms rather than causes of tension, but they can certainly exacerbate existing frustrations.

Behavior or discussions of procedure are often little more than routine, but in the event that someone chooses to beat what everyone else considers a dead horse or to push the limits of acceptable behavior, the matter can jar like the scraping of fingernails on a blackboard. If one or another member of the Court is already feeling a degree of tension with respect to colleagues, the behavior can fuel a smouldering fire.

For example, Justice Frankfurter began almost every term with a memorandum to the conference suggesting procedural changes. The memoranda grew like Topsy over the years, but they commonly spoke to similar themes—in some cases precisely the same arguments Frankfurter had been making each term for a decade. In 1951 his memorandum was a scant four pages long, but by September 1960 his annual missive had reached ten type-set pages. Time and again Frankfurter lectured his colleagues on the need for more reflection before votes were cast and more deliberation before opinions were handed down. He called for exchanges of memoranda before opinions were prepared, delays in responses to circulations until dissents and concurrences had also been circulated, and holding over cases without reargument to allow more time for consideration.

Such lectures would not have been welcome from virtually any member of the Court, but Frankfurter's pedantic attitude and condescension were particularly unbearable. Eventually, Douglas took to answering Frankfurter, in part at least because he knew it infuriated him. Responding to the 1951 annual Frankfurter lecture on Supreme Court procedure, Douglas wrote:

> We are not first-year law students who need to be put under strict restraints. In the great bulk of cases our minds are fixed at the end of oral argument. One who is not prepared on a case passes and does not cast a vote. His vote is cast when he is ready. . . . The blowing of whistles, the counting to three or ten, the suspension of all activity for a stated time may be desirable and necessary on playgrounds or in sports. But we are not children; we deal not with trivia; we are not engaged in contests. School room procedures are not fit for our tasks.[123]

Frankfurter had also proposed more extended memoranda prior to circulation of full draft opinions, a suggestion that sent Douglas around the bend. He insisted, "The proposal for assigning cases to two Justices for the writing of their separate views *in extenso* would launch the Court into the law review business, multiply our volumes, and load them with irrelevancies."[124]

In fact, Douglas went after Frankfurter, Black, and others for failing to return circulations promptly to the authors, thereby delaying the issuance of opinions. He wrote of Frankfurter's suggestions: "Promptness in making returns to circulated opinions by those whose minds are made up is a desirable practice. Those in dissent may want a delay in the hope that their views will carry the day. (I have even seen flying squadrons of law clerks used for that purpose.) But here again, we are not teenagers."[125]

Frankfurter continued to press for more consideration of issues but simultaneously argued for limiting conferences to four hours to avoid fatigue.[126] It has been argued that the length and lack of structure in the Stone Court's conferences of the 1940s exacerbated tensions, as frustrated and drained judges said things that triggered harsh responses,[127] which then unfortunately stayed with some of the justices after they left the conference.

Chief Justice Hughes's biographer noted that the amount of time that the justices spent together in close quarters caused occasional friction.

> The snug courtroom itself was so poorly ventilated as to be a source of friction. Within their own restricted circle the judges passed down

a story of how Justice Gray, a large and full-blooded man, insisted on keeping a window open behind the screen. One day frail Justice Brown, feeling the draft, asked a page to close the window. Justice Gray, overheated, arose from the bench and went behind the screen to confirm his suspicions. "What damn' fool told you to close that window?" he asked the frightened page. "Mr. Justice Brown," the page admitted. "I thought so," sputtered Gray as he stormed back to the bench.[128]

When the new Court building was opened, the justices spent even more time together, since previously each had worked out of an office in his home and saw the others only at conferences and when the Court sat.

Small things, in themselves trivial, may form a basis for tension over the years. There is the story of how Chief Justice Burger appropriated two footnotes, essentially verbatim, from the first draft of Justice Powell's dissent in *TVA v. Hill*[129] and used them in his majority opinion. Powell's clerk visited Burger's chambers to inquire about the matter and was told in essence that the Chief Justice could use whatever he thought should be included in the opinion for the Court. The clerk suggested to Powell that some kind of rebuke would be appropriate in his own opinion, but Powell is reported to have replied, "It's no time to get into a pissing contest with a skunk."[130] Powell did, however, write a note to Burger to raise a "flag of gentle protest," but Burger did not get the point, telling Powell to "Relax!"[131] As Powell's biographer rightly observed, anyone who knew Lewis Powell would see this as considerably more than a small matter. Jeffries referred to this injury as "a kind of emotional paper cut," but added, "Multiply such trivialities many times over, pile them up for years on end, and one has some understanding of the way Burger's personality undermined his leadership."[132]

Everyone occasionally trips over something that creates a small tension with co-workers, particularly if one is new to an office. Justice Sandra Day O'Connor has been enormously grateful over the years for the assistance and support of Justice Powell. However, early in her tenure, Justice O'Connor dissented from a Powell majority draft. She felt so strongly about it that she wanted to have the case held over for reargument so that others would have a chance to see how problematic Powell's approach was. As she described it: "That upset Lewis dreadfully. It was the only time I've seen him upset."[133] As soon as she was informed that a dissenter who tried to hold a case over would be regarded as engaged in an unfair tactic, O'Connor apologized to Powell and all was well.

Burger did not understand that such missteps are hard to forgive if they are frequent and long-standing and the way he operated the conferences, assessed votes, and assigned opinions reflected his insensitivity. These were not small matters, and Burger's colleagues felt that his behavior was not merely insensitive but intentional.

Justice Marshall felt slighted by Burger on a number of occasions. In April 1972, Marshall wrote his colleagues to protest the fact that a conference had been held in his absence.

> I am deeply disturbed as a result of the conference on argued cases being held in my absence. I know that this has not occurred during my few years here except where the Justice involved was ill and unable to be present and, even then, it was with the consent of the Justice involved. I had assumed that this was the usual practice here.
>
> I am not worried so much about this particular conference as I am that it may become a precedent for some future time. Like the late John Harlan I, for one, am worried about changing some of the time-honored practices of the Court. . . .
>
> As matters now stand I could not in good conscience participate in any opinion coming out of that conference. This is further highlighted by the fact that it places the responsibility on the absent Justice to call for another conference. I, for one, do not appreciate that weight being put on my shoulders and do not request another conference. Rather, I prefer that I just be listed as not participating in any opinions coming out of yesterday's conference. I will leave it to the press to speculate as to why I am not earning my salary.[134]

One of Burger's most divisive behaviors was the manner in which he handled assignment of opinions for the Court. The chief justice, of course, assigns the writing of the opinion for the Court if he or she is in the majority, but if the chief voted against the majority, then the opinion is to be assigned by the senior justice in the majority. For much of Burger's career, that meant that either Douglas or Brennan was most often the senior on the other side of the case.

On several occasions Douglas asserted that Burger simply miscounted conference votes in order to control the assignment.[135] Nor was Douglas the only person who had difficulties with Burger's assignments. Potter Stewart wrote Burger on December 29, 1970, citing four assignment errors in a single assignment list.[136] In *Rosenbloom v. Metromedia,* Stewart found that he had been assigned an opinion in which he was one of three justices on the losing side with five justices in the majority.

The clash over the assignment in *Lloyd v. Tanner,* an important case involving claims for free speech in shopping centers, caused Douglas to vent some of his frustration with the Chief. Douglas discovered that in spite of his assignment of the opinion to Marshall on April 21, Burger had issued a new assignment three days later. An outraged Douglas prepared a reply to the chief.

You apparently misunderstand. *Lloyd* is already assigned to Thurgood and he's at work on an opinion. Whether he will command a majority, no one knows.

Under the Constitution and Acts of Congress, there are no provisions for assignment of opinions. Historically, Chief Justice has made the assignment if he is in the majority. Historically, the senior in the majority assigns the opinion if the Chief Justice is in the minority.

You led the Conference battle against affirmance and that is your privilege. But it is also the privilege of the majority, absent the Chief Justice, to make the assignment. Hence, *Lloyd* was assigned and is assigned.

The tragedy of compromising on this simple procedure is illustrated by last Term's *Swann.* You who were a minority of two kept the opinion for yourself and faithfully wrote the minority position which the majority could not accept. Potter wrote the majority view and a majority agreed to it. It was not circulated because we thought you should see it. After much effort your minority opinion was transformed, the majority view prevailed, and the result was unanimous.

But *Swann* illustrated the wasted time and effort and the frayed relations which result when the traditional assignment procedure is not followed.

If the Conference wants to authorize you to assign all opinions, that will be a new procedure. Though opposed to it, I will acquiesce.

But unless we make a frank reversal in our policy, any group in the majority should and must make the assignment.

This is a two-edge sword. Byron might well head up five members of the Court, you, Bill Brennan, Potter Stewart and I being the minority; and we might feel very strongly about it. But in that event it is for Byron to make the assignment. It is not for us in the minority to try to outwit Byron by saying "I reserve my vote" and then recast it to control the assignment. That only leads to a frayed and bitter Court full of needless strains and quarrels.

Lloyd stays assigned to Thurgood.[137]

One of the most dramatic clashes came over the abortion cases, *Roe v. Wade*[138] and *Doe v. Bolton*.[139] Douglas took issue with Burger's discussion of an assignment in *Doe,* the Georgia case, on grounds that the alignment was Brennan, Stewart, Marshall, and Douglas to strike elements of the law and Burger, White, and Blackmun to uphold it.[140] Burger disagreed, claiming that "there were, literally, not enough columns [in the docket sheet] to mark up an accurate reflection of the voting in either the Georgia or the Texas cases."[141] The stakes were raised considerably when Harry Blackmun called for reargument in both abortion cases[142] and issued his memorandum in *Roe v. Wade,* suggesting that the Court could avoid the direct constitutional question on abortion and strike the state bar on grounds of vagueness.[143] Douglas and Brennan tried to persuade Blackmun to take on the issue directly and disputed the need for reargument.

When, on June 1, the recently appointed justices Powell and Rehnquist decided to vote for reargument in the case, Douglas was outraged. He warned Burger that he would "file a statement telling what is happening to us and the tragedy it entails" if the Court held the cases over to the next term.[144] He immediately set to work on a memorandum that he had printed and sent to Brennan.[145]

The Douglas memorandum charged that Burger improperly assigned the cases despite requests from Douglas not to do so. Douglas insisted that "the matter of assignment is not merely a matter of protocol." He recalled the tradition of assignment by senior associate in cases where the chief was not in the majority and warned that "When a Chief Justice tries to bend the Court to his will by manipulating assignments, the integrity of the institution is imperiled."[146] He wondered in print if "perhaps the purpose of the Chief Justice . . . was to try to keep control of the merits. If that was the aim, he was unsuccessful."[147]

Brennan told Douglas that he had "serious reservations" about Douglas publishing any of that material but suggested specific deletions if Douglas was determined to go ahead with it. Douglas decided not to publish, but a copy nevertheless found its way to the *Washington Post*. When Douglas, then at his summer home in Goose Prairie, Washington, learned of the leak, he wrote Burger to assure him that he was not the source. "I am upset and appalled. I never breathed a word concerning the cases, or my memo, to anyone outside the Court."[148] But Burger decided to answer Douglas's memo "to keep the record straight, and to allow any future scholar who may peruse the current press accounts or papers of Justices to have the 'due process' benefit of all the facts in context, as I have tried to place them fairly."[149] Although Douglas answered in a more conciliatory tone, he maintained his original position on the assignment question.[150]

Burger's habit of attempting to use passes and delayed vote counting to get control of assignments and his efforts to encourage reargument to buy time caused considerable frustration. In the first major northern school desegregation case, *Keyes v. School Dist. No. 1*,[151] Burger tried to delay the opinion by calling for reargument in the next term when the Court would be facing the Detroit case. "Brennan shot back a short but devastating letter. 'If you have canvassed the Detroit issues, as I have, you might agree that none of them is even remotely connected with any decided in Keyes.' When Burger responded in turn, the bickering proved too much for Blackmun."[152] At that point, Blackmun cast the deciding vote for Brennan's opinion.

The manner in which process is handled can foment trouble in a host of other situations. The suspicion of a plain lack of fairness or respect makes matters worse. Thus, as noted previously, Thurgood Marshall was outraged by the fact that Chief Justice Burger wanted to press to deliver the Detroit school busing case despite the fact that Marshall had requested more time to complete his dissent.[153] More recently, Marshall publicly chastised his colleagues for using summary judgment, in some instances based upon nothing more than petitions for certiorari, to decide important cases.[154]

Some of these questions of internal Court practice are closely related to differences in style. Justices Powell and White experienced some early tensions of this sort. "Once White grew so exasperated with Powell's carefulness that he snapped his pencil in Powell's face and said he should make up his damn mind."[155] White's clerks treated Powell to lunch to make up for the bad feelings. "Powell 'graciously—but pointedly—replied that it would take more than one lunch to do that.' "[156]

Powell's biographer points out that Scalia and Powell were "like oil and water."[157] Scalia has had the same effect on some of his other colleagues, even ones who do not completely oppose his ideas. Marshall reacted to Powell in about the same way as the latter did Scalia. When Justice Ginsburg arrived on the Court and plunged immediately into active questioning of counsel in oral argument, some justices responded as Powell had to Scalia, when the Virginian leaned over and asked Marshall, "Do you think he knows that the rest of us are here?"[158]

Eventually, people who work together get used to new additions and their modes of behavior, as long as they remain within tolerable limits. The newcomers learn the ropes and the taboos. Working together closely can generate friction, but it can also build understanding. In the end, though, the conduct of members of the Court can promote as much conflict within the Marble Temple as the substance of their views.

CONCLUSION

At the end of the day, it's no wonder that there is conflict in the Court or that it takes so many different forms. It can emanate from so many causes. Those forces that shape conflict can be tied to things that happened even before one reached the Court. They can be based in ideology or early political experience. They can come from strongly held issue positions or the forces of change within the Court, even competing understandings of the very nature of the Supreme Court as an institution. They can emerge in small things, like differences over ways of working and procedural rules. They can also be larger issues like ego clashes or competition for leadership. They can even emanate from incompatible personalities and styles of interpersonal behavior on the bench or from tensions that come from the way one's colleagues reportedly behave off the bench.

It is, then, no surprise that there has been conflict among members of the Court over the years. It is useful to understand the motivations for that conflict not only because doing so might help those who seek to reduce it in the future but also because it helps us learn how members of the Court clash with one another and what difference that conflict can make. In the end, though, it is still amazing how well the members of the Court are able to monitor, constrain, and control these potential causes of battle, and to maintain their effectiveness and public image. Just as it is crucial to understand why they fight, it is also important to understand how they do it.

THREE

HOW DO THEY FIGHT?
THE PROFESSIONAL FIGHTS

A quite extraordinary event occurred on the last day of the Supreme Court's October 1988 term.[1] Justice Antonin Scalia issued a stinging, pointed, and seemingly quite personal attack on a colleague in the form of a concurring opinion. The case was a suit against a Missouri statute that was adopted as a deliberate challenge to the Court's 1973 *Roe v. Wade*[2] decision that recognized a right to abortion. What made Scalia's opinion so unusual was that it was not a criticism of the Court, or even a response to a dissenter. It was, rather, a public upbraiding of another concurring justice, Sandra Day O'Connor.

What made it worse was the public perception that Scalia was attempting to intimidate O'Connor into providing the crucial fifth vote that would reverse *Roe v. Wade*. That impression was reinforced because the *Webster* clash came just six months after a ruling in which Scalia had issued another stinging concurrence, this one aimed at the majority opinion prepared by O'Connor. Just to make certain that the point of his criticism was not lost, Scalia's *Webster* concurrence took O'Connor to task and cited her own opinion in the earlier case, *Richmond v. Croson,*[3] back to her.[4]

In both cases, Scalia implied that O'Connor lacked the courage of her convictions. In the *Richmond* case, she had struck down the particular minority preference in city contracting but did not hold that any such preference was per se unconstitutional for violation of the equal protection clause of the Fourteenth Amendment. Even so, her opinion made it nearly impossible to construct a satisfactory set-aside program at the state or local level. Scalia found exactly the same situation in *Webster*. He wrote: "I share Justice Blackmun's view . . . that it effectively would overrule *Roe v. Wade*. . . . I think that should be done, but would do it more explicitly."[5] He then promptly added that "today we contrive to avoid doing it, and indeed to avoid almost any decision of national import."[6] Just to make certain that there was no mistaking his point, no thought that Justice Rehnquist, author of the plurality opinion in *Web-*

ster, was the target, Scalia directed all but two brief paragraphs of his opinion directly at Justice O'Connor by name, not simply in footnotes but in the text of his opinion.

Scalia rejected the idea that O'Connor's refusal to cast the fateful vote to reject *Roe* could have been based on an attempt to avoid deciding constitutional questions unnecessarily. He also dismissed the notion that O'Connor's approach could be explained by "the quite separate principle that we will not 'formulate a rule of constitutional law broader than is required by the precise facts to which it is to be applied,' "[7] the argument advanced by O'Connor in her separate concurrence in *Webster.*[8] If that principle was so important, he asked, why was it that Justice O'Connor had done exactly that in two previous cases that term and two other cases in recent years?

Scalia then considered what he regarded as the consequence of O'Connor's lack of courage. He asserted that it

> preserves a chaos that is evident to anyone who can read and count. . . . We can now look forward to at least another Term with carts full of mail from the public, and streets full of demonstrators, urging us—their unelected and life-tenured judges who have been awarded those extraordinary, undemocratic characteristics precisely in order that we might follow the law despite the popular will—to follow the popular will. Indeed, I expect we can look forward to even more of that than before, given our indecisive decision today.[9]

Rejecting O'Connor's approach, Scalia insisted that "we should decide now and not insist that we be run into a corner before we grudgingly yield up our judgment."[10]

Scalia also pointedly dismissed as frivolous the question whether Missouri's abortion statute could be reconciled with *Roe.* "That question compared with the question whether we should reconsider and reverse *Roe,* is hardly worth a footnote, but I think Justice O'Connor answers that incorrectly as well."[11] Although he hardly thought the matter worthy of footnote, Scalia's note carried over to a substantial portion of the following page, in which he expressed reasons for doubting that the Missouri law could be said to pass muster under *Roe.* He then observed:

> To avoid the question of *Roe v. Wade*'s validity, with the attendant costs that this will have for the Court and for the principles of self-

governance, on the basis of a standard that offers "no guide but the Court's own discretion." . . . merely adds to the irrationality of what we do here today.

Similarly irrational is the new concept that Justice O'Connor introduces into the law in order to achieve her result, the notion of a state's interest in potential life when viability is possible.[12]

Of course, O'Connor had not invented that idea. It had been a part of the discussion of the basis for restrictions on abortion in the third trimester at the heart of *Roe*.

The bottom line, for Scalia, was that O'Connor was effectively holding the country hostage to an impossible legal situation. He wondered aloud what possible set of circumstances would be sufficient for the Court, clearly meaning O'Connor, to take on the clash between state antiabortion statutes and *Roe*. It appeared that engagement could not happen "unless one expects State legislatures to adopt provisions whose compliance with *Roe* cannot even be argued with a straight face."[13] He proclaimed that, of all of the possible ways to resolve this matter, the Court, once again clearly meaning O'Connor, had chosen "the least responsible."[14] Interestingly, Scalia concluded by concurring with the judgment of the Court but "strongly dissent[ing] from the manner in which it had been reached."[15]

Disagreement is one thing, but this type of public display of pique is another. It was not Scalia's position but the manner in which it was presented that was so problematic. There had never been any question of his position on the issue. It was equally clear that O'Connor was not prepared to support that position. Scalia's published opinion served apparently little purpose beyond ridiculing a colleague.

This chapter, then, considers the manner in which members of the Court conduct their disputes. What options are available? What weapons have been used in various circumstances? Consider the matter using the professional versus personal and internal versus external framework discussed earlier.

There is nothing new about hard-fought clashes between the Court's majority and dissenters. That history includes the important dynamic that authors of dissents or even concurrences have the freedom to write with a hardness of tone that would be unavailable to the writer of the majority position who must hold a coalition together. Nevertheless, the manner of public dispute has changed. Moreover, there are a number of means by which such contests are waged.

FROM THE BROADSIDE TO THE BATTLE OF THE FOOTNOTES AND BEYOND

Certainly the tradition of dissent is not new. The Court has witnessed, however, a movement from traditional dissents, which themselves could be quite harsh, to dissents that attack other justices in a particularly direct manner, though without naming the target, to dissents that speak directly to the wayward colleague in footnotes, and, most recently, to opinions (whether dissents or counter-concurrences) that attack a colleague by name in the text of an opinion, such as Scalia's diatribe against O'Connor.

The Dissent

The tradition of dissents began shortly after Chief Justice John Marshall guided the Court into the habit of delivering a unified opinion for the entire Court majority rather than seriatim opinions (delivered by each judge one at a time as in the British system). Justice Johnson filed more than two dozen separate opinions, mostly dissents, between 1825 and 1835, a time modern observers tend to think of as the period of Marshall's dominance.[16] Even Marshall, the great unifier, was known to dissent.[17]

Justice Henry Baldwin was a thorn in Justice Story's side for years because of his harsh dissents. In fact, Baldwin went so far as to write a general dissent to Story's *Commentaries* in the pages of the Court's official reports. "Story was so indignant that such a work had been published in the reports that he even upbraided his old friend Peters for letting it happen."[18]

Justice Peter V. Daniel was another early perennial dissenter.[19] "The first conspicuous quality of the new Justice was firmness in resistance to change, bullheaded intransigence, if one wishes to be charitable about it."[20] Daniel dissented more often than the Court's three other leading dissenters combined and more than twice as often as any other single member of the Court.[21] The character of his broadsides was best described as "ferocious, unyielding, and utterly humorless in dispute."[22]

Until relatively recently, discussions of dissents in the Court usually elicited recollections of Justices Holmes and Brandeis. Indeed, the mention of these justices often elicited a kind of word association with the answer being "Brandeis and Holmes dissenting." And there were indeed many times when the two found themselves taking on their brethren. Holmes's biographer recalls how contentious those days were.

> Fewer cases were decided, and more dissenting opinions were issued. Important matters were determined by narrow votes, statutes were struck down by votes of five to four, with bitter dissents, and no single view commanded a majority. When Holmes, for five members of the Court, upheld the constitutionality of a rent-control law, McKenna dissented in such violent terms, for a minority of four, that it was difficult to remain civil afterward. . . . In his dissent in *Block v. Hirsh,* 256 U.S. 135 (1921), McKenna asserted that the position Holmes had taken opened to the door to socialism.[23]

The dissents during the Stone era sometimes reflected the tensions within the Court. The frustrations felt by Frankfurter, Jackson, Murphy, and Black became increasingly obvious. Even during World War II, in such cases as the Japanese exclusion order ruling, *Korematsu v. United States,*[24] the dissents were strong, with Murphy and Jackson attacking Black's opinion for the Court as giving official sanction to historic racism and permitting gross unfairness in the form of irrational group punishment. Of course, Frankfurter's passionate and personal dissent in the flag salute case, *West Virginia Board of Education v. Barnette,*[25] was a defining moment in his relationships with other members of the Court.

Much to Harry Truman's chagrin, Chief Justice Fred Vinson's arrival did nothing to curb the conflict. Indeed, Vinson exacerbated it. By this point, Frankfurter had long since labeled Black and Douglas as "the Axis" and used every opportunity to wage war against them. That Frankfurter was clearly no longer an effective leader only intensified the tension at the Court.

As the Red Scare cases concerning prosecution of alleged Communists began to emerge, led by *Dennis v. United States*[26] in 1951, the tenor of the opinions made the interpersonal dynamics more apparent to observers outside the Court. Frankfurter's side triumphed in *Dennis,* but Douglas issued a ringing dissent. He was joined by Black, who added a brief opinion expressing sadness at the low ebb to which the Court had fallen and looking to a better day in the future. Frankfurter could not contain himself, and issued a concurrence—really an attack that the professor thought put the nails in the coffin of Hugo Black's absolute theory of the First Amendment.

Still, there prevailed a general tendency to avoid direct mention of an opponent's name in dissent. Although the knowledgeable observer knew beyond doubt the identity of the target, there was something calming about the formalism that one kept the clash impersonal. To cynics, that naive nicety might be regarded as silly, but, like so many modest informal structures, it reminded the members of the Court of outer boundaries.

As the work of the Court expanded, political tensions grew and membership on the Court brought different types of people to the bench. External signs of internal pressure became more apparent. One of the more obvious examples was the rising level of tension in the opinions by Fortas and Black as they squared off in a variety of cases. One of the battle-grounds between the two men was the so-called speech-plus cases in which parties asserted that the Constitution protected demonstrations and symbolic speech as well as more traditional expression. Black's literalist sensibilities were offended by interpretations of the language of the First Amendment that expanded it well beyond what he regarded as the common-sense understanding of speech.

Moreover, there were two more personal dimensions to the speech-plus fight, since Black himself had been the target of vigorous protests after his appointment to the Court when it became known that he had formerly been a member of the KKK. So intense were these attacks that Black and his wife felt it necessary to leave their home until calm had been restored. Then there was the fact that a number of protest cases arose in connection with civil rights demonstrations in the South, from the Freedom Riders to the lunch counter sit-ins. For Black these cases raised the specter of an attack by federal officials, including the Supreme Court, on southern states in particular, and a more general assault on the ability of all states to protect property and maintain the good order of the community.[27] Describing a case involving sit-ins in segregated libraries, one of Fortas's biographers observed that Fortas's opinion protecting the demonstrators

> drove Hugo Black to distraction. In an extreme and intemperate draft dissent, Black accused Fortas of being prejudiced against the

South. When he saw it, the chief justice tried to apologize to Fortas: "I am somewhat saddened by Hugo's dissent. It does not reflect the better part of his nature." While Black later tempered his dissent to secure the agreement of three colleagues, his final opinion still displayed to the world his growing displeasure with his new colleague. "I am deeply troubled," he wrote, "with the fear that powerful private groups throughout the Nation will read the Court's action, as I do—that is, as granting them a license to invade the tranquility and beauty of our libraries whenever they have a quarrel with some state policy which may or may not exist."[28]

This kind of clash between Fortas and Black continued and intensified in case after case. Black saw Fortas as the very embodiment of the kind of loose and personal interpreter of the Constitution that he had opposed since his days in the Senate. Fortas's views on the First Amendment, the due process clause of the Fourteenth Amendment, and several areas of constitutional criminal procedure were anathema to Hugo. For his part, Fortas rapidly came to resent what he regarded as a personal attack. The clash between the two men over the case brought by comedian-turned-civil-rights-leader Dick Gregory, who had been arrested in a Chicago protest, was an obvious example of their tensions. "Fortas began complaining that Black's early draft in the Gregory case had been nothing more than a direct attack against his own opinion. And he was right."[29] Eventually, the two men broke completely.

During the period of the Burger Court, the dissents intensified and the tone became increasingly bitter. The fact that President Nixon ran against the Court and promised to change it raised the level of visibility of the Court. Nixon's appointment of Chief Justice Warren Burger, the failed attempts at confirmation of Haynsworth and Carswell, the resignation under pressure of Justice Fortas, the impeachment attempt against Douglas, and the arrival of Justices Powell and Rehnquist all increased public awareness of the political complexity of the Court and its members.

The several commentaries that suggest that there really was nothing radically new or counterrevolutionary about the Burger Court[30] are not very helpful for understanding what was taking place within it. No, the Court did not directly overturn (and the word directly matters mightily) a raft of Warren Court rulings in the early going. Yes, they even issued rulings that expanded some areas of constitutional protection. By 1973, however, it was clear to Douglas, Brennan, and Marshall, at least, that the Nixon justices were willing to make dramatic changes. In the area of desegregation rulings, constitutional criminal procedure, civil due process requirements, constitutional protections available to government workers, establishment of religion cases, standing (and other Court access rules), and protection against discrimination for aliens and illegitimate children, this was a very different Court. Whereas White and Stewart increasingly joined the Nixon appointees, Douglas, Marshall, and Brennan more often found themselves in vigorous, though frequently futile, dissent. For example, from 1960 through 1970, Douglas published 171 dissents, or just over 15 per year. From 1971 through his departure from the bench in 1975, he authored 200, or 40 dissents per year, and that number includes his last year, during which his illness kept his total opinion production below what it had been previously.

Justice Brennan assumed the mantle of lead dissenter from Douglas and held it, along with Thurgood Marshall, through the 1970s and 1980s until his departure from the Court. During these years the Nixon appointees were joined, or in some cases replaced, by those named to the Court by Presidents Reagan and Bush. Brennan fought open battles in his dissents to protect the right to due process for those injured by government,[31] challenged the Court's changing position on First Amendment issues,[32] attacked the Court's efforts to curb access to abortion services,[33] and, most ardently of all, resisted with all his might the Court's inexorable move to support the death penalty.[34]

As indicated in Chapter 2, Thurgood Marshall spent the Burger and Rehnquist Court periods battling what he saw as a clear backward movement in many areas, not the least of which was the opportunity for aggrieved persons to prove that they had been victims of discrimination[35] and the ability of those victims or communities that sought to do so to craft remedies for past discrimination.[36] Actually, Marshall became reasonably adept at the fine art of judicial counterpunching, a tactic in which one cites the arguments of one's opponents against them. In *Bell v. Wolfish*, Marshall observed that the treatment of detainees in the Metropolitan Correctional Facility "is so unnecessarily degrading that it 'shocks the conscience.' " His language harkened back to Felix Frankfurter, who had originated it, and Rehnquist's willingness to set limits only where the shocks the conscience standard was satisfied. In effect, Marshall was challenging Rehnquist to actually apply the standard he said he was using to judge the case.

A more telling example occurred in a setting unrelated to civil rights. In a case involving judicial review of Occupational Safety and Health Administration standards for workplace exposure to benzene,[37] Marshall not only attacked the plurality opinion written by Stevens but also the concurring positions taken by Burger and Rehnquist. Marshall repeatedly cited the Court's unanimous opinion in *Vermont Yankee Nuclear Power Corp. v. Natural Resources Defense Council,*[38] which had been authored by Rehnquist. Rehnquist's *Vermont Yankee* opinion had lectured one of the Burger's and for that matter Rehnquist's least favorite judges, Judge David L. Bazelon of the D.C. Circuit, on the evils of interfering with agency decision making. In the Benzene case, Marshall accused the plurality and concurring justices of being guilty of precisely the same thing, except that they had favored nuclear power and opposed regulation to protect workers by the Occupational Safety and Health Administration (OSHA). In the end, he dramatically pinned the dreaded label of activist on these conservative justices who so often criticized their colleagues for their "activist" behavior. He likened them to Justice Peckham in the infamous case of *Lochner v. New York,*[39] quoting Justice Holmes's famous attack on conservative "activism." So often himself the target of conservative critics calling for "restraint" and attacking "activism," Marshall now used the same language to return the attack.

There is a current tendency to think of liberals like Marshall, Brennan, and Douglas as the type of justices who are usually dissenters. This trend derives in part from a historical clash within the Court during the pre-1937 years when reactionary justices like the infamous "four horsemen," Sutherland, Van Devanter, Butler, and McReynolds, sought to repeal the Progressive era and impose a rigid laissez-faire capitalism on all public policymaking at all levels of government. It was an effort, as Holmes put it, to enact "Mr. Herbert Spencer's social statics."[40] The tradition of dissent, however, is by no means limited to those who would be termed liberals today. Certainly Justice John Marshall Harlan kept the tradition of conservative dissent alive during much of the Warren Court period.[41]

The Devolution to Caricature and Cynicism

It was, in fact, a conservative who raised the ante in terms of the language and personal targeting of dissents. Justice Rehnquist was a dissenter long before he came to the Court. He was an ardent conservative in a less conservative age. He had never been reticent about voicing public and vigorous dissent. In Arizona, Rehnquist had risen in public meeting to protest desegregation efforts.[42] When he lost that fight, he wrote articles publicly attacking the movement. And when Rehnquist came to the Court, he was perfectly prepared to stake out a position on the far right of the Court and pull the center of gravity toward him if possible. He not only lashed out at the liberals when they were able to scrape together a majority, but he also went after his conservative colleagues when they seemed to compromise conservative principles.

Burger was willing to follow suit, though he was less adept than brother Rehnquist. Lewis Powell's biographer relates the story of Burger's reaction to the Williams murder case, in which the police effort to convince the suspect that his victim, a young girl, deserved a "Christian burial" was rejected by the Court as an acceptable means to obtain a confession.[43]

Burger was furious. He lashed out in an opinion so intemperate that his fellow dissenters (White, Blackmun, and Rehnquist) refused to join it. Burger expected this kind of nonsense from bleeding-heart liberals but not from Powell. He gave Powell "unshirted hell" about his vote—and not just in private. He took the unusual step of delivering his opinion orally, glaring down the bench at Powell as he read excerpts from his dissent. . . . The Chief's performance was so obviously personal that Powell's staff tried to pick up his spirits with a note to the bench saying they had "sent out for a bushel of rotten tomatoes."[44]

But it was Rehnquist who really set the tone, and in more ways than one. Rehnquist can be extremely warm and gracious in person, but he takes on an entirely different character when he writes. He is perfectly willing to be harsh and abrasive and to do it in a way that makes it difficult for his target, or anyone else for that matter, to avoid seeing the attack as pointed at the author of the offending ideas and not simply at the ideas themselves. Rehnquist was in large part responsible for the increasing tendency toward name calling during the 1970s that laid the groundwork for what has been termed "the battle of the footnotes," initiated, somewhat surprisingly, by Sandra Day O'Connor.

One of the most obvious early examples of name calling was Rehnquist's attack on Brennan's opinion for the plurality in the *Weber* case.

In that case Brennan wrote for the Court, arguing that Title VII of the Civil Rights Act was never intended to stand as a barrier to voluntary efforts by employers to redress existing discrimination. "Writing in 1979, [Rehnquist] suggested that the majority opinion 'could more appropriately have been handed down five years from now, in 1984, a year coinciding with the title of a book from which the Court's opinion borrows, perhaps subconsciously, at least one idea.' "[45] Rehnquist built his attack on Brennan on the theme that Brennan was using Orwellian logic. The civil rights act was, Rehnquist said, intended to bar all discrimination on the basis of race whether it was intended to help a disadvantaged group or hurt it, and no amount of "newspeak" (the Orwellian notion that with a sweep of the pen one can change history) should be permitted to confuse that purpose. Brennan replied that the entire point of the civil rights act was to remedy the sorry history of racial discrimination. To prevent good faith efforts to achieve that end was a perversion of the purpose of the law. But Rehnquist seemed to enjoy the sarcastic plays on words. In the end, Rehnquist charged that Brennan's opinion was " 'a tour de force reminiscent not of jurists such as Hale, Holmes, and Hughes, but of escape artists such as Houdini.' "[46] In another case, Rehnquist concluded that "the Court's opinion would make a very persuasive congressional committee report arguing against the adoption of the limitation in question."[47]

Brennan was by no means Rehnquist's only target. In the Columbus school desegregation case,[48] "He denounced the 'superficial methodology' of Justice White's opinion, calling it a 'lick and a promise' approach to the issue of racial balance."[49] "Finally, he likened the Court's majority to Pontious Pilate in washing its hands of 'disparate results' in school cases, and compared his colleagues to 'a bevy of Platonic Guardians' who ignored the public will. 'Whether the Court' result be reached by the approach of Pilate or Plato,' he concluded, 'I cannot subscribe to it.' "[50]

Similarly, Rehnquist took out after a plurality opinion prepared by White in *Florida v. Royer*,[51] a case involving a search and seizure of a man at Miami International Airport based upon a "drug courier profile." Rehnquist again unleashed a barrage of sarcasm, launching his dissent with a nursery rhyme.

The King of France
With forty thousand men

Marched up the hill
And then marched back again[52]

He declared that "the plurality's meandering opinion contains in it a little something for everyone"[53] and added: "The opinion nonetheless, in my view, betrays a mind-set more useful to those who officiate at shuffle-board games, primarily concerned with which particular square the disc had landed on, than to those who are seeking to administer a system of justice whose twin purposes are the conviction of the guilty and the vindication of the innocent."[54] When the plurality explained what the officers might have done that would have made the search consensual, Rehnquist replied, "All of this to my mind adds up to little more than saying that if my aunt were a man, she would be my uncle."[55] Suggesting that the plurality's attempt to explain the nuances of this sort of search merely masked a lack of real substance in its opinion, Rehnquist concluded: "If the plurality's opinion were to be judged by standards appropriate to Impressionist paintings, it would perhaps receive a high grade, but the same cannot be said if it is to be judged by the standards of a judicial opinion."[56]

Rehnquist's penchant for overblown rhetoric and ad horrendum argumentation has the effect of appearing to deliberately belittle his opponent. An example is found in Rehnquist's dissent in the flag burning cases, *Texas v. Johnson*.[57]

In his impassioned dissent, Rehnquist responded as if the Court were personally responsible for the death of the marines who died on Iwo Jima, fighting "hand to hand against thousands of Japanese." Rehnquist, who reportedly glared at Brennan when he read portions of his majority opinion from the bench, accused the senior justice in his dissent of giving a "patronizing civics lesson" to the Court. But the Chief Justice delivered his own civics lecture, devoting six pages to quotations from patriotic literature and poems, spanning American history from the Revolution to the Vietnam War. He again quoted Emerson's tribute to the "embattled farmers" who stood at the Concord bridge and "their flag to April's breeze unfurled." He sang the first verse of "The Star Spangled Banner," and recited all sixty lines of John Greenleaf Whittier's epic poem, 'Barbara Frietchie,' including her immortal—and apocryphal—words, "Shoot, if you must, this old gray head, But spare your country's flag."[58]

Rehnquist's overblown and often cynical rhetoric made the next step in the escalation of dissents appear relatively modest. Some of the first shots were fired by Sandra Day O'Connor in what is now considered the beginning of the battle of the footnotes. During her confirmation process there was discussion of just how the first woman on the Court would respond to the give and take, and there were questions about whether she would be tough enough. Anyone who knew anything about O'Connor's political and legal record before coming to the Court would have had few doubts. She was and is a tough-minded person who gives as well as she gets.

O'Connor by no means embodied the "freshman phenomenon," according to which the new justice maintains a relatively low profile within the Court and in public statements during the first year or two, learning the many unwritten rules of life in the Supreme Court. The new Justice O'Connor came out swinging in some of her first opinions, significant dissents that hammered the author of the majority.[59] In one case, O'Connor said of Justice White's opinion for the Court: "In short, if the Court hopes to support its result on the basis that a straightforward interpretation of statute 'makes little sense,' the Court errs, unless, of course, the 'sense' to which the Court refers is to be found, not in logic, but in the Courts view of what makes 'sense' as a matter of public policy."[60] White answered:

We would agree with much of Justice O'Connor's dissenting opinion if we accepted its premise that the language of the statute is "plain" in the sense that it can reasonably be read only as the dissent would read it. But we do not agree. . . . Given our view . . . much of Justice O'Connor's dissent is rhetorical and beside the point.[61]

Not surprisingly, O'Connor's footnote warfare included cases involving questions of federalism, issues about which she had firm convictions plainly at odds with several other members of the Court. O'Connor went after Blackmun in *FERC v. Mississippi,*[62] attacking his positions generally, but hammering Blackmun by name in her footnotes. Blackmun, not surprisingly, replied in equally direct terms. For his part, Blackmun had said in a televised interview that if "someone is going to play hardball with me, I'm going to play hardball back."[63]

Blackmun commented on O'Connor's version of constitutional history, which concluded that the power of the federal government was dramatically less than what is generally understood today: "If Justice O'Connor means this rhetorical assertion to be taken literally, it is demonstrably incorrect."[64]

After citing precedents against her position, Blackmun added: "Justice O'Connor's partial dissent finds each of these cases inapposite. Yet the purported distinctions are little more than exercises in the art of ipse dixit."[65] He challenged her repeatedly in footnote after footnote. Blackmun, like White in the *Abramson* case, called her on her rhetoric.

> Justice O'Connor's partial dissent suggests that our analysis is an "absurdity," . . . and variously accuses us of "conscript[ing] state utility commissions into the national bureaucratic army," of transforming state legislative bodies into "field offices of the national bureaucracy," of approving the "dismemberment of state government," of making state agencies "bureaucratic puppets of the Federal Government," and—most colorfully—of permitting "Congress to kidnap state utility commission." . . . While these rhetorical devices make for absorbing reading, they unfortunately are substituted for useful constitutional analysis. For while Justice O'Connor articulates a view of state sovereignty that is almost mystical, she entirely fails to address our central point.[66]

Not content to make his point and move on, Blackmun picked up each piece of loose rhetoric in O'Connor's opinion and hammered away: "Justice O'Connor . . . accuses us of undervaluing National League of Cities [v. Usery], and maintains that our analysis permits Congress to 'dictate the agendas and meeting places of state legislatures.' . . . These apocalyptic observations, while striking, are overstated and patently incorrect."[67]

O'Connor's clashes and the tendency of her colleagues to wade into the battle of the footnotes were not limited to federalism.[68] She provided an unusually candid public commentary on the battle of the footnotes in an interview with Bill Moyers.

Moyers: Are you deferential to each other?

O'Connor: Yes, very much so. Very courteous, always. I think every justice holds every other justice in very high regard and has great respect one for the other. It's a very civil group.

Moyers: But some of the opinions that go back and forth, I've heard of dueling banjoes and dueling swords, but some of the opinions are dueling as well.

O'Connor: The battle of the footnotes and so forth, yes.

Moyers: Are you writing those opinions for the other justices?

O'Connor: Yes, quite often. You know the real persuasion around here isn't so much done at our oral conference discussion as it is in the writing. . . . Having been here a while I understand why that's so. Because I think when you have time to sit down with pen in hand and reflect on these things and to spell out in writing with all the authorities mustered and set out, then you can be more persuasive than you could just giving oral thought off the top of your head at the oral conference.

Moyers: Do you have another justice in mind when you write?

O'Connor: Absolutely, sometimes you do. . . .

Moyers: Do you frame your language with him in mind. . . .

O'Connor: Sometimes.

Moyers: But they sometimes antagonize some of your colleagues, don't they?

O'Connor: That can happen too.

Moyers: One of your brethren scolded you a little bit for some of your language.

O'Connor: That can happen too.

Moyers: Did you answer him back?

O'Connor: Oh, I think there have been occasions when I've taken a stab at responding and others when I don't.[69]

Beyond the Battle of the Footnotes

It was a short jump from the battle of the footnotes to direct attacks by name in the body of the opinions. And although Justice Scalia has come to be the best-known practitioner of that form, its principal architect was William Rehnquist.

One of the harshest early examples came in 1982, a testy period. In *Is-*

land Trees Bd. of Ed. v. Pico,[70] which concerned the attempt to ban books from a high school library, Rehnquist blasted the plurality written by Brennan. In so doing, he directed his attack specifically and by name at Brennan, lashing out at him on almost every page (and nearly every paragraph) of the dissent. Rehnquist began, "I disagree with Justice Brennan's opinion because it is largely hypothetical in character, failing to take account of the facts as admitted by the parties . . . and because it is analytically unsound and internally inconsistent."[71] Only then did he take off the kid gloves. Rehnquist found that Brennan's opinion "first launches into a confusing, discursive exegesis" of the constitutional issues. "When Justice Brennan finally does address the state of the record, he refers to snippets and excerpts of the relevant facts. . . . Justice Brennan's combing through the affidavits, school bulletins, and the like for bits and snatches of dispute is therefore entirely beside the point at this stage of the case." Although he dismissed the constitutional argument as hypothetical and unnecessary to the case, Rehnquist challenged Brennan in that substantive area as well.

> But it is not the limitations which Justice Brennan places on the right with which I disagree; they simply demonstrate his discomfort with the new doctrine which he fashions out of whole cloth. It is the very existence of a right to receive information, in the junior high school and high school setting, which I find wholly unsupported by our past decisions and inconsistent with the necessarily selective process of elementary and secondary education.[72]

Each step, from references to "the Court" or "the dissent" to named attacks in footnotes to direct attacks in the body of opinions, seemed a more or less logical progression—an understandable escalation from the simpler, more formal and polite battles of an earlier time to the judicial street fights (or literary muggings) of the 1990s. Taken in their entirety, however, these transformations mark a substantial change in tone and an erosion, rather than an occasional breach, of unwritten but well understood rules of civil discourse on the Court. Passages written by justices like McReynolds that were regarded as scandalous at an earlier time are tame by comparison with contemporary public debate among the justices.

Dissents from Denials of Certiorari and Denials of Stay Petitions

Some of these impassioned exchanges have moved from the more or less standard dissent to the less common but recently popular filing of dissents from denials of petitions for certiorari and dissents from denials of stays of execution (or other kinds of orders).

Hugo Black jumped into his role on the Court quickly, so quickly in fact that Chief Justice Stone was shocked by his atypical behavior, particularly his readiness to dissent. Stone went so far as to write then-Professor Frankfurter to offer some tutoring to Black.[73] Among his more shocking tendencies was to offer dissents when the Court refused to grant review to cases Hugo thought meritorious, a practice he started in the 1940s and accelerated in the 1950s, when he was joined in the habit by William O. Douglas. Douglas later explained that the practice spread to other justices, as well.[74]

David O'Brien studied the patterns of these dissents from denial and concluded that the growth of the practice was both dramatic in numbers and pervasive in the sense that nearly all members of the Court participated.[75] Not surprisingly, O'Brien found that

the most ideologically opposed justices are likely to write opinions dissenting from denials. In 1980–1981 Rehnquist wrote 32 percent of the dissents from denials, whereas Brennan wrote 22 percent. By contrast, in 1987–1988, as the Court became more conservative because of Reagan's appointees. Brennan wrote 44 percent of all the dissents from denial of certiorari, while Rehnquist issued only three, or less than 1 percent, of all the dissents from denial. All the justices joined in one or more dissents from the denial of cases. But, after Brennan and Marshall left the bench and the conservative majority grew further with the arrival of Justices Souter and Thomas, the number of dissents from the denial of certiorari declined.[76]

During Brennan and Marshall's last years on the Court, they issued increasingly harsh dissents from denials of stays in death penalty cases. They did so principally because of their fundamental opposition to the death penalty itself, but also because they came to feel that there was a rush to judgment in which important issues and cases were simply ignored.[77] In his last year on the Court, Blackmun came to a similar conclusion and issued two intensely written dissents. In the first, Blackmun announced that after his many years of support for the death penalty, he had reached a point where he could no longer uphold it. In the second, a stay sought to block an execution by hanging in Washington State, he issued a dissent from denial very like the kinds of opinions for which Brennan had become known.[78]

Chief Justice Warren was generally opposed to dissents from denials,[79] but neither he nor any of his successors have been able to put a stop to the practice or even to curb its expansion.

Although legal scholars read such arcane essays as dissents from denials, few others do. Still, they are a device by which justices can vent their frustration and at least record the intensity of their anger at the unwillingness of the Court to undertake critical decisions that are in the dissenters' view essential. Today, however, even this equivalent of primal scream therapy is an occasion for conflict.

For example, in the last few months of his tenure on the bench, Justice Harry Blackmun concluded that he could no longer support the death penalty. In a dissent from denial of certiorari rendered in February 1994, Justice Blackmun wrote what was clearly an anguished personal statement. He declared:

> Twenty years have passed since this Court declared that the death penalty must be imposed fairly, and with reasonable consistency, or not at all, . . . and, despite the effort of the States and courts to devise legal formulas and procedural rules to meet this daunting challenge, the death penalty remains fraught with arbitrariness, discrimination, caprice, and mistake.[80]

Blackmun explained that his agonizing journey to this conclusion could be dated from the Court's decision in *McCleskey v. Kemp*,[81] decided in 1987, when he joined Brennan's dissent from the Court's rejection of the claim, based upon on the now-famous Baldus study, that the administration of the death penalty was fraught with racial bias. As he worked through this rending personal reckoning, Blackmun admitted with great pain the fact that "I voted to enforce the death penalty, even as I stated publicly that I doubted its moral, social, and constitutional legitimacy."[82] "From this day forward," he announced, "I no longer shall tinker with the machinery of death. . . . I feel morally and intellectually obligated simply to concede that the death penalty experiment has failed."[83] Hoping for the day when the Court would take the more difficult but, in his view, proper position, he concluded: "I may not live to see that day, but I have faith that eventually it will arrive."[84]

Scalia simply could not let it pass. He had to issue a concurring opinion that attacked Blackmun's dissent from denial of certiorari, specifying his anguished colleague by name. Unwilling to acknowledge the wrenching personal character of Blackmun's opinion, Scalia twice quoted with derision Blackmun's reference to his "intellectual, moral, and personal" obligation to enter his statement, however ineffectual. Then, as if to drive home his position of power in the midst of a majority firmly committed to the rapid enforcement of the death penalty, Scalia concluded by throwing what amount to needlessly defiant words at his soon-to-retire colleague. "If the people conclude that such more brutal deaths may be deterred by capital punishment; indeed, if they merely conclude that justice requires such brutal deaths to be avenged by capital punishment; the creation of false, untextual and unhistorical contradictions within 'the Court's Eighth Amendment jurisprudence' should not prevent them."[85] As in his attack on O'Connor in the Missouri abortion case, Scalia punished his colleague for a perceived character flaw.

CLASHES IN OPEN COURT

Readers of the published opinions might have been spared some of the truly rough edges of the relationships within the Marble Temple, but those present in the courtroom saw life on the Court in the raw. There were two different settings for these clashes. Sparks flew as a result both of behavior during oral argument and of broadsides in the form of the presentation of opinions, particularly dissents.

Presentation of Dissents

Taft found McReynolds's reactions to draft opinions and his manner of delivering dissents from the bench aggravating.

> Of his performance in the Carroll case, Taft reported: "McReynolds delivered himself without reference to his written opinion" in a

grandstand play to the galleries. Turning to the new member of the Court, Harlan Stone, Holmes remarked "that there were some people who could be most unmannerly in their dissenting opinions."[86]

Holmes's biographer, Sheldon Novick, recalled that "McReynolds . . . bitterly overruled a constitutional decision that Holmes had written for the Court, a precedent of twenty-five years' standing, angrily denouncing Holmes's decision as Holmes sat calmly beside him."[87]

Justice Murphy had little use for Justice Roberts, and the feeling was mutual. After one particularly harsh attack from the bench on one of Murphy's opinions, Roberts told Murphy that it was "nothing personal." Murphy responded that he did not like "some of the things Roberts was doing to the Court in his dissents."[88] It was a bitter time for Roberts, who dissented in 52 out of 156 cases in which there was a full opinion during that term.[89]

Others joined the fray as well. One of Murphy's biographers reported that

Murphy considered December 20, 1943, "an historic day" because of two "bitter dissents" by Black. . . . These dissents, which Black read in the court-room with 'fervent intensity,' were a prelude to the explosion that occurred on the next decision day, January 3, 1944. A journalist who attended the session reported that "everybody was going off in all directions, with concurring opinions, dissenting opinions, and philosophic dissertations coming thick and fast." There were twenty-nine separate opinions in the fourteen decisions announced that day, the Court speaking without concurrence or dissent in only two cases.[90]

Earl Warren may have been a considerably more skillful politician than Stone or Vinson, but he still had a temper. And it would have been asking the impossible to expect Warren to avoid losing his temper at the intemperate Felix Frankfurter. Frankfurter had a well-known tendency to deliver speeches from the bench that were purportedly announcements of dissents but often departed significantly from his published text. Bernard Schwartz reported on several such occasions.

Departing from his opinion's text, [Frankfurter] caustically complained, "I know what the court has said but I don't understand the meaning of it." Warren, evidently stung by Frankfurter's words, said that, "since so much has been said that was not in any written opinion," he wanted to explain why he joined the majority. After explaining extemporaneously, the Chief Justice invited Frankfurter to respond; the latter declined saying, "The Chief Justice urges me to comment on what he said, but of course I won't."[91]

Of course, Frankfurter was always in fine form when he thought he could get a rise out of one of his colleagues, since it allowed him to both go at his opponents and then play the innocent victim. Warren would have none of it. When, shortly after the last incident, Frankfurter again delivered himself of an extemporaneous harsh rebuke in the courtroom, he set Warren off. Warren, as Schwartz recounts the story, insisted that

Frankfurter was "degrading the court." "This is a lecture," the Chief Justice asserted. "This is a closing argument by a prosecutor to the jury. It is properly made in the conference room, but not in the courtroom. As I understand it, the purpose of reporting an opinion in the courtroom is to inform the public and is not for the purpose of degrading this court." Frankfurter then limply said, "I'll leave it to the record."[92]

Warren was clearly not Frankfurter's only target. Felix had seen Black as the leader of the opposition for years. Black felt the sting of Felix's barbs, but his experience of the rough and tumble of the Senate often allowed him to control his reaction in public. Douglas had no such tolerance. He wrote Hugo Black about what had occurred when he had presented one of Black's opinions while the author was away.

I handed down your dissent in Shotwell and your opinion for the Court in McGee and Green yesterday, and I hope I did them justice. The Green case got our friend from Harvard extremely excited. He went to great lengths on the bench to denounce it, departing from his printed dissent.
    At first he covered himself with ashes by pointing out that he was bitterly opposed to capital punishment and therefore viewed all these cases very compassionately. Having made that bow in the direction of the defendant, he then turned resolutely to the law and felt abso-

lutely compelled to follow the indistinguishable Trono case, on which he lectured for some time.

He denounced your opinion as containing falsehoods. He said your reference to the fact that the great majority of cases in this country have regarded the jury's verdict as implicit acquittal on a charge of first degree murder is false unless 16 equals 19.

When he got around to Lambert he also went hogwild. He said it would take a book to list all the criminal statutes which this decision held unconstitutional. Therefore, he did not want to clutter up the law books with all these hundreds or thousands of citations.

Since the announcement of his dissent, I have been writing him asking him to give us just one citation of one other statute which would be held unconstitutional.

It is now 11:40 AM, December 17th, and this has been going on for nearly 24 hours. He has not yet sent me any citations, but if he does I will rush it all down to you, because I know you must be as worried about the devastating effect of Lambert and Green as I am.[93]

Of course, Douglas absolutely relished the opportunity to catch Frankfurter in hyperbole and then to drive the point home with a demand for proof.

Despite the fact that Black had considerably more public composure than one might have imagined given his passionate commitment to principle, he could and did cut loose on occasion. And few members of the Court had the ability to set Hugo off like Abe Fortas. He was, for Black, the very symbol of what was wrong with the Court. Nowhere were their differences more pronounced than in the area of First Amendment protection for demonstration. One of Fortas's biographers described Black's response to Fortas's opinion for the Court in the library sit-in cases.

[Black] took the opportunity to express his outrage by delivering a thirty-minute oral tirade on the case. According to one reporter who heard it, Black's speech "made his strongly phrased written dissent seem pale by comparison." Trembling with rage, and periodically shaking his finger at the courtroom audience as he spoke, Black scorched Fortas with charges that his decision would lead "misguided" civil rights demonstrators to think that they would be "automatically turned loose, so long as whatever they do has something to do with race."[94]

By the Burger Court era, the practice of reading opinions, much less dissents, had declined sharply, replaced by relatively brief summaries presented from the bench on opinion days. Still, when their blood was up, some justices felt the need to make their point in public. Justice Blackmun explained his own decision to blast the Court from the bench in the Georgia case upholding sodomy statutes, *Bowers v. Hardwick:* "Well, about once a year, a dissent is announced from the bench. I've had it done against me. It was done against me in *Roe v. Wade.* And I can remember Justices Black and Harlan doing this, on occasion."[95] He let fly at his colleagues that day and felt not a little vindicated shortly thereafter when newspaper cartoonists around the country depicted variations on the theme of nine robed members of the Supreme Court banging on bedroom doors in the middle of the night.

Oral Argument Clashes in Court

Presentation of opinions represents a kind of blast at the end of a debate over a case. The frustration often occurs precisely because the battle has already been lost and there is nothing left for the losing side but to vent its anger and point out the errors of the majority. The situation is quite different, however, with respect to oral arguments.

Conflict during oral argument is in a sense an opening salvo in a clash that is unfolding, and the dynamics can be complex. It is certainly true that justices use the opportunity to ask counsel questions from which they may gain guidance for the drafting of opinions that will follow. There are, however, other dynamics at work as well. As a number of justices have pointed out, their behavior during oral argument is often intended to serve other ends and influence colleagues rather than simply to allow members of the Court to pose inquiries to an attorney in the case.[96]

The justices know when they come to the bench which four justices voted to hear the case. Usually, justices will not vote to take a case if they think it was properly decided below, with the exception of cases in which they wish to make a point. For the most part there is not enough time to hear cases where there is nothing to correct. In fact, over 70 percent of cases granted a hearing produce a decision to vacate, reverse, or remand the ruling in the court below.

Given that dynamic, justices can assume the preliminary position of four justices going into oral argument. They often also have a reasonably good sense of which of their colleagues have serious commitments to the other side of some of the issues. In many cases, then, the most astute members of the Court know who will likely be the one or two crucial votes if the outcome promises to be close. With that knowledge in mind, they can use questions to obtain information that will persuade a wavering colleague as the justices contemplate moving into conference and drafting opinions. By the same token, a justice may attack the positions of his or her adversaries by attacking the argument of the counsel presenting that case. As Justice Douglas put it, "I soon learned that . . . questioning from the bench was . . . a form of lobbying for votes."[97]

Apart from tactical uses, some justices have used oral argument to act out publicly some of the usually unseen conflicts within the Court. Far from planned tactical skirmishes, these public spats may sometimes simply be matters of the moment. Others are part of an ongoing pattern.

One example of the continuing public spectacle is the clashes between Frankfurter and Douglas. Frankfurter was a tempting target because, as Douglas saw it, he often treated lawyers arguing before the Court like law students who had to be taken down to size. During one argument, Douglas passed a note to Frank Murphy. "Why in hell don't you choke that torrent on your right? We shouldn't carry free speech too far."[98] When he was not too disgusted by Frankfurter, Douglas enjoyed needling him. There is a famous story of what looked like a tennis match between the two men. Each time Frankfurter would pose a question, Douglas would reply without hesitation. Finally, Frankfurter snapped, "I thought you were arguing this case." The somewhat dazed lawyer answered, "I am, but I can use all the help I can get."[99] On another occasion, Frankfurter blasted an attorney and repeatedly insisted that he provide "one case that stands for that proposition!" Justice Douglas looked over and replied, "Don't bother to send Justice Frankfurter the list he wants; I'll be happy to do it myself."[100] Douglas enjoyed the game, even when there was no particular reason for it. "When some incompetent soul was wasting our time trying to present a case, I often sent a note to Felix Frankfurter. Sometimes it read: 'I understand this chap led your class at Harvard Law School.' Sometimes it read: 'Rumor has it that this lawyer got the highest grade at Harvard Law School you ever awarded a student.' Almost always Felix would be ignited, just like a match."[101]

Douglas was not alone in his response to Frankfurter's public performances. Earl Warren became increasingly frustrated by the professor's courtroom behavior. During one argument, "Frankfurter interrupted Warren and reworded a question which the Chief Justice was putting to counsel. Warren angrily said: 'Let him answer *my* question! He is confused enough as it is.' Frankfurter bitterly retorted, 'Confused by Justice Frankfurter, I presume.' "[102]

Black had encounters with Frankfurter on the bench as well. Frankfurter recorded one such episode in his diary:

> I followed that question up by asking Fahy [then solicitor general], "Is it suggested that the Communist party has no principles?" At which Black turned to me with blazing eyes and ferocity in his voice and said, "The Hearst press will love that question." I replied, "I don't give a damn whether the Hearst press or any other press likes or dislikes any question that seems to me relevant to the argument. I am a judge and not a politician." "Of course," replied Black, "you, unlike the rest of us, live in the stratosphere." I made no further comment but resisted the impulse to say that in any event I do not change my views and votes on cases before this Court because of newspaper criticism.[103]

One of the reasons why Frankfurter's behavior in oral argument became the focus of so much frustration was because it consumed valuable time. As the workload increased over the years,[104] the pressure grew to move through the cases quickly. A thirty-minute argument for each side leaves each of the nine justices precious little time to ask questions. Hence the rumors of tension over Justice Ruth Bader Ginsburg's tendency to wade into the middle of the argument with numerous questions. Similar comments have emerged concerning Justice Scalia.[105] Scalia answers playfully that it is the academic devil within him that makes him do it.

BATTLE BY SURROGATE

While courtroom clashes and published arguments have tended to dominate attention, professional contests have been waged by other public mechanisms, including battle by surrogate. Surrogate conflict is a way of waging a battle indirectly, and it is in some respects at least a natural product of the institutional characteristics of the Supreme Court. The surrogates who do battle for their principals may be law clerks, former clerks, academics, journalists, political figures, or even other justices. Although there have been members of the Court who have intentionally rallied their champions to the cause, other justices have had surrogates whether they deliberately mustered them out for a fight or not.

Law Clerks: Today's Foot Soldiers and Tomorrow's Professional Leaders

There are few more ardent supporters of a justice than his or her law clerks. They are also among those most willing to take on that justice's adversaries. Years after they have left the service of the justice, they can still often be counted upon to take the field in the law reviews, in the classroom, or even on the bench, to champion their mentor's cause.

It is not that law clerks cannot be critical or that they are the mindless minions of a crafty judge. Indeed, the clerks are among the brightest graduates of the most prestigious law schools in the nation. In recent years, most have already successfully completed a clerkship in a lower court and often come to the Supreme Court with the sponsorship of a judge of a federal district court or U.S. Circuit Court of Appeals. They are bright, quick, strong, opinionated, and have enough stamina to make them ready to try to keep up with men and women more than twice their age who have already adapted to a work schedule that would kill many a younger lawyer.

They have been hired through a screening process unique to each justice often with the advice and support of law school professors, practitioners, and other judges. The application often carries not only an established respect for the justice in question, but a desire that the would-be clerk might develop a mentor/apprentice relationship with the judge. There is also the unspoken assumption that a successful intern can count on sponsorship from the justice after the clerkship year has ended. The fact of a clerkship and the existence of fulsome recommendations from a member of the Court are valuable professional tickets whether the clerk is headed for a faculty position at a leading law school, a government position, or private practice.

From the justice's point of view, important forces tend toward a close and supportive relationship. In the first place, the justice very much needs the help and effective performance of the clerks. Their work keeps a justice's chambers operating. From review of cert petitions, to bench memos, to research, to opinion drafts, to debate over positions the justice is contemplating, the clerks are extremely helpful. Although the clerks are only at the Court for a year, the working environment is intense, and it is very common for the justices to form friendships as well as good working relationships with their junior colleagues. Moreover, a justice who is willing to do so might easily develop a sense of parental concern (in the best sense) for the young person they have come to know.

Frankfurter, Black, Warren, and Brennan became particularly known over the years for the warm relationships they formed with their clerks. Black and his wife referred to the clerks as members of the family ("the boys,"[106] since most were young men). Frankfurter was well known as an ardent supporter of his best and brightest, with such luminaries as Philip Elman and Alexander Bickel able to boast his support. Warren's clerks found themselves with a great deal to do, since Warren often called upon them for opinion drafting even in very important opinions and before that practice was common at the Court. Bernard Schwartz told the story of how Warren nonetheless would occasionally decide that a particular afternoon absolutely demanded that his clerks join him at the stadium to take in a professional baseball game. It is no wonder, then, that the clerks often formed close supportive working relationships with their justices. Neither should it be surprising to find that they sometimes saw the chambers of their justice's adversaries as the enemy camp while they were at the Court and in the years to come.

As in most areas of intra-Court battle, Frankfurter became known for what Douglas called his use of "flying squadrons of law clerks," sometimes also known as "Felix's Happy Hot Dogs."[107] Frankfurter's adversaries cautioned their clerks that the Happy Hot Dogs would be sending their bosses messages and seeking intelligence about what was going on in other chambers.

When a new clerk joined Murphy for the 1943 term, he was "quickly indoctrinated" into the differences between his boss and Frankfurter. "How he hates Frankfurter!" the clerk observed of Murphy.

"FM referred to FF today as 'shit,'" the clerk recorded in his diary at the end of December 1943.[108]

More moderate justices were nevertheless known to warn their clerks about Frankfurter's gift of flattery and charm when the mood struck him.

Law clerks, even those working for the enemy, became accustomed to periodic visits and needling questions from Frankfurter. Most, like Justice Black's clerk, Marx Leva, listened politely but held to their loyalty and support of Justice Black. Rarely, with a Black clerk, like Max Isenbergh, Frankfurter was successful. The conversations between Frankfurter and Isenbergh developed into a rich, lifelong friendship. When Isenbergh joined the academic ranks, he did so as an avid proponent of Frankfurter's philosophy of judicial restraint. He even criticized his former boss, Justice Black, in terms that echoed Frankfurter's.[109]

Eventually, Frankfurter was no longer surprised to find that clerks from other chambers had been told to steer a wide birth around Frankfurter's chambers and to keep their mouths shut around his clerks.

After the early Warren-Frankfurter relationship had begun to change, the Chief became very concerned about what he saw as Frankfurter's attempts to subvert his clerks. As one clerk recalls it, "we were enjoined from falling under that sway and he as much as said, 'I know you're all quite young fellows from law school and here's this great professor, but don't let him sell you any beans.' And it took the form of a mild paranoia about contacts between his law clerks and Frankfurter, or even Frankfurter's law clerks.' For his part Frankfurter was, of course, also well aware of the Warren attitude. One time during the 1957 Term, Frankfurter asked one of the Warren clerks to come into his office, "unless, of course, I've been quarantined."[110]

Academics

Clerks often go on to become law professors and are then ideally situated to challenge their mentor's enemies in print. Some justices have called upon academics, former clerks or otherwise, to support their efforts on the Court. Consider just three examples.

The Frankfurter-Black battle was conducted off the Court as well as within it. The story of the relationship between Hugo Black and Alexander Meiklejohn is illustrative. It is a relationship for which, ironically, Frankfurter was in part responsible.

Professor Meiklejohn's interest in defending dissent was a longstanding concern that grew in the post–World War I years and intensified in the post–World War II period when he saw a reemergence of the same sort of reaction against dissent that had marked the Red Scare of the 1920s. Indeed, Meiklejohn was not only a scholar but a person of conviction who was discharged as president of Amherst College during the first Red Scare for defending free speech. As World War II came to an end, Meiklejohn began work on a defense of freedom of expression with the hope that he might head off another round of repression. His efforts culminated in a series of lectures fashioning a theory of First Amendment absolutism, later published in 1948 as *Free Speech in America and Its Relationship to Self-Government*.[111] Meiklejohn's work came at the same time that Black was developing his own absolutist view of the First Amendment as a member of the Court, articulated most clearly in its early manifestation in 1950.[112] Both concluded that the First Amendment posed an absolute prohibition to governmental interference with freedom of speech, including speech thought to be dangerous. For Black, the protection stemmed from the absolute language of the First Amendment and his understanding of history.[113] Meiklejohn believed it was a derivative right, the most important prerequisite to self-government.

The First Amendment views expressed by Black and Meiklejohn were, however, very much minority opinions. The Court's ruling in *Dennis v. United States*[114] upholding the convictions of the Communist Party leaders for expression of their ideology and association as a party (albeit with no specific alleged acts of subversion) presented the issue of the meaning and limits of the First Amendment in such stark terms that it virtually compelled members of the Court to confront their own fundamental views of the freedom of speech. Justices Black and Douglas dissented, with Douglas writing the lead dissent. Black added a short note to the effect that the Court would one day come to its senses and sweep the *Dennis* ruling into the ash heap of history.

Frankfurter contributed a counter-concurring opinion, intended not so much to speak to the majority ruling but to reply to Douglas and, more important, Black. Rejecting the notion that the First Amendment was intended to add any protections for speech beyond those available to Englishmen,[115] Frankfurter concluded that the determination of the limits of political freedom should be left to the legislature, whose decision should be upheld so long as it was not patently unreasonable.

The manner in which Frankfurter chose to attack Black forged the alliance between Black and Meiklejohn. Frankfurter criticized Black's approach indirectly, by chastising Meiklejohn, using what Meiklejohn later referred to as criticism by caricature.[116] Moreover, Frankfurter cited criticisms of Meiklejohn from a book review by Zechariah Chafee in the *Harvard Law Review*.[117] Frankfurter knew full well that what appeared to be a mere reference to an academic commentary was far more. His old friend from Harvard Law faculty days, Zech Chafee was a party at interest. Chafee was the author of *Free Speech in America*,[118] in which he criticized the First Amendment approach taken by the Court during the first Red Scare and advocated the "clear and present danger" standard announced by Justice Holmes in *Schenck v. United States*.[119] Criticism of that standard and of Chafee's argument in support of it was at the core of Meiklejohn's argument. The decision to have Chafee write the review guaranteed the attack. Frankfurter knew exactly what he was doing when he used Chafee's critique to assail Meiklejohn and, by clear implication, Hugo Black.

Meiklejohn's answer was to attack Frankfurter's *Dennis* concurrence in the pages of the *University of Chicago Law Review*.[120] Among other things, he pointed out that the same Frankfurter who so dramatically condemned absolutes with respect to free speech had no difficulty advocating an absolute separation of church and state.[121] Meiklejohn was saddened by what he saw as a breach of constitutional faith by Frankfurter, the same Felix who had helped him when he was under attack at Amherst: "May I add as a final summary, that I find it hard to understand how my good friend, the Justice who so steadfastly guards from usurpation the authority of the legislature, can so easily overrule the authority of the Constitution itself, can substitute for its wisdom the wisdom of the Court of which he is a member."[122]

Meiklejohn battled Chafee and Frankfurter in the journals, in the pages of the *Harvard Crimson,* and even before Congress as he brought a petition for a redress of grievances against the abuses of the House Un-American Activities Committee.

Black dissented in part in *Yates v. United States* in 1957, the second of the Communist Party leadership cases. By that time the composition of the Court had changed, and there were sufficient votes to substantially undermine the *Dennis* opinion, though the *Yates* majority avoided admitting a direct intention to overturn the earlier ruling. Black, however, insisted that the Court face directly the need to eliminate the political speech prosecutions. In the process, he cited Meiklejohn's interpretation of the First Amendment over Chafee's.[123] Meiklejohn wrote Black:

> May I send just a note to tell you that it gave me great pleasure to see your reference to me in your concurring-dissenting opinion in the Yates case? Even though I can do it only as an amateur, I delight to be travelling the road which you have followed with what seems to me clear and steadfast vision. For whatever it may be worth, I make a guess that the tide of Constitutional battle has turned your way and that more decisive victories will come soon.
> P.S. I'm glad you brought Chafee in too. I wish it were not too late to get you to arbitrate between him and me.[124]

Meiklejohn then sent Black a copy of his petition for redress of grievances to the Congress. Black's *Barenblatt*[125] dissent lambasting the abuses of HUAC paralleled Meiklejohn's petition. Meiklejohn, who was in New York City when excerpts from the just-announced decision were published in the *New York Times,* wrote Black to express pleasure with his rendering. In conversations with Black, Meiklejohn encouraged him to deliver the James Madison lectures at New York University. In those lectures, Black, like Meiklejohn in his *University of Chicago Law Review* piece, issued pointed criticisms of Frankfurter's reasonableness approach with its overlay of legislative primacy in matters of the First Amendment.[126] In the end, Black said, "The phrase, 'Congress shall make no law' is composed of plain words, easily understood. The Framers knew this."[127]

When he received a copy of the address from Black, Meiklejohn applauded the "direct and forthright denunciation of F.F.'s denial of the absoluteness of the First Amendment," which "will do a lot of good where such goodness is sorely needed."[128]

It was not long before Justice Frankfurter's leading champion, Alexander Bickel, responded. He published his critique of Black's Madison lecture entitled, "Mr. Justice Black: The Unobvious Meaning of Plain Words," in the *New Republic*.[129] Bickel cast the argument between those who agreed with Black's approach to constitutional interpretation and those who preferred Frankfurter's. In the end, he argued that Black was really using his insistence on the absolute language of the First Amendment to hide his creation of First Amendment protections that never existed. He concluded: "The question remains, in a sense, one of candor, but it is more complicated than that. I should say that it is a question . . . of the utility of illusions and of the justifications for creating them."[130]

Meiklejohn knew precisely what was going on between Felix and his former clerk. He immediately proposed to Black that he would write a reply to Bickel's article and asked Black's leave to proceed.[131] Black indicated that he had no objection but that he personally was not about to read Bickel's article, let alone be involved in any reply to it. "I can well imagine what Professor Bickel would say. He was Justice Frankfurter's clerk and at present his intimate friend and advisor. The result of this is that he largely reflects Felix's views. I respect those views very much but prefer to hear them discussed by the man who originates the concepts."[132]

It was, in the end, unnecessary for Meiklejohn to reply, for John P. Frank, one of Black's former clerks, issued a response that was about as direct as was decently possible. "Professor Bickel," he wrote, "could not have done less justice to the thread of Black's argument if he had set after it with a hatchet. . . . The Black view is and has been a minority view. The law is as Professor Bickel and his judicial heroes would have it."[133]

Then came a piece in the *New York Times Magazine* by Anthony Lewis that characterized Black as the leader of the minority "activists" against Frankfurter's group. At the time, William O. Douglas was livid. He was absolutely convinced that Lewis had been supported for a Newman Fellowship at Harvard Law School by Frankfurter and that he was repaying his mentor with this attack on Black. Later, in his autobiography, Douglas softened his views somewhat, though he gave Lewis a kind of backhanded compliment.

Frankfurter's drive was to get newsmen to study law at Harvard, and some did, notably Anthony Lewis, one of the ablest journalists of my time. Newsmen who study law usually become advocates of a particular type of jurisprudence that dominates the law school where they went, so they are apt to bring to their reporting the prejudices of one school of thought or another. Tony Lewis grew out of that stage; some never did.[134]

Black knew what his champions were doing, but he did not enlist soldiers and sometimes even called them off. John Frank once sent Black a draft copy of his review of Samuel Konefsky's biography of Frankfurter. The review contained comments about Frankfurter's obnoxious behavior on the Court, but Black warned him off. Black replied, "I am compelled to state that if left up to me, I should prefer that it not be published."[135] He added: "New situations are developing which I think you should bear in mind in connection with the publication. There are ominous signs that Justice Frankfurter is about to be made the target of powerful forces gathering strength from the present national hysteria. Should these forces not be arrested, I have no doubt that you would be 100 percent on the side of the Justice."[136]

What made Frankfurter's use of surrogates so troublesome was that his colleagues knew exactly what he was up to.[137] Justice Brennan, who was about as controlled as any member of the Court could be, came to "a parting of the ways" over his behavior.[138] "When Felix didn't get his way, he was like a child. In his letters to friends like Hand and Burlingham he would unburden his soul about those who didn't agree with him. But his views were distorted. And yet right afterward, when we saw eye to eye, he believed we saw the light of day."[139] This commentary came as a result of the battle over *Trop v. Dulles*.[140] The day on which the opinion was announced was a difficult one. Anthony Lewis referred to the justices' remarks in the courtroom as "bitter, even waspish."[141] Warren delivered the opinion for the Court and, although the point was not made in his published opinion, argued that the Court's ruling was justified by eighty-one cases in which the Court had struck down legislation. Frankfurter responded in presenting his dissent, though no such comment appears in the published version, that "these eighty-one cases are nothing to boast about."[142] Frankfurter then wrote to his surrogate, Alexander Bickel, suggesting that it would be a good idea to study the eighty-one cases to which Warren referred with the obvious intention of generating another piece critical of Warren and company.[143]

Brennan's biographer, Kim Eisler, tells the story of a battle between the two men in conjunction with *Irvin v. Dowd*.[144] Brennan had written for the Court, managing to attract the essential fifth vote from Justice Stewart. Frankfurter not only wrote a stinging dissent but enlisted the aid of surrogates in the academic community to attack Brennan. "He then encouraged a distinguished Harvard professor, Henry Hart, to focus on the case in the 1959 edition of the *Harvard Law Review*."[145] Warning that "first-rate lawyers are losing confidence in the Court,"[146] Hart went after Brennan's *Dowd* ruling as a primary example of the lack of quality and craftsmanship that was causing the concern. Eisler explained that although Brennan was not inclined to reply, his friend Judge David L. Bazelon convinced him that a response was necessary. Bazelon then offered to arrange for someone at Arnold, Fortas, and Porter to do the job. Bazelon and William O. Douglas prevailed upon Thurman Arnold to act as Brennan's champion with an article to be published in the *Harvard Law Review*. In his critical essay, Arnold referred to Hart's charges against Brennan as "fantastic" and insisted that the matter had more to do with conservative lawyers opposed to any change than with competence.[147]

There is little doubt that Frankfurter was the most active surrogate warrior in the history of the Court, but he was far from the only one. Professor Charles Fairman sent justices Jackson and Frankfurter, Black's leading opponents on the Court, advance copies of an article he was about to publish in the *Stanford Law Review* attacking Black's interpretation of the Due Process clause of the Fourteenth Amendment.[148] Jackson wrote back, congratulating Fairman on his historical work on the Fourteenth Amendment, which had, in his view, thoroughly discredited Black's argument.[149] Jackson went so far as to solicit Fairman's assistance as an advisor in *Sweatt v. Painter* and other civil rights cases then before the Court. In asking Fairman's help, Jackson saw himself as doing nothing unusual. He wrote:

> I know of no one who had made so thorough and disinterested a study of the origins and history of the Fourteenth Amendment as you have done. The work of the Court leaves no time to begin to approach your research. Yet we are probably faced with as important Fourteenth-Amendment decisions as any that have been rendered. Frankly, I should like to draw upon your store of knowledge. I suppose you have no interest in the litigations other than the intellectual interest which any legal scholar would have. It is considered quite permissible for a Justice to rely on the knowledge and opinion of a boy just out of law school to contribute to his judgment. I know of

no reason why one should be foreclosed from consultation with more experienced and matured minds, if they are disinterested.[150]

Jackson knew that he was not only fostering a surrogate relationship for battle outside the Court, but obtaining the assistance of an outside consultant who could help wage the war within the Court.

These communications with others outside the Court, even when they were not requests for surrogate battle, did serve to bolster justices in their own fights. Frankfurter's correspondence with Harold Laski and Learned Hand are classic examples.[151] Justice Stone's correspondence with Professor Thomas Reed Powell furnishes another instance. "The acerbic Thomas Reed Powell wrote Stone that Homer Cummings had said that, with Murphy's appointment, the number of justices would be increased to twelve since Murphy would 'bring with him as colleagues Father, Son, and Holy Ghost. With those Three and the Constitution itself as mentors,' Powell observed, 'we ought to get some fine constitutional law in the future.'"[152]

The final variation on surrogate battle is the encouragement of one's colleagues within the Court to undertake a fight. Again, Frankfurter was the leading, but by no means the sole, practitioner of this brand of warfare. One of the most divisive examples was Frankfurter's encouragement of Jackson's clash with Black over the *Jewel Ridge* case and the alleged effort by Black to block Jackson's elevation to the center chair. Frankfurter wrote Jackson, "I want you to know, that the facts as you set them forth in your Nuremberg statement gives an accurate account in every detail of what actually took place."[153] After a book entitled *The Truman Merry-Go Round* charged that Frankfurter had informed Jackson of the newspaper story that set off the storm, Felix wrote to Black denying that he had been involved or that he had encouraged Jackson. Although Black responded that Frankfurter should not be concerned about the book's claims, he told his son that he was sure that Frankfurter had been behind it.[154]

THE PUBLIC PRESS CAMPAIGN

Several members of the Court have maintained good relationships with particular reporters or publishers. These relationships have precipitated correspondence over coverage of Court activities and opinions. There have even been occasions when members of the Court have attempted to use the press to support their internal battles. Melvin Urofsky tells the story of how Felix Frankfurter launched a publicity campaign in support of his dissenting opinion in the flag salute case. "He wrote friends in the press such as Bruce Bliven of the *New Republic* and Frank Buxton of the *Boston Herald,* and pointed out that Learned Hand and Louis Brandeis had agreed with his Gobitis opinion."[155]

Perhaps the most obvious effort was Justice Stone's engineering of a criticism of Hugo Black not long after his arrival. Among other things, Stone disliked the fact that Black did not act like a junior justice. Black immediately launched a career as a dissenter, issuing eight such opinions in as many months.[156] "Audaciously, Black had even dissented from an unsigned opinion supported by all eight of his colleagues. By tradition, that simply was not done."[157] Stone began the habit of taking morning walks with Marquis Childs of the *St. Louis Post-Dispatch,* explaining the problems he saw with Black and worrying that President Roosevelt might make other such appointments. Childs published those concerns in January 1938.[158] Stone told Childs that his article was "what is needed to educate the public," but he asked why the journalist did not go further and publish the message more broadly. He did, in an article in *Harper's* in May. Writing of Black's transgressions in even greater detail than in the newspaper articles, Childs said of Hugo: "It is as though a comparatively inexperienced player had stepped into a fast game, say tennis or pelota, and, ignoring the rules, made vigorous passes at every ball with a piece of board."[159] It was clear that Childs had an informant in the Court, and it became increasingly obvious that it was Stone.

William O. Douglas was accused on several occasions of leaking information to the press, though he consistently denied having done so.

TAKING THE BATTLE TO ANOTHER POLITICAL INSTITUTION

Members of the Court have sometimes become involved with other branches in ways that represent a kind of argument in another quarter. One of the more obvious contemporary examples is the involvement of Chief Justice Rehnquist in the death penalty debate in Congress.

Chief Justice Rehnquist is a long-time supporter of the death penalty. By the late 1980s, he and his other pro–death penalty colleagues appeared not only to have obtained a more or less unbeatable majority supporting the penalty, but also to have swept away a number of the last remaining barriers to substantial numbers of executions. Those victories, however, had come at the cost of serious disagreements within the Court. Whereas Brennan and Marshall had been continuous opponents, a number of cases heated up the debate and began to shake members of the Court who had been supporters, like Blackmun and Powell. The most important of these cases was the 1987 *McCleskey* ruling,[160] which rejected the Baldus study showing the prevalence of racial discrimination in the application of the penalty. The number of death penalty cases before the Court was increasing as the population of death rows around the country approached 3,000 and virtually everyone, supporters and opponents alike, were thoroughly dissatisfied by the lack of well-organized means for addressing various types of appeals. In summer 1988, Rehnquist appointed a committee chaired by then-retired Justice Powell to look into the process. A deal had been struck between those who wanted a thorough study and Senate advocates of strong legislation limiting federal habeas corpus review of death penalty cases. Under the arrangement, the chair of the Senate Judiciary Committee would wait for the transmittal by the chief justice of the United States of the Powell report. At that point the chair was required to introduce legislation in three work weeks or less.

Powell's report went public in August 1989, but the Judicial Conference (the national governing body of the federal judiciary) voted not to transmit the report to Congress until its March 1990 meeting.[161] That delay would allow time for consideration of the report before triggering a fast-track legislative process. After the conference action, Rehnquist simply took it upon himself to transmit the report in any case, concluding he was not bound by the conference (nor, obviously, by the reaction he had to know would be aroused in some of his Supreme Court colleagues).

Around the nation outraged judges exploded against Rehnquist's patent disregard of collegiality. His behavior undermined the report in Congress as well, and its recommendations went down to defeat.[162] The turmoil surrounding this misadventure, the nature of the opinions in death penalty cases, and a refusal by the Court to grant certiorari in several potentially important cases pushed Blackmun into opposition to the death penalty. For his part, Powell told his biographer in 1991 that he regretted

his vote in *McCleskey* and indeed had come to believe "that capital punishment should be abolished."[163]

THE ATTACK BY ADMISSION OF PRIOR ERROR

At the other end of the spectrum from the extremely public clash is the
more subtle but quite effective technique in which a justice attacks his or
her opponents by admitting, and redressing, former error. It is an interesting tactic, a kind of passive art of battle.

Justice Douglas offers a classic example. He admitted that he had been
wrong to think that it was possible, as Hugo had argued in *Everson v. Bd.
of Education in 1947,* to maintain an effective separation of church and
state while finding ways for there to be some kind of support for church-
related activities. Douglas wrote in *Walz v. Tax Commission:* "The *Everson* decision was five to four and, though one of the five, I have since had
grave doubts about it, because I have become convinced that grants to institutions teaching a sectarian creed violate the Establishment Clause."[164]
To make the point even more strongly, Douglas appended to his *Walz* dissent a copy of James Madison's "Memorial and Remonstrance." Madison had contended that even so much as "three pence" worth of support
was too much. Justice Rutledge had used the same text in his *Everson* dissent, attempting to hit Black over the head with just how wrong he was by
using the admonitions of a hallowed founding father.

Brennan, meanwhile, had spent a great deal of time and effort during
the ruling in *Abington School Dist. v. Schempp,* 374 U.S. 203 (1963), attempting to find vehicles of accommodation. The resulting concurring
opinion was the length of a small monograph and considered ways to
avoid head-on clashes over religious practices. In *Marsh v. Chambers,*[165]
Brennan repudiated his prior optimism about the possibility of finding
ways around the separation barrier. "He wrote in 1983 that, 'after much
reflection, I have come to the conclusion that I was wrong' in approving
those 'forms of accommodation' he surveyed in his Schempp concurrence."[166]

In 1972 Brennan had done something similar in the obscenity area
when he produced his voluminous memorandum on the history and development of obscenity statutes. At the end of his study he concluded
that it was not possible to develop a sufficiently clear standard that

avoided First Amendment interference with protected expression. He announced his intention in the future to rule against obscenity convictions unless they concerned sales to minors or were cases in which the materials were thrust upon unwilling recipients.[167] The fact of his considered switch lent power and credibility to his position.

CLASH OVER COURT OPERATIONS

Disputes over doctrinal positions have gone public since the earliest days of the Supreme Court. Most disputes over the operation of the Court itself have tended to remain internal. Recently, however, even these disputes have been taken to the public arena.

During the Burger Court years, in particular, the debate over the work load of the Supreme Court and how to deal with it occurred outside the Court as well as within it. The docket debate was fought out at two very different levels. At one level, the docket question was in fact what it appeared to be, an argument about how the Court was to handle a burgeoning case load, particularly the huge number of prisoner appeals brought in the form of petitions for certiorari.

At another level, opponents argued that Burger's efforts to reduce the docket and handle the business of the Court more efficiently were anything but a relatively neutral administrative project. Douglas, Brennan, and Marshall considered Burger's attempt part of an overall effort to make the Court less available to the poor and the disenfranchised. Efforts to screen cases, reduce or eliminate three judge federal district courts with direct appeals to the Supreme Court, move most review of certiorari petitions to a certiorari pool made up of law clerks, tighten standing rules, and reduce federal habeas corpus attacks on state convictions were not neutral for people like Douglas, Brennan, and Marshall. These innovations reflected, in their view, a distinct bias against the poor, the weak, and the members of racial minorities. Brennan had served with Frankfurter, and he knew about what Gerald Gunther has referred to as "the Subtle Vices of the Passive Virtues,"[168] the ability to obtain conservative outcomes by simply finding ways to avoid ruling on the cases.

Support for Burger's recommendations for a mini–Supreme Court was, therefore, far from unanimous. Douglas argued that the docket was manageable and draconian measures unnecessary.[169] Brennan took the high ground, arguing that to have a meaningful effect on the docket, the mini-Supreme Court ideas would present serious constitutional difficulties, because they would, in effect if not in terms, challenge the Article III requirement that there be "One Supreme Court."[170]

One device for disposing of cases that has provided a focus for continuing dispute is the use of summary dispositions to decide important cases. The use of summary dispositions increased during the Burger Court period when the Court decided important issues on summary dispositions without even receiving briefs on the merits of the case. Parties are prohibited from arguing the merits of their case in their certiorari petitions; they may only argue why the Court should take the case. Nevertheless, the Court's first significant ruling on gay rights[171] and a major ruling on free press questions was resolved by summary judgment.[172] Brennan, like Marshall and others, reacted strongly against the use of summary judgments to avoid a full treatment within the Court of difficult cases.[173] He wrote: "No spectre of increasing caseload can possibly justify today's summary disposition of this case. The Court's erosion today of [an important principle] without even plenary review reaches a dangerous level of judicial irresponsibility."[174] He continued, "The increasingly alarming penchant of the Court inappropriately to invoke its power of summary disposition could not be more evident than in this case."[175] He was frustrated by the fact that the Court had issued a very important ruling in a brief per curiam opinion with "the benefit of neither full briefing nor oral argument."[176] He observed further that this case was a significant, but by no means the only, example of a growing practice.

> Today's decision is profoundly disturbing not only because the Court has misused precedent . . . , but also because it represents yet another instance of this Court's "growing and inexplicable readiness . . . to dispose of cases summarily. . . ." I am, of course, cognizant that, because of an ever-increasing docket, the Court has come under extraordinary pressure to accelerate its disposition process. But I do not believe that summary disposition on the basis of the certiorari papers is a proper response to such pressure where, as here, it is employed to change or extend the law in significant respects. Here, the Court reverses the judgment of the Court of Appeals, which had the benefit of our decisions, a concrete record, and a thoughtful District Court opinion. . . . I can only believe that the Court perceives this

case as one in which the narrow Rummel ruling . . . can be extended
to new terrain without the necessary exertion of argument and briefing. . . . I dissent from this patent abuse of our judicial power.[177]

Marshall also used this specific issue to vent his frustration with a number of efforts by his Burger Court colleagues to close the doors.

I write separately to underscore my disapproval of what I perceive to
be a growing and inexplicable readiness on the part of this Court to
"dispose of" cases summarily. Perhaps this trend is due to what is
often lamented as our "increasing caseload." Whatever the reason
for this trend, I believe that it can only detract from this Court's decisions in deserving cases by consuming time and energy better spent
elsewhere.[178]

Interestingly, the publicity generated around some of the speeches and
articles by Marshall, Stevens, and Brennan drew attention to clashes
within the Court and brought some journalists to say of the Burger Court
that "it became a contentious Court for a contentious society."[179]

CONCLUSION

There is a rich history of conflict in the Court. Even in matters of external
professional clashes, there is a wide choice of weapons and a host of strat-
egies and tactics. Although some warriors have been particularly note-
worthy for their energy and aggressiveness, the process of conflict traces
itself to the earliest days of the Court's history and has involved a wide
range of personalities and ideologies.

It does seem to be true, however, that the nature of conflict has esca-
lated and changed, at least by degrees, over the years. The moves from attacks on one's adversaries but without reference to them by name, to battle by surrogate, to the relatively harsh and even cynical language about
"the dissent" or "the majority," to the battle of the footnotes, to the
head-on clash by name in the text of opinions, to public statements criticizing colleagues mean that conflict is different now.

Frequently, the public clashes reflect internal disputes or, in some instances, are made more intense by internal but perhaps unrevealed ten-

sions. The internal professional conflicts are what most scholars of the Court consider common. With effort, those disputes might remain unseen unless the need were truly pressing for appropriate and careful disagreements in the writing of opinions. It is clear, however, that internal disputes are part of the working life of the Court, even when they remain professional rather than personal in character. When they do turn personal, then life at the Court may become more complex and difficult than it would otherwise be. It is to the ways in which these internal professional and personal conflicts are waged that we now turn.

FOUR

HOW DO THEY FIGHT?
INTERNAL AND PERSONAL BATTLES

Internal disputes among the justices over professional matters are at the very core of collegial decision making. Moreover, personal disagreements are inevitable features of an institution made up of strong-willed, independent, successful men and women who are appointed for life to an important position in national government. It is not at all uncommon for professional and personal tensions to blend in any particular dispute; indeed it is not always clear that even the justices themselves know precisely where the professional ends and the personal begins. One of the most difficult situations for the Court as an institution arises when the clashes become both personal and public.

INTERNAL PROFESSIONAL DISPUTES

Notwithstanding the many public professional clashes among the justices, the internal battles have been more numerous and, in a number of respects, more vigorous. The general categories of conflict that have been with the justices through the years include conference contests, management of alliances, leadership battles, clashes over workways, and threats to go public.

Conference Battles

A certain irony inheres in the fact that the conference—perhaps the best-known symbol of collegiality within the Court, dating back to the days of conversation after dinner at the boarding house where John Marshall and his associates resided—became in later years an arena for conflict. This evolution, however, should come as no great surprise. After all, in the days before construction of the Supreme Court building, the justices maintained chambers in their homes and only saw each other when they sat in court or when they met in conference. Since it was generally regarded as poor form to wage a fight in public, the conference was the logical forum for conflict. Thus it became something different than an after-dinner conversation. In the modern age, members of the Court have often remained surprisingly aloof from one another, except in sitting for arguments and opinion delivery or in conference.

There are in fact two conferences, the sitting conference and the continuing conference. The sitting conference is the actual meeting of the Court. After that meeting ends, however, the conference continues in the form of circulating memoranda and draft opinions. Indeed, such documents are often labeled "Memorandum to the Conference." On some occasions, the reactions to drafts lead to another conference on a case, as members look for ways to get beyond impasse to a majority, or at least a strong plurality opinion.

Rarely do justices change their positions substantially as a result of the conference discussion. More often, the conference serves as an opportunity to hear arguments from all positions that will probably surface up in the draft opinions to come. It also allows a justice contemplating the writing of an opinion to do some reconnaissance on the other justices in order to craft the opinion that will command the maximum number of votes.

Furthermore, conference battles can range from crude and harsh to subtle and sophisticated. They do not always arise where one might assume. For example, there is little doubt that one of the more contentious cases of the past half-century was the *Dennis* case, involving the conviction of Communist Party officials, decided in 1951. Douglas registered surprise at how little discussion occurred at conference.[1] Everyone had made up his mind before conference, and the disputes were left for the opinions. In other words, the battle was left for the continuing conference. Chief Justice Burger's protest that he had never heard a voice raised in anger at the conference,[2] then, tells us relatively little about the amount of conflict or its intensity.

The urbane and sophisticated Justice Holmes was one of the Court's regular conference contestants. Holmes came to the Supreme Court after an eminent career as a scholar of the law and a distinguished justice of the Supreme Judicial Court of Massachusetts. Even earlier, Holmes was literally a warrior, a battle-tested veteran of the Civil War. In the Court, he met a John Marshall Harlan who was just as fully prepared to engage.

"John Harlan was never close to Holmes. Perhaps he disliked having his own intellectual leadership of the Court usurped. Holmes, for his part, was distinctly patronizing toward the senior justice, which must have made Harlan furious at times."[3] Harlan did not appreciate Holmes's jurisprudence or the manner in which he expressed it. Holmes "liked to refer to Harlan as the last of the tobacco-spittin' judges and insisted that the old man's opinions were verbose and demagogical."[4] Holmes knew exactly how to launch Harlan, and he did so very effectively. Nothing got to Harlan faster than a deliberate snub based upon Holmes's view of his own intellectual superiority. "On one occasion he said that Harlan's mental processes were 'like a great vise, the two jaws of which cannot be closed closer than two inches of each other.' "[5]

Holmes was always ready to needle Harlan in conference. When the latter exploded, Holmes would add fuel to the fire, referring to him as "my lion-hearted friend."[6] Worse, Holmes would remain calm when Harlan lost his temper. "When Harlan was haranguing, Holmes coolly interrupted, 'That won't wash.' In the silence that followed, as Harlan grew apoplectic, the chief justice interposed himself gently, making a gesture as if at a washboard, and said, 'Still I keep scrubbing and scrubbing.' "[7]

Holmes was not the only one who set Harlan off. Harlan and White disliked one another from the moment they sat together.[8] And, of course, Harlan was not the only one whom Holmes inflamed. As Holmes's biographer, Sheldon Novick, observed, Justice McKenna "would be humble and deprecatory in the conference room, but when criticized he would flare out in violent anger. He lost his temper and his self-control entirely at Holmes one Saturday, but Holmes remained cheerful, and it passed over."[9] Indeed, writing of the period just before the 1921 term, Novick observed:

> The conferences of the Court had grown bitterly acrimonious and emotionally exhausting. White had no longer been able to manage their work, and they had fallen farther and farther behind their docket. McKenna was embittered and would strike out at random. Justice McReynolds, a difficult and irascible man, had taken a violent personal dislike to the other Wilson appointees, Brandeis and John H. Clarke, and did not try to conceal his dislike. He wrapped his animosity toward Brandeis in anti-Semitic barbs, refused to visit houses where Brandeis had been invited—"I do not dine with the Orient"—and was bitterly contemptuous of Brandeis's opinions. In conference he would rise and leave the room while Brandeis spoke.

Holmes, his courtesy once failing him, called McReynolds a "savage."[10]

McReynolds was not the only member of the four horsemen (Butler, McReynolds, Sutherland, and Van Devanter) who was a problem in conference. Merlo Pusey, Charles Evans Hughes's biographer, concluded that "Butler was the most difficult man on the court. Tough-minded and unshakable in his convictions, he was always ready for intellectual battle. At the conference table he argued with typically Irish tenacity and force, sometimes with thrusts of wit and eloquence."[11]

The period of the Stone Court was a difficult time within the Court as well as without. His colleagues disliked Stone's management of the conference, ironically enough at least partly because he exercised no control over the justices' sniping. As Justice Murphy put it, "the chief was unable to act speedily and efficiently ('lets all talk and they get nowhere') and sat back helplessly while the justices threw 'brickbats' at one another. 'What we need is a new chief justice.' "[12]

Notwithstanding his reputation for allowing the others to discourse ad horrendum, ad nauseam, Stone often enough waded into the fray. In one case in 1943, Stone indicated that he would not recuse himself because it would create quorum problems for the Court. "Roberts exploded and said that 'he would write and tell the world about Stone.' The chief justice 'turned white' and responded that no one would tell him in what cases he should disqualify himself."[13] Even his former student, William O. Douglas, could ignite Stone. Douglas loved to tell the story of those occasions. He quoted Stone: " 'Douglas, I can understand why some of the Brethren went astray. But I never thought you would.' I would reply, 'Chief, all the law I ever learned I learned from you.' That would always steam him up. He would hit the table with his fist and say, 'You never learned *that* from me.' "[14]

The 1942 term of the Court is often cited as one of the most hostile and divisive in the Court's history, a fact that bothered Stone no end. " 'I have had much difficulty in herding my collection of fleas,' Stone reported at the close of the term. He complained that he had been compelled to write an excessive number of opinions since his brethren were 'so busy disagreeing with each other.' "[15] Not surprisingly, Frankfurter, Black, and Douglas were at the heart of many of the clashes. Frankfurter often wrote his many correspondents about Black's unwillingness to see the light and about his manner in debate. "Commenting on a conference discussion in the 1942 term, Frankfurter wrote, 'Black at his worst, violent, vehement, indifferent to the use he was making of cases, utterly disregardful of what they stood for, and quite reckless when challenged once or twice regarding the untenability of what he was saying.' "[16] Frankfurter's diary records outrage at Black's behavior at conference. He observed, for example, that he was subjected to " 'harangue' by Black at conference, 'worthy of the cheapest soapbox orator.' "[17]

Of course, Douglas and Frankfurter went at each other regularly in conference, but the basis for their clashes was at least as much personal as it was professional. They were not, however, the only members of the Court in those days to lose control in conference. Douglas recalled an occasion when Chief Justice Vinson came to the end of his rope with Frankfurter. "At last Vinson left his chair at the head of the Conference Table, raised his clenched fist and started around the room at Frankfurter shouting, 'No son of a bitch can ever say that to Fred Vinson!' "[18]

Although Warren could hold his composure with most members of the Court, he too reached his limit with Frankfurter, and Felix felt the same way. Hard words passed between the two of them on several occasions. At one point at conference, Frankfurter "screeched" at Warren, "Be a judge, god damn it, be a judge!"[19]

One might wonder, in fact, why there is not actually more conflict in conference at certain points in the Court's history. Chief Justice Burger's manner of conducting conferences had all the elements necessary to engender battles. His colleagues were frustrated by the apparent lack of preparation. He regularly launched into case summaries at the beginning of discussions that were either inaccurate or not focused on the crucial issues. Furthermore, he sometimes offered ideological speeches rather than summaries of facts and issues. "Brennan said that Burger would 'drive us all crazy—including Lewis—with the same law-and-order speech in every damn criminal case.' According to another Justice, once others began to speak, Burger would freely 'interject his own comments and views . . . which might or might not be relevant.' "[20] That habit, plus his penchant for interrupting his colleagues (a violation of a long-standing informal norm of the conference) and his tendency to pass on his vote so that, as some of his colleagues saw it, he could control the majority and assign the opinion, tended to make conferences difficult, even when everyone else held their fire.

The Use of the Chief Justiceship

Other members of the Court felt that Chief Justice Burger used his formal powers to advance his own agenda. The use of these powers also affected understandings about informal norms concerning habits of work
within the Court. Burger's authority and control over some of the important work patterns of the Court became a means of waging conflict. He
attempted to employ these tools even though his control was more illu-
sory than real.

Burger's tendency to hold his vote to control assignment (discussed at
length in Chapter 2) is the most frequently noted example of this kind of
behavior. Although Powell's biographer, John Jeffries, attributes some of
the apparent manipulation to a lack of preparation,[21] certain members of
the Court, particularly Douglas, simply did not accept that view. For example, in the clash over the assignment of *Roe v. Wade* and *Doe v. Bolton,* Douglas was convinced that Burger was managing the decision and
assignment of the case with an eye toward the upcoming 1972 presidential
election. There were even times when Burger pulled the rug out from under his colleagues, though it is not at all clear whether these actions were
deliberate or the result of thoughtlessness.[22]

Similarly, Burger threatened Lewis Powell with the use of a special session to force his hand in a major case. Jeffries explains that Powell was
affected by doubts when he prevailed on the death penalty in *Gregg*.[23] He
hesitated when Anthony Amsterdam filed for a stay pending reconsideration in the Supreme Court. According to Jeffries, Powell wanted to grant
the stay so that the entire Court would be in session and share the responsibility when the executions began.

> At this point Burger intervened. . . . Burger threatened to call the
> Court into special session to vacate any stay Powell might grant.
> Powell's hurried telephone consultations elicited support from Stew-
> art and Stevens and advice from Brennan to show some "back-
> bone." On July 22 Powell granted the stay. The Chief did not call a
> special session, but, as he anticipated, the stay was vacated when the
> petition for rehearing was eventually denied.[24]

Burger supported the death penalty and was unwilling to recognize the
danger to the internal tenor of the Court if this difficult issue were not

handled sensitively. Indeed, "the war of the stay memos got very heated, even to the point of questions about bad faith."[25]

In 1984 John Paul Stevens found himself at odds with Burger about the management of opinions in a very important case, *Garcia v. San Antonio Metropolitan Transit Authority*.[26] The case was significant because it reversed an opinion in *National League of Cities v. Usery*[27] that had attempted to draw a new line to protect states and localities against federal commerce clause powers. The Court had been moving away from *Usery* and it appeared likely that this case would provide the opportunity for reversal of the precedent, a rare event in the Court and one that went to the heart of the states rights commitments of Burger, Rehnquist, O'Connor, and Powell.[28] As was so often the case, Burger waited until after the conference to weigh in with his vote, making it five votes to affirm the lower court, and assigned the opinion to Blackmun who was on that side but not strongly committed. The obvious ploy was to pull his vote when a strong ruling by one of the other four might very well push Blackmun onto the other side of the case. Ever since *Usery*, it had been clear that Blackmun was the crucial vote.

It did not work. On June 11 Blackmun wrote his colleagues: "I have spent a lot of time on these cases. I have finally decided to come down on the side of reversal. I have been able to find no principled way in which to affirm. . . . The enclosed draft of a proposed opinion reflects my views."[29] Burger immediately replied: "At this stage—almost mid-June—a 30-page opinion coming out contrary to the Conference vote on a very important issue places those who may dissent in a very difficult position. I think we should set the case over for reargument."[30] O'Connor, Powell, and Rehnquist promptly favored reargument, but Brennan and Marshall quickly opposed that approach. Stevens saw no reason for it other than the obvious one that the pro-*Usery* forces wanted more time to get Blackmun back or at least to avoid a direct overturn of the *Usery* ruling. He wrote an extensive memorandum to Burger and his colleagues the day after Burger's reargument move. Stevens suggested that it was time the justices agreed on standards for such a procedure. He reviewed the Court's recent behavior and concluded that unless there were not five votes by the end of June, there was no time for dissenters to prepare opinions, and that even if a pivotal voter were uncertain, there was no reason for reargument. He added, "Another possibility, of course, is the thought that the membership in the Court might change over the summer and thereby produce a different outcome. In my view, this would not be a proper ground for reargument."[31] There had been speculation that either Brennan or Marshall or both might leave the Court now that President Reagan had been reelected and the chances of holding out for a Democratic president to replace them seemed remote. The case was reargued, but Burger and his allies lost nevertheless.

Thurgood Marshall was clearly angered by many of Burger's proclivities, including the holding of a conference in his absence[32] and the manipulation of assignments. But among the more frustrating actions was the move to publish the Detroit desegregation case, *Milliken v. Bradley,* before Marshall had had enough time to complete desired changes in his dissent.[33] The Court, which was in the throws of the Watergate tapes case, had given *Milliken* short shrift, badly misstating the facts and the record. In truth, most of the crucial arguments over the issues raised in *Milliken* had been decided at the time of the *Richmond* case (discussed in Chapter 2). For Marshall, there was a crucial battle to be fought, and the chief's refusal to permit him to fully express himself was a slap in the face.

The repeated efforts by Burger to assert a leadership that he had not earned by intellectual or political skill was awkward for members of the Court, even for those justices who had no wish to fight. In addition to the conference tactics, assignment debates, and his tendency to self-assignment, Burger occasionally decided to force a confrontation in ways that were difficult to address without creating tensions. The classic example is the debate between Burger and Brennan over the obscenity standard.

In 1972 Brennan more or less resigned as the Court's obscenity expert, a position he had occupied since his early years on the Court. He announced that he had become frustrated by his inability to find an acceptably clear standard for judging the boundaries of First Amendment–protected expression in sexual matters.[34] Chief Justice Burger wrote a memorandum countering Brennan's and called for "a division of the house" among his colleagues. He told them plainly that they must indicate whether they were with him in favor of tougher obscenity standards, which would allow greater flexibility to local communities to prohibit what they regarded as pornographic materials, or with Brennan in his far more permissive view.[35] Burger ultimately got enough votes to prevail, and the Court announced a tougher standard in the 1973 *Miller v. California* ruling.[36] It was a needlessly confrontational approach to a foregone conclusion.[37]

The Threat to Go Public

Members of the Court react in very different ways when they believe they or their views have been badly treated. One reaction is to work on their own internal alliances, another is to threaten to go public.

One device employed over the years is the rump conference, a gathering outside of the normal Court conference of a few judges who share similar views. One of the first things Felix Frankfurter received upon arrival at the Court was an invitation from Stone that read " 'You are invited to join the party at Brandeis home at 6 P.M. today.' "

> "That evening, at L.D.B.'s, I met Stone and Roberts and the four of us went over the cases that had been argued the week of February 6. We agreed on all." At the end of the 1941 term, Frankfurter added: "This practice continued at Stone's house, after Brandeis' retirement. When Douglas came on he was invited to join. Roberts dropped out the following fall, that is, October 1940. Thereafter Douglas and I went to Stone's and that was discontinued after Stone became C.J."[38]

Douglas's description of these sessions centered on his view that Stone enjoyed playing "de facto Chief Justice" and going over the cases for the next day at length without the discipline imposed by Hughes.[39]

The four horsemen had been holding their own rump conferences for years. During Warren's years with Brennan, the two of them often held a meeting prior to conferences in which they reviewed matters before the Court and how they might be handled.

In addition to these ongoing groups, rump conferences have been held on an ad hoc basis. Frankfurter helped to organize the group he called the "Anti-Everson" lads to oppose Hugo Black's approach to establishment of religion cases. They caucused on the *McCollum* case[40] beginning on January 6, 1948, and worked together on revisions of the draft concurrence among themselves.[41] Frankfurter harbored dreams of turning the concurrence into a majority if he could only convince Murphy not to join Black. Murphy had agonized over *Everson* and in the end gave Black the needed margin of victory, but he remained uncomfortable about the opinion. Justice Burton, meanwhile, hoped to use the existence of the bloc and Black's support on the other side to allow him to forge a compromise.

A rump conference allowed several members of the Court to agree on a strategy to move the opinion in *United States v. Nixon* once it had bogged down.[42] A rump conference also broke a logjam in the effort to build a base for opinions on the death penalties that had been adopted by several states after the Supreme Court had struck virtually all of them down in *Furman v. Georgia.*[43] Over lunch, Powell and Stewart brought Stevens into an understanding that allowed each of them to support each other on critical issues but to maintain their individual objections to specific parts of individual state plans.[44]

If, however, a justice does not have the opportunity to form a coalition that can fend off a challenge or if he or she feels that there is a power move that appears likely to be successful, he or she may threaten to go public. There is, of course, a difference between threatening to take a problem into the public view and actually doing it. As Walter Murphy observed years ago, there are two important determinants of whether the threat to go public will be a useful device. The first is the skill and stature of the person making the threat. Murphy summarizes the second: "The threat of airing disputes in public is effective to the extent that it is never actually applied."[45] There is also a third determinant—the identity and character of the justice against whom the threat is leveled.

Because Louis Brandeis was such a skillful dissenter, his threat to go public with an argument that would weaken the majority was usually taken seriously. There were, however, some colleagues with whom he simply could not use that threat to gain a better end. Justice Frankfurter quoted Brandeis to the effect that " 'Van Devanter and Clarke would not be moved by threatened dissents: Clarke practically never changes his views.' Day was not to be bargained with: 'Day couldn't be persuaded by anybody but himself. He does not change his own views; he is a fighter, a regular game cock.' "[46]

Douglas was a threat for a time, since he held critical votes in many cases in the 1940s and 1950s, but he used the threat so often, wrote so much criticism of the Court's position regardless of colleagues' attempts to accommodate him, was so well known for switching his votes, and dissented so often that his threats became less potent.

At times the threat to go public is more powerful because it is linked to a set of relationships that are important. Powell's biographer explains how sensitive other members of the Court became to Justice Blackmun's concerns about what seemed to some a modest case. Blackmun had an important vote in the *Bakke* case, but was, at the time, frustrated by an apparent lack of respect by some of his colleagues.

> Then the trouble started when Brennan decided to withhold his vote until argument of a related case. Blackmun was outraged. At Conference in late March, he erupted in bitter recrimination about the delay in handing down the Montana elk-hunting case and the damage it did to his reputation. A law review had said that he was the Court's slowest author, but, as the Montana case showed, that was not his fault. He even threatened to have a press conference to refute the charge of slowness. No one dared mention Bakke.[47]

Brennan and Powell ran afoul of Blackmun and both tried hard to be responsive, in part at least to move the *Bakke* discussion along.[48]

Switched Votes, Lost Courts, and Lines Drawn in the Sand

When tension rises, working relationships are tenuous, and justices feel under attack, the Court can be less stable around particular opinions than it might otherwise be, as when several cases "lost courts" between the conference and the final opinion during the 1988 and 1989 terms.[49] Instability and uncertainty in voting patterns enhance the ability of a justice to employ a variety of weapons to block an effort to build a court, but, by the same token, a justice faces the same difficulty in getting a majority as his or her opponents.

There is another facet to the threat dynamic, one that arises particularly when a member of the Court sees an area of possible change: "the warning of considered position-taking." One example was Hugo Black's decision to stake out a position on the incorporation of the Bill of Rights into the Fourteenth Amendment, in effect putting Frankfurter on notice. In March 1945 Black wrote a memorandum to the conference during discussion of *Malinski v. New York,* making his position vis-à-vis Frankfurter very clear.

> Mr. Justice Frankfurter has filed a concurring opinion which construes the Due Process Clause as authorizing this Court to invalidate state action on the ground of a belief that the state action fails to set "civilized standards." This seems to me to be a restoration of the

natural law concept whereby the supreme constitutional law becomes this Court's views of "civilization" at a given moment. Five members of the Court, including Mr. Justice Frankfurter, have expressed their assent to this interpretation of the Due Process Clause.

I disagree with that interpretation. Due Process, thus construed, seems to me to make the remainder of the Constitution mere surplusage. This Due Process interpretation permits the Court to reject all of those provisions of the Bill of Rights, and to substitute its own ideas of what legislatures can and cannot do. In the past, this broad judicial power has been used, as I see it, to preserve the economic status quo and to block legislative efforts to cure its existing evils. At the same time, the Court has only grudgingly read into "civilized standards" the safeguards to individual liberty set out in the Bill of Rights. While the case under consideration unquestionably involves the admissibility of compelled testimony, the concurring opinion is careful to point out that this question must not be resolved by reliance upon the constitutional prohibition against compelled testimony.

I think this is an improper case to debate this question. The case could be decided without it. When the matter does hereafter arise in a proper case, I shall discuss it and shall also explain why I did not write about it here.[50]

This kind of action is rare, but it can be an important way to frame a conflict if a justice thinks that he or she can attract enough potential votes. Like all approaches that smack of drawing lines in the sand, however, this device puts potential adversaries on notice, allows them to mount a counterattack, and can make compromise extremely difficult.

THE PERSONAL BATTLES

It is truly surprising that the justices could face all of these professional battles inside and outside the Court and still have positive personal relationships. As Justice Blackmun once put it:

Well, I like to get away. As a matter of fact, I think I have to get away from Washington and this building, once in awhile, just to maintain my sanity. This is a very close intimate association that the nine of us have. We're working constantly with each other under conditions of a certain amount of agreement, and a very definite amount of disagreement.[51]

The situation is even more complex than it may appear. Like all organizations, the Court spawns varying types of interpersonal relationships. They range from the polite, arms-length association that barely goes beyond the purely professional, to the close friendship, in which a relatively small jab can be painful and in which little nettlesome behaviors can build up over time.

Historically, many members of the Court have been able to maintain strong personal relationships with other justices whose views on the cases before the Court have been anathema. When a difference of opinion becomes a battle, it becomes difficult to maintain that desirable mix of personal and professional relationships. One sometimes influences the other.

Pressures to personalize disputes must be resisted if members of the Court are to disagree without being disagreeable. The small size of the Court and the coequal status of its members cuts many ways. Although the size and need for regular interaction remind the justices that unnecessary conflict is too expensive a luxury to tolerate, the Court's organizational character also fosters personal clashes. In a large organization and particularly one that is relatively hierarchical in character, it is possible to blame the unseen "them" "out there" or "up there" for problems. In the Court, by contrast, the guilty party, if there is one, is sitting at that conference table twice a week and on the bench regularly. Given the nature of things, the identities of the conflicting parties are known not only to the combatants but, generally speaking, to everyone else as well.

The other institutional characteristic that makes a sense of personal injury relatively easy to accept is that the justices serve together for a long time. A justice cannot escape the frustrating habits of colleagues. Small things can become extremely irritating over time. The scars of past battles may fester and break open. Even friends of long-standing can reach a point where the strain is severe, particularly if one or both of the participants hangs on too long and suffers the effects of age and debilitation.

Personal clashes, then, are every bit as much to be expected as the professional variety. Chief Justice Warren likened life on the Court to a marriage; one cannot tolerate it if it is one battle after another. Conversely, living in close proximity inevitably means an occasional clash. The challenge is to recognize personal clashes for what they are, control them so they do not exceed reasonable boundaries, and to bring them to resolution, so they do not fester and cast a continuing shadow on the work of the Court.

INTERNAL PERSONAL CLASHES

Members (and for that matter, students) of the Court prefer to see it as a place where, as Justice O'Connor put it, "every justice holds every other justice in very high regard and has great respect one for the other."[52] But it has not always been so. Indeed, justices have engaged in a variety of personal conflict, from shunning colleagues, to clashing over irreconcilable ideology, to openly criticizing and abusing one another's characters.

The extent and intensity of the personal conflict is linked to the widely varying ability of individual justices to maintain the separation between personal and professional on which most members of the Court rightly pride themselves. Some, like Hugo Black, a battle-tested veteran of the Senate, can face a vicious attack and walk away as if nothing had happened. The members of the Court were extremely anxious about what would happen when Black and Bob Jackson encountered one another for the first time after Jackson had launched the most vicious public attack on a colleague in the Court's history from Nuremburg. When Black entered the conference room on October 10, 1946, he immediately walked over to Jackson and shook his hand. " 'Good morning, Hugo,' said Jackson, and the dreaded moment of awkwardness was averted. The two joined in the conference discussion with controlled geniality, giving no hint of their earlier hostilities."[53] That is not to say that Black did not feel anger. Black wrote a former clerk saying that he had been sent him an editorial entitled "Jackson is an Unmitigated Ass." Black added that there was also an article on that same page "by John Temple Graves on the same subject. I have nothing but sympathy for John Temple."[54] For his part, Jackson, who was not as effective at maintaining the distinction between professional and private hostility, wrote to Frankfurter, "I simply give up understanding our colleague and begin to think he is a case for a psychiatrist."[55]

Shunning, Caricature, and Other Direct Insults

One of the worst examples of interpersonal personal conflict was Justice McReynolds's abuse of Justice Brandeis, mentioned briefly in Chapter 2. It is an extreme example of a more common phenomenon, the shunning of one justice by another. Alpheus T. Mason describes McReynolds's behavior.

In 1922 Taft proposed that members of the Court accompany him to Philadelphia on a ceremonial occasion. "As you know," McReynolds responded, "I am not always to be found when there is a Hebrew aboard. Therefore my 'inability' to attend must not surprise you." McReynolds even refused to sit next to Brandeis for the Court photograph. "The difficulty is with me and me alone," McReynolds wrote the Chief Justice in 1924. ". . . I have absolutely refused to go through the bore of picture-taking again until there is a change in the Court and maybe not then." The Chief Justice had to capitulate; no photograph was taken in 1924.[56]

Brandeis was not the only target of McReynolds's misanthropic behavior, however. Justice Clarke found McReynolds's personality and conduct so obnoxious that it became an important factor in his decision to retire from the Court, much to the chagrin of Woodrow Wilson who had appointed McReynolds as well as Brandeis and Clarke. Clarke explained in a letter to Wilson just how serious the situation was.

McReynolds as you know is the most reactionary judge on the Court. There were many other things which had better not be set down in black and white which made the situation to me deplorable and harassing to such a degree that I thought myself not called on to sacrifice what of health and strength I may have left in a futile struggle against constantly increasing odds. . . . It was in some respects as disillusioning a chapter as Washington could afford.[57]

Chief Justice Taft, too, found McReynolds a serious problem. Although he thought the man capable, Taft found him "selfish to the last degree, . . . fuller of prejudice than any man I have ever known, . . . one who delights in making others uncomfortable. He has no sense of duty.

He is a continual grouch; and . . . really seems to have less of a loyal spirit to the Court than anybody."[58] Taft also found others of his colleagues troublesome.

Taft thought Brandeis dangerous on ideological grounds, but his distrust went well beyond the simply political. Given Taft's commitment to judicial reform, the Chief Justice was wounded by information that convinced him that Brandeis had worked behind the scenes with members of Congress to oppose what became the Judiciary Act of 1925. That legislation, which granted the Court discretion over most of its docket, was at the heart of Taft's efforts to improve administration of the Court's business. He also concluded that Brandeis was working against him when Taft moved to support reform of bankruptcy proceedings. Taft complained, "The truth is that when we make rules that interfere with the young Russian Jews [who composed the bulk of the bankruptcy petitioners] . . . we find him a real obstructionist."[59] Beyond that, he was frustrated by what he saw as Brandeis's control over Holmes. Holmes was "so completely under the control of Brother Brandeis that it gives to Brandeis two votes instead of one."[60]

The feud with Brandeis predated appointment to the Court. Indeed, "Brandeis and Taft were old antagonists."[61] Brandeis hurt the Taft administration badly when he served as special counsel to a congressional investigation of the so-called Glavis affair. Louis Glavis was an Interior Department employee under Secretary Richard Ballinger who charged that the secretary, at the behest of the administration, was giving mining leases to political friends. Glavis was fired after attempts to squelch his accusations failed, and documents were manufactured in a cover-up attempt.[62] Brandeis's work in the hearings that followed forced Ballinger's resignation and "the President himself was made to appear either foolish or corrupt. The original charges seemed to lack foundation, but efforts to hush them up had crippled the administration."[63] There was no love lost between Taft and Brandeis from that point forward.

Brandeis had his own evaluation of his colleagues. Philippa Strum summarizes his views as follows:

If Brandeis was cooly objective about people he liked, he was devastating about those he did not. Sutherland was "a mediocre Taft"; Sanford "thoroughly bourgeois"; McReynolds "lazy," moved by the "irrational impulses of a savage," a man who "would have given

Balzac great joy" and who looked at times like "an infantile mo-
ron"; Pitney was "much influenced by his experience and he had had
mighty little" . . . ; Pierce Butler had "given no sign of anything except a thoroughly mediocre mind." Worst of all was Joseph Mc-
Kenna: the "only way of dealing with him is to appoint guardians
for him."[64]

Although Justice McReynolds is generally regarded as the most obnoxious person to sit on the Court in modern history, others have had a talent
for alienating colleagues. Felix Frankfurter clearly ranks in this group.
Frankfurter was one of the classic examples of a justice who had great
difficulty separating the personal from the professional, in part at least
because so much of his personal identity was wrapped up in his professional persona.[65] The same man who had praised a colleague to the skies
promptly turned to sarcasm and gossip with other justices as though they
were unaware of his modus operandi. Harsh comments about Justice
Murphy's reputation as a playboy, such as Frankfurter's oft quoted remark mimicking imaginary showgirls, "Us girls call him Murph," along
with frequent suggestions that Murphy was a rather simple-minded
would-be "priest" led to a sad, sour relationship.[66] Murphy was badly injured by the battling of the Court as a whole during the Stone era and was
frustrated by the fact that he knew some of his colleagues undervalued
him.[67] He did not take it as a compliment when Frankfurter tried to get
him appointed to a political job to get him off the Court.[68]

Frankfurter was a master at the use of ridicule, what Meiklejohn referred to as criticism by caricature, but there is no evidence that it did anything but alienate his colleagues. Walter Murphy cites Frankfurter's mock
Black opinion:

> I greatly sympathize with the essential purpose of my Brother's . . .
> dissent. His roundabout and turgid legal phraseology is a *cri de
> coeur.* "Would I were back in the Senate," he means to say, "so that I
> could put on the statute books what really ought to be there. But
> here I am, cast by Fate into a den of judges devoid of the habits of
> legislators, simple fellows who have a crippling feeling that they must
> enforce the laws as Congress wrote them and not as they ought to
> have been written."[69]

Frankfurter singled out colleagues he found particularly weak for extremely harsh criticisms, rather than simply dismissing them. In a letter to Judge Learned Hand, Frankfurter said, "Reed is largely vegetable—he had managed to give himself a nimbus of reasonableness but is as unjudicial-minded, as flagrantly moved, at times, by irrelevant considerations for adjudication as any of them [the justices]."[70] Frankfurter was not alone in employing caricature. Asked if he thought Justice Murphy was growing on the bench, Chief Justice Stone replied, "He can no more grow than that stone."[71] Still, no one was more devastating in criticism than Frankfurter.

The feud between Frankfurter and William O. Douglas was among the most vicious and long-standing in the history of the Court. It was both professional and personal. Douglas had once admired Frankfurter and tried to build a good relationship with him. When he was engaged in studies of corporate bankruptcies, Douglas issued a variety of criticisms of proposed market reforms, including the Securities Act of 1933 of which Frankfurter had been a major architect and of which Max Lowenthal was a supporter. He wrote to Frankfurter, explaining his view and attempting to soften his criticism. He wrote that it caused him "great suffering . . . that some of the things that I said might be taken as an effrontery to you and the noble cause you serve."[72] Frankfurter would not let him off the hook and told Douglas that "you ought to bring your head and heart into alignment."[73]

However, Frankfurter never took Douglas very seriously in part because of his manner. Besides, Douglas was in appearance and age more like one of his students than a colleague. Douglas had been among the upstart advocates of legal realism at Columbia and became one of its leaders while at Yale during a period when many Harvard purists viewed the realists as marginal at best and heretics at worst. Frankfurter was erudite and sophisticated, whereas Douglas, who could easily have behaved likewise, deliberately chose to poke fun at the Washington establishment, with too much strong language and ribald humor and just enough use of strong spirits to shock the blue bloods. His iconoclasm, not to mention his history of polio, was precisely what attracted Roosevelt to Douglas— and what drove Frankfurter to distraction. When Douglas refused to place himself under Frankfurter's tutelage on the Court, the end was at hand. The final break came with the decision by Douglas to join Black in admitting error in supporting Frankfurter's opinion for the Court in the first flag salute case.

For his part, Douglas had tried to impress Frankfurter but had been treated with the kind of derision that he had experienced earlier in his life as a poor, sickly child. He was no longer either poor or sickly and was not about to accept Frankfurter's dismissal. He also knew Frankfurter from New Deal days and was more than ready to spot Frankfurter in action behind a variety of events. When Justice Black was not appointed to follow Charles Evans Hughes as Chief Justice, Douglas had no trouble blaming Frankfurter.[74] Douglas knew Frankfurter would have been much happier if Douglas had left the Court and was equally certain that Felix had been trying to find ways not only to get him, but others as well, off the Court.[75]

Frankfurter gave as good as he got, blasting Douglas for using the Court as a political springboard to the White House. He wrote Learned Hand that Douglas "is the most cynical, shameless immoral character I've ever known."[76] He recorded in his diary the now-famous conversation with Justice Murphy in January 1943 in which Frankfurter declared Douglas guilty of violating the sanctity of the monastery because of his assumed desire to run in 1944. Frankfurter never seemed to be aware how often he himself violated the supposed principle of political celibacy.[77]

Douglas was just as capable as Frankfurter of alienating colleagues, though he could be gracious and every bit the life of the party when he wanted to be. Although specific behaviors antagonized some of his brethren, others were put off by his general personality and demeanor. Justice Goldberg tells the story of a year-long tension between Earl Warren and Douglas during 1964 and 1965 when they basically did not speak to one another.[78] One of Douglas's colleagues reported that his friend Hugo Black interceded with angry justices on Douglas's behalf on a number of occasions. After Black's departure from the Court Justice Brennan played the mediating role, though it was neither an easy nor a pleasant task.[79] Justice Powell had mixed views of Justice Douglas and "privately thought Douglas 'a real SOB.' "[80]

If Black and Frankfurter clashed because they disagreed, Douglas and Frankfurter battled because they could not stand one another. Douglas often deliberately baited Felix. He had a number of techniques for sending Frankfurter into apoplectic rage. Douglas sometimes pricked his nemesis by leaving the conference room when Frankfurter began to speak. Justice Stewart remembered that Douglas, who spoke after Frankfurter in conference, would wait for the professor to conclude one of his lengthy speeches and then observe: " 'When I came into this conference I agreed with the conclusion that Felix has just announced; but he's just talked me out of it'—which used to drive Felix Frankfurter crazy."[81] Bernard Schwartz recounted the story of the day Fred Rodell was waiting for Douglas to emerge from conference when he received a note from the justice that read, "That little S.O.B. knows you're here and he's filibustering."[82]

The Reliable Anti-Authority

On a more serious note, Douglas quickly tired of his former idol's arrogance and assumed superiority, not to mention his double-dealing and backstabbing. Furthermore, he could not abide Frankfurter's continuing efforts to turn the Court into what Douglas saw as an academic debating society. If he caught Frankfurter in what was obviously a throwaway line in conference during a debate with him, Douglas would demand evidence in support of the hyperbole, knowing full well that Frankfurter was not going to respond.[83] Finally, Douglas wrote a memorandum in which he concluded that he would no longer participate in conferences where Frankfurter sat, though he ultimately did not send it on the advice of Chief Justice Warren.[84]

> The continuous violent outbursts against me in Conference by my Brother Frankfurter give me great concern. They do not bother me. For I have been on the hustings too long.
>
> But he's an ill man; and these violent outbursts create a fear in my heart that one of them may be his end.
>
> I do not consciously do anything to annoy him. But twenty-odd years have shown that I am a disturbing symbol in his life. His outbursts against me are increasing in intensity. In the interest of his health and long life I have reluctantly concluded to participate in no more conferences while he is on the Court.[85]

Things deteriorated to a point where each man became the other's most reliable antiauthority. The mere fact that Douglas favored a position was virtually enough in itself for Frankfurter to disagree, and the feeling was mutual. Black and Frankfurter reached a similar stage, as did Frankfurter and Murphy. Black was rapidly approaching the same position with Abe Fortas. Douglas reached nearly the same point with Burger and Rehnquist, although despite his overwhelming disagreement with both men, Douglas had moments in which he and Burger could share a cup of tea, Burger's afternoon libation for visiting colleagues. Douglas managed a positive personal engagement with Rehnquist, though he despised the man who appointed the future chief justice and rarely found himself voting on the same side with Rehnquist.

The Sense of Betrayal

It is not uncommon for personal disputes to begin or continue because of a sense, justified or not, that one justice has betrayed another. Clearly, Frankfurter had that view of Black, Douglas, and Murphy, who abandoned him in the flag salute cases.[86] Murphy thought Frankfurter guilty of betrayal in the sense of double-dealing, for Frankfurter ridiculed Murphy behind his back while flattering and feigning friendship to his face.

Justices have felt betrayal more subtly. Hugo Black said toward the end of his years on the Court that Douglas had "left him." The two men had shared so much for so long, and yet they had reached a time when they were regularly on opposite sides of very important issues. To the degree that the concept of betrayal signifies a sense of loss, the process of moving away from an ally can generate basic, if quiet, tensions. This characterization of betrayal, of course, implies that the feelings can be asymmetrical. Clearly, Black had a stronger sense of Douglas's movement away from him than Douglas possessed about Black's positions.

Insensitivity or Discrimination

There were times during the Burger and Rehnquist years when Thurgood Marshall felt strongly that he was not being treated with the respect due a full colleague on the Court. It was not simply that he repeatedly lost in equal protection cases coming to the Court. His memoranda and dissenting opinions from 1973, beginning with *San Antonio Independent School District v. Rodriguez,* through *Milliken v. Bradley, Memphis v. Greene, Regents v. Bakke, Spallone v. United States,* and the several major battles of the 1988 and 1989 terms of the Court, reveal an anger that seems more than merely professional. Marshall had given a very substantial portion of his life, indeed had risked his life, to bring major civil rights actions to court, not only in Washington but in the deep South.[87] Too much of himself was wrapped up in the battles that he saw being undone for Marshall to avoid feeling the losses deeply. Conferences like the *Bakke* discussion, cited in Chapter 2, in which other justices seemed to display severely limited and stereotyped understandings of the results of the civil rights efforts of the post–World War II years were painful to Marshall. It grated on Marshall that Justice Powell, a southerner, seemed to think that he understood Marshall's experiences. The conferences and memoranda that he distributed display some of the frustration he felt. When Marshall lashed out in some of these fights, he was clearly waging a personal as well as a professional battle.

Basic Personality Clashes

Quite apart from everything else, justices have had to deal with personality clashes, more or less inevitable consequences of long-running working relationships among diverse, strong-willed colleagues. Some members of the Court simply do not like others very much, and that dislike can only be disguised or hidden for so long. In the case of Douglas and Frankfurter, neither man even tried to hide the tension. Black talked to his son and to Douglas about Frankfurter, but he was generally careful about what he wrote and said. Frankfurter did not reciprocate. Frankfurter recognized Black's native intellect, but he simply could not tolerate him. Frankfurter took every opportunity to cast Black in the worst possible light. James Simon quotes a letter from Felix to Harlan concerning Black's plans to attend an ABA convention.

> For members [of the Court] and their wives to go out there as guests of the Association—except a Justice who had an active share in the program—strikes me as a bit shabby. And the excuse that their presence will generate good will for the Court strikes me as reliance on fatuous notions. . . . I almost puked when I heard Hugo say that if it would be good for the Court, he'll go. Gosh! For nearly twenty years I have heard his uniform condemnation of the A.B.A. and his contempt for their views. And now he puts on that noble act. The truth of course is, I have not a particle of doubt, that this will afford a pleasant trip for his young wife. He is not the only old Benedick I know who is

more eager to please his new bride than ever he was his first wife (Josephine Black was an uncommonly lovely person). I have little doubt that Hugo now believes it will help the Court, for he has infinite capacity—beyond anyone I've known—for self-deception.[88]

Black was perfectly happy to set Frankfurter off. Elizabeth Black, who was then his secretary, recalled the day that Hugo came back to chambers after conference and declared, with an obvious twinkle in his eye, that he thought Felix was about ready to hit him at one point during the conference.[89]

Warren Burger clashed with several members of the Court, often in connection with his style and manner. Even Powell found his high-handedness annoying.[90] Jeffries points out that Burger would have had difficulties with certain members of the Court in any event, since he was appointed to replace the very popular Earl Warren and because he was named by Nixon precisely to oppose the positions taken by members of the Court. "To this predictable incompatibility, Burger's personality added an unfortunate irritant."[91]

Powell, as much a gentleman as one could ever expect to encounter, nevertheless found Scalia irritating, as well.

> Politically Powell and Scalia were not so far apart, but personally they were like oil and water. Scalia's cheerful lack of deference rubbed his senior colleague the wrong way. His volubility struck Powell as bad manners. . . . Scalia's quick dismissal of conventional wisdom seemed to Powell more suited to an academic than to a judge. Scalia's boundless energy and pugnaciousness, which his many friends admitted, struck his quiet, self-deprecating older colleague as almost uncivil. Even Scalia's wit and charm were largely wasted on Powell.[92]

Powell's biographer quotes a clerk, " 'Those two wouldn't agree on whether the sky was blue.' After a pause, he added, 'On second thought, they would agree, but for different reasons.' "[93]

The Battle to Retain Identity and Protect a Legacy

Ironically enough, personal tensions can emerge from the dynamics of retirement from the Court. Fundamentally, of course, the decision to retire is an intensely personal decision. Unlike the decision by many in the wider population to enjoy a reduced work schedule, to move to a desired residential area, or to undertake new projects, the decision to leave the Court calls upon a strong person to decide that it is time to leave what is often a second full career at an advanced age. Many justices come to Court in their mid- to late fifties. In recent years, they have tended to leave in their late seventies or eighties, often because they were forced by medical condition to give up their grueling work schedule. A third element of the retirement decision is a willingness to give up a title and role that often becomes a central part of the justice's identity. The decision to leave can therefore be wrenching. If that decision is not completely voluntary but a result of pressure by colleagues, a clash can result. As other members of the Court, particularly the more senior members, watch that process, they realize that they could be next.

Justice Douglas argued at an early point in his judicial career for a mandatory retirement but later found himself with a brilliant mind locked in a body debilitated by the effects of age and a severe stroke. Though he tried to press on, it became clear that he had to leave. Justice Holmes participated in more than one discussion of whether a colleague should retire, but at his advanced age, it was not a subject he liked to address.

The classic case of the justice who had to take his own medicine was Justice Stephen Field. Justice Field had served as a member of a committee that asked Justice Grier to retire. He was reminded of his role when it came time that he was no longer able to continue in an active and productive role. Chief Justice Hughes recalled the experience.

Justice Harlan was deputed to make the suggestion. He went over to Justice Field, who was sitting alone on a settee in the Robing Room apparently oblivious of his surroundings, and after arousing him gradually approached the question, asking if he did not recall how anxious the Court had been with respect to Justice Grier's condition and the feeling of the other Justices that in his own interest and in that of the Court he should give up his work. Justice Harlan asked if Justice Field did not remember what had been said to Justice Grier on that occasion. The old man listened, gradually became alert and finally, with his eyes blazing with the old fire of youth, he burst out:
"Yes! And a dirtier day's work I never did in my life!"[94]

One dynamic of the politics of retirement is the tendency of an aging justice to suspect one's colleagues or others outside the Court of attempting to force a resignation. Chief Justice Taft found that Justice McKenna, whose vote was crucial in a number of settings, "interpreted polite criticism as thinly veiled attempts to force him off the bench. 'He is exceedingly sensitive,' the Chief Justice noted, 'and loses his temper and at times creates little scenes in the conference.' "[95] The Court went so far as to try to avoid ruling on cases in which McKenna would have the critical vote with the hope that he would soon retire. McKenna maintained that "when a man retires, he disappears and nobody cares for him."[96] Taft had difficulty obtaining agreement from his colleagues to approach McKenna and ask for his resignation. Justice Holmes was older than McKenna and did not want to be implicated in Taft's move. The Chief Justice concluded that Brandeis resisted the effort to pressure McKenna to leave because "he would like to have a Democratic President appoint" the successor.[97]

The decision to resign can engender serious disagreement because the justices, who remember how they came to the Court in the first place, know that their action will set in motion a new political dynamic that could very well help a president alter the balance in the Court. Justice Douglas was fully aware that his resignation would mean that Gerald Ford, the man who had led the impeachment effort against him only a few years earlier, would be in a position to appoint his successor. Thurgood Marshall was constantly hounded by Reaganites and Bush supporters to retire and give the Republican presidents an opportunity for an additional appointment. Marshall was determined to stay put: "For all those people who wish very dearly for me to give up and quit and whathave-you. . . . I hope you will pardon me for saying it, but . . . 'Don't worry, I'm going to outlive those bastards.' "[98]

The justice is also aware that retirement means giving up important battles that he or she has waged within the Court. Thus, it was clear that Justice Black had a difficult time making the decision to retire, even though his eyesight had deteriorated and he had suffered a stroke, largely because he had been engaged in an increasingly hard fight over what he saw as the Court's abuse of due process and inappropriate willingness to create new rights.[99] And the mere fact that the end is approaching may cause the justice to feel the increased urgency of ongoing conflicts within the Court. Douglas and his wife and staff waited in the justice's chambers until confirmation came from the White House that the president had received his letter of retirement. As they departed, Douglas left a poem for his staff.

Keep the faith in the rule of law not only for our
own people but for the people of the world.
Keep the faith in a unity of mankind irrespective of
race, intellect, color, religion, or ideology.
Keep the faith in the informed citizenry who can
govern wisely and justly.
Keep the faith in the system that allows a place for
every man no matter how lowly or how great.
Keep the faith in a system which does not leave
every issue of human rights to the ups and downs of
the political campaigns.[100]

Members of the Court sometimes lash out in their last days, but other
justices may also get into conflicts surrounding retirements. One such
battle was, surprisingly, an important part of the hard internal dynamics
of the Court in the late 1940s. Justice Roberts resigned from the Court in
August 1945. A battle ensued over the normally innocuous business of
the proper content of a farewell letter from colleagues to the departing
justice. Chief Justice Stone drafted a letter that, among other things, said
that his departure was met with a "sense of regret, that our association
with you in the daily work of the Court must now come to an end." After
speaking of his diligent efforts, the letter observed, "You have made fidel-
ity to principle your guide to decision." Hugo Black indicated that he
could not sign a letter containing either of those two passages.[101] He wrote
Douglas at his summer home in Lostine, Oregon: "If the letter is signed
and sent to Roberts, he may, and will if he follows the course he did last
year, simply take advantage of the opportunity to say something mean
about us. If the letter is not signed, this information is certain to be
adroitly passed to the public, together with invidious implications."[102]
Stone agreed to a recirculated letter but Frankfurter then objected that he
would not sign the letter if the changes were made.[103] By this point it was
clear that the battle was rapidly becoming another clash between Black
and Frankfurter. Black wrote Douglas explaining that Frankfurter had
convinced Stone to recirculate the original letter for decision by the justices, a course of action that seemed only calculated to push the matter to
a public clash. Douglas replied: "It's all a goddam tempest in a teapot.
FF is looking for trouble—some opening so R[oberts] can let go a
blast."[104] In the end, no letter was sent.

EXTERNAL PERSONAL DISPUTES

Although every serious scholar of the Court knows that they exist, personal conflicts among the justices have always been uncomfortable subjects for discussion. The discomfort is in a way surprising, for virtually all organizations have those dynamics and there is absolutely no reason to assume that the Court would be immune from them. Perhaps it is a tribute to the justices that we expect them to be above the kind of behavior of which we ourselves are guilty. It is also, however, unreasonable and unrealistic. What does present serious concern are situations in which these personal disputes spill over into the public—and they have.

The Attack on Integrity

Although fortunately extremely rare, it has happened that justices, either directly or through surrogates, have challenged others on grounds of character. The best-known example was Robert Jackson's "war" against Hugo Black in 1946.

Jackson took the position that one could not disagree with Black, one had to go to war with him. The tough, eloquent former attorney general was more than ready to do just that. While still in Nuremberg serving as the U.S. war crimes prosecutor, Jackson, over the objection of President Truman, simultaneously released a lengthy written broadside against Black to the newspapers and the Congress.

The battle began over two portal-to-portal pay cases seeking to determine exactly when workers were to be deemed at work for pay purposes. It was the second case, *Jewell Ridge*, that provided the basis for the Jackson challenge.[105] A sharply divided Court found Black in the majority upholding the miners' claim and the chief justice in dissent. Black assigned the opinion to Murphy. The employers sought a rehearing, arguing among other things that Justice Black should recuse himself on grounds the attorney for the miners, Crampton Harris, had been his law partner in Birmingham. The Court unanimously rejected the rehearing petition, but the discussion of the case brought difficulties. The chief justice suggested that the Court might wish to add a statement, indicating that the decision whether to recuse was one to be made by the justice alone and that the Court would not question that judgment. Black was adamant that nothing be said of the matter, but Jackson decided to write a concurring opinion indicating that it was up to each justice to determine what he would do in such circumstances. Frankfurter joined Jackson's opinion. As some of the justices feared, that opinion issued in June 1945 was taken to be a suggestion that Black should have removed himself from the case. Jackson left for his assignment as Nuremburg War Prosecutor, where he was when Chief Justice Stone died.

Jackson had a promise from Roosevelt to name him to the center chair when the opportunity presented itself, but Harry Truman was now in the White House. The level of conflict within the Court was widely discussed and clearly played a role in Truman's decision to name Vinson chief justice. Before the decision, a May 16 story by Doris Fleeson in the *Washington Star* received wide play. Fleeson reported that there was a "blood feud raging on the Supreme Court which has caused the court's anxious friends to urge an outsider as Chief Justice."[106] After recounting the *Jewell Ridge* battle of the previous year, Fleeson added that "Justice Black reacted with fiery scorn to what he regarded as an open and gratuitous insult, a slur upon his personal and judicial honor. Nor did he bother to conceal his contempt. An already marked coolness, especially between Messrs. Black and Frankfurter froze into impenetrable ice."[107] Then she presented what became the fateful interpretation. She indicated that the information about the Court feud had been presented to Truman in the form of an ultimatum by Hugo Black. Fleeson quoted an unnamed senator's claim that Truman had told him, "Black says he will resign if I make Jackson Chief Justice and tell the reasons why."

Jackson reacted to the Fleeson article with rage at the idea that Black would have done such a thing, even though there was no evidence beyond the third-person quotations in news reports that he had actually approached Truman. Jackson was also doubly devastated that he was being held up to ridicule in the press and that he did not gain the chief justiceship. There was no small irony in the fact that his ally Felix Frankfurter had played a role in denying him the center chair in 1941 when he advised Roosevelt that, for a variety of reasons, Stone was the better choice.[108]

On June 7 Jackson cabled Truman to congratulate him on the selection of Vinson and to inform the president of his intention to provide what he considered to be a full accounting of Black's misdeed and a defense of his own actions to the public and congressional leadership. He recalled the events surrounding the *Jewell Ridge* case and particularly the conference discussion at which he informed Black and the others of his intention to file the concurrence.

> Mr. Justice Black became very angry and said that if I wrote any opinion which discussed the subject at all, it would mean a "declaration of war." I told Justice Black . . . that I would not stand for any more of his bullying, and whatever I would otherwise do I would now have to write my opinion to keep my self-respect in the face of his threats.[109]

Truman replied immediately in a classified memorandum warning Jackson that he had been "grossly misinformed." He had not been in touch with Black or any other member of the Court and the story was absolutely false. He implored Jackson not to make the matter public. "The reputation and the position of the Court are of paramount interest to me and no purpose can be served by making this controversy public."[110]

But Jackson would hear none of it. He sent the story to the newspapers and the House and Senate Judiciary committees. The mess was immediately spread throughout the nation. In fact, the version that he sent for publication was in some respects even tougher than the one he sent to Truman. He spoke of an ultimatum in which the justices were required to "join in covering up the fact or have war."[111] Jackson went on to declare, "If war is declared on me, I propose to wage it with the weapons of the open warrior, not those of the stealthy assassin."[112] It was, of course, completely predictable that the tactic would backfire, and it did.

A lack of respect by a member of the Court for the institution or its justices has sometimes been taken to be a character flaw, a lack of civility. Carl Brent Swisher tells the story of the public challenge by Justice Joseph Story, the guardian of the Marshall Court tradition, to the Jackson appointees who were to make up the Taney Court. The clash grew out of the fact that the Court had heard arguments in *Briscoe v. The Bank of the Commonwealth of Kentucky*[113] under Marshall and had been strongly of the view that this case involving notes issued by the Kentucky bank was squarely within the coverage an earlier case[114] that had held that notes issued by Missouri violated the constitutional prohibition against state issuance of bills of credit. The fact that the Kentucky notes were issued by the bank rather than by the state made no difference since the bank was owned by and operated for the state. However, the decision was not delivered until after Marshall had left, and the new court rejected the preliminary reading and upheld the bank practice on grounds that the paper was issued by the bank and not the state. The opinion was written by Justice McLean rather than by Chief Justice Taney, but it was clear that Story felt himself and his former colleagues under siege by the new Court. Swisher describes the events:

> Story's lone dissent reveals starkly the tenaciousness with which he clung to a regime and a personnel which had gone. A majority of the judges who heard the first argument had been of the opinion that the act in question was unconstitutional. "Among that majority was the late Mr. Chief Justice John Marshall—a name never to be pronounced without reverence." The second argument, he declared, had been upon precisely the same grounds as the former. After explaining at length his reasons for believing the decision to be wrong, he declared that he did so because of his belief that the public had a right to know the opinion of every judge who dissented from the opinion of the court on a constitutional question. "I have another and strong motive," he continued; "my profound reverence and affection for the dead. Mr. Chief Justice Marshall is not here to speak for himself; and knowing full well the grounds of his opinion, in which I concurred, that this act is unconstitutional; I have felt an earnest desire to vindicate his memory from the imputation of rashness, or want of deep reflection."[115]

The Public Snub

The deliberate snub conveys a very definite message to those who watch the Court closely, but it is more subtle than other expressions. It was not a good sign, for example, when Justices Reed, Black, and Douglas attended Justice Murphy's swearing-in ceremony at the White House, but Hughes, Stone, Roberts, and McReynolds refused to come.[116] Melvin Urofsky describes the 1944 term as follows: "Frankfurter complained to Rutledge near the end of the term about an increasing tendency on the part of members of this Court to behave like schoolboys and throw spitballs at one another.[117] Similarly, when Hugo Black received the Thomas Jefferson Award given by the Southern Conference for Human Welfare in the spring of 1945, Murphy, Rutledge, Reed, and Douglas attended, but Stone, Frankfurter, and Jackson did not.[118]

Overlapping Public and Private Tensions in the Public Arena

In the current era of pervasive media coverage, it is far more complex than it was even a decade ago to hide conflicts within the Court or to avoid the appearance of personal conflict. Thus efforts by Justices Thomas and O'Connor during 1994 to play down the idea that there is conflict, some of it personal, within the Court have not convinced very many observers.[119] Moreover, there is too much evidence to the contrary in published opinions, articles, interviews, and speeches to ignore the obvious tensions that even untutored citizens can observe. Particularly during the especially turbulent period from 1984 to 1986, the number of press reports of public statements by the justices criticizing each other and the Court focused attention on what were obviously sharp disagreements among the justices. This series of open debates in the public arena, along with the published clashes in opinions, led the *New York Times* to observe that the Burger Court "became a contentious Court for a contentious time."[120]

These observations have not been limited to talk shows or magazines. Judge Robert Henry of the U.S. Circuit Court of Appeals asked Justice Ginsburg about the reported disputes during a presentation by Justice Ginsburg in Denver in August 1994. At her presentation to the Ninth Circuit Judicial Conferences in 1994, Justice O'Connor was asked about "civility among judges." The question obviously arose not only because of the reports, but also because of Scalia's harsh attack on O'Connor (discussed in Chapter 3). She replied, "'Sticks and stones will break my bones, but words will never hurt me.' Then she bluntly added, 'That probably isn't true.'"[121]

CONCLUSION

Clearly, many of the conflicts that have arisen in the Court over the two hundred years of its existence have taken a variety of forms quite apart from external professional clashes in published opinions. A variety of weapons have been used by justices against each other, whether the focus of the clash was internal professional, internal personal, or external personal. Indeed, it is time to treat disputes among justices as dynamics to be expected rather than aberrant behavior. On the other hand, there are dangers that can arise from internal disputes that get out of hand or from an excessive spillover of conflicts into public arguments among the justices.

Ironically, it has become clearer over time that external professional battles sometimes reveal the existence of internal personal disputes, notwithstanding the fact that trained observers know how attorneys and all members of the Court who are indeed trained advocates, use sharp rhetoric. At some point, the ability to simply write off harsh words as so much posturing is no longer credible.

FIVE
WHAT DIFFERENCE DOES IT MAKE?

When Justice O'Connor observed that it "probably isn't true" that "words will never hurt me," she posed a word picture with which everyone can identify and also captured some important nuances regarding the impact of clashes on the Court. Words do hurt, and when they come from peers and colleagues with whom one must work every day and on whom one must depend for support, they hurt even more. When there are informal norms that are supposed to prohibit taking those tiffs to friends and others outside the workplace, they can fester and become more hurtful still. If small injuries occur often enough over a sufficiently long time, the hurt can transform into bitterness, resentment, and even retribution. Speaking of the relationship between Earl Warren and Felix Frankfurter, Bernard Schwartz observes, "If, according to Bryce's noted truism, 'judges are only men,' the Frankfurter papers show that they behave as such on matters about which they feel strongly enough."[1]

IT SHOULD NOT HURT THAT MUCH, BUT IT DOES!

One answer is simply to dismiss conflict in the Court as part of the territory. After all, judges are trained advocates whose legal careers involved accepting money for taking harsh action against others, usually strangers, on behalf of a client. In the process, attorneys regularly exchange barbs. Lawyers associated with the plaintiff bar may even end up forming alliances with others on the same side against the defense bar, and so on. Beyond all that normal pull and haul of the business there is the fact that these are seasoned professionals with years of practice, in one form or another, who know better than to take everything seriously, or at least personally.

Life on the Court is different, however. Judges may be lawyers by training, but their profession is supposed to be judging, not serving as advocates for clients. The Court does not take cases because of an obligation to parties or their lawyers but because the issues presented by the cases are so important that the nation needs answers. The justices' task is not to choose up sides but to find answers to those questions.

Moreover, justices are not young men and women. They are senior members of their profession, at least middle-aged, if not substantially older. Most people do not become more flexible with age, particularly if they have been subjected to aggressive behavior from someone over an extended period. The wisdom of age, notwithstanding, there is a limit to flexibility and diplomacy.

Indeed, diplomacy is part of the problem. Not only are justices constrained, at least by custom, to keep the fights inside the Court, they are also restricted as to what they can do even within the institution. Because of the basic rule that one needs the votes of others and cannot compel them to give those votes, it is not wise to vent all the anger one feels, even if doing so would be fully justified.

There is also the felt obligation to maintain a level of civility within the Court. Although some members of the Court, like Douglas, Frankfurter, and Scalia, have never been particularly constrained by that idea, other members of the Court have. If there is a public sense that the Court is engaged in petty squabbling, all of the ringing declarations by justices on the hustings to the contrary, as in Justice Thomas's 1994 circuit address, will not eliminate the concern.

In general terms, then, it should not be surprising that words can and do hurt. Neither is it unexpected that the kinds of people who sit on the Court feel and to some extent fear the problems of conflict more than they sometimes admit. But what about particular instances? How do clashes among the justices affect the institution and the actions it takes? There are several answers, including departures from the Court, loss of the ability to compromise, decline of collegiality, changes in the nature of dissenting and concurring behavior, the creation of new patterns of dispute, barriers to effective Court operations, and damage to the public perceptions of the Court.

DEPARTURE OF MEMBERS OF THE COURT

As strange as it may seem, battles on the bench have played a role in more than one justice's decision to leave and have influenced the decisions by others not to go.

Enough Is Enough

It is difficult for most outside observers to think of a justice of the United States Supreme Court leaving the bench because of the effects of internal strife, but it has happened. One of the first members of the Court who left at least in part because of clashes on the bench was Justice Curtis.

In addition to the infamous majority ruling in Dred Scott penned by Chief Justice Taney, Justices Curtis and McLean also issued separate opinions that were distributed to the newspapers before the Taney opinion. Curtis requested a copy of the Taney opinion so that those who sought to publicize the opinions would have the entire collection.

> Taney, under the written endorsement of approval from Justices Wayne and Daniel, the only two Justices then in the city, directed the clerk not to give a copy to Curtis. Curtis was thus in the position of not being able to obtain a copy of an important opinion of the Court of which he was a member. The resultant personal tension was a factor—though only one—in his resigning shortly thereafter.[2]

Story's biographer, Newmyer, reports that Story "resigned, angry at the direction the Court had taken and rendered powerless by the strength of the remainder of the Court against his own positions."[3]

Justice Clarke made it quite clear that he was leaving the Court because he had had enough strife. Taft had been concerned because of the extremism of McReynolds and the behavior of other members of the Court, and Clarke saw no likelihood that the situation would improve. His resignation in 1922 disappointed Woodrow Wilson, who had appointed him. Wilson wrote:

> It has deeply grieved me to learn of your retirement from the Supreme Court. I have not the least inclination to criticize the action, because I know that you would have taken it from none but the highest motives. I am only sorry—deeply sorry. Like thousands of other liberals throughout the country, I have been counting on the influence of you and Justice Brandeis to restrain the Court in some measure from the extreme reactionary course which it seems inclined to follow.

Clarke replied a few days later in a letter that made the point in stark terms. It is worthy of lengthy quotation.

Unless you have much more intimate knowledge of the character of work which a Supreme Judge must do than I had before going to Washington you little realize the amount of grinding, uninteresting, bone labor there is in writing more than half the cases decided by the Supreme Court. . . .

I protested often, but in vain, that too many trifling cases were being written, that our strength could be conserved for better things, and that no amount of care could avoid hopeless confusion and conflict in the decisions. It resulted from all this and from court conditions which I cannot describe in writing that for 2 or 3 years the work kept growing more and more irksome to me. . . .

Of one, and by no means the least distressing of the conditions I must write in answer to a suggestion in your note.

Judge Brandeis and I were agreeing less and less frequently in the decision of cases involving what we call, for want of a better designation, liberal principles. It is for you to judge which was falling away from the current standards. . . .

There is much more, but this will suffice to show that in leaving the Court I did not withdraw any support from Judge Brandeis. One or the other of us was shifting or had shifted his standards so that in critical or crucial cases we were seldom in agreement. Our personal relations, of course, continued entirely cordial.

McReynolds as you know is the most reactionary judge on the Court. There were many other things which had better not be set down in black and white which made the situation to me deplorable and harassing to such a degree that I thought myself not called on to sacrifice what of health and strength I may have left in a futile struggle against constantly increasing odds. Sometime I should like to tell you of it all. It was in some respects as disillusioning a chapter as Washington could afford—I am sure I need not say more than this to one who has differed as you have in the recent past.[4]

By 1945 Justice Murphy was thoroughly aggravated by the tension that he had felt for the past three years. He had let it be known before Roosevelt's death that he would be happy to accept another kind of high-level appointment, but nothing ever came of it. "Frankfurter's continued digs got under Murphy's skin,"[5] and he was tired of the derision of others, like Roberts, who made no secret of their disdain for him.

You Can't Get Rid of Me That Easily!

However, Murphy was one of those who, though more than ready to leave in terms of physical condition and attitude, felt a need to hang on precisely because of the struggles within the Court. He had been hospitalized more than once and missed the start of the 1948 term. J. Woodford Howard observes:

> Politically the tight power balance on the Court made retirement even less palatable. . . . Rutledge and Murphy's clerks improvised a system of communication and opinion production which enabled the absent Justice, who kept up with written briefs, to give Rutledge his vote in November conferences and not to fall behind. . . . Returning to the bench in January 1949 he was hospitalized again for short spells in February, April, and June.[6]

Many justices have hung on to continue the good fight for their views and to resist perceived efforts by those outside the Court to get them out, only to be forced out in the end by physical condition. In the modern era, examples include Felix Frankfurter, Hugo Black, Thurgood Marshall, and William Brennan. One of the more interesting examples is William O. Douglas.

When Douglas came to the Court as one of the youngest men ever appointed, fresh from behind-the-scenes support (despite his later denials) of President Roosevelt's Court-packing plan, he was of the opinion that there should be a mandatory retirement age. But like others who have come to the Supreme Court, he changed his views over the years. Starting in the late 1940s, there were several attempts to get him off the Court, including an attempt to impeach him after he granted a stay of execution to Julius and Ethel Rosenberg, in the infamous atomic spy case, and again after his statement to the press on a return from abroad that the United States should recognize the government of the People's Republic of China.

By the early 1960s, Douglas had had a bellyful of Frankfurter, had worked up a thorough dislike for Earl Warren,[7] and was utterly disgusted with what he saw as the Court's timidity in the face of important issues ranging from the First Amendment to important constitutional criminal procedure questions. He said so in no uncertain terms in his Madison lecture, "The Bill of Rights Is Not Enough," which was nothing less than an indictment of the Court on which he served.[8]

Then things improved. Frankfurter left, Brennan was coming into his own, Goldberg and then Fortas joined the Court, and many of the rulings Douglas had hoped for in the late 1950s and early 1960s came to pass. By the late 1960s, he had seen many things change, his health was not good, and he had taken a great deal of heat in the press and from right-wing politicians in Congress because of his three divorces and his marriage to Cathleen, a woman much younger than he. By 1969, he had decided that he would retire shortly,[9] but when pressures began to build both inside and outside the Court, he changed his mind.

The Court had been a major target in the 1968 presidential race. There was a clear intention to replace people like Douglas with conservative Republicans, and to have Richard Nixon, a man Douglas hated, make the selections. Abe Fortas became a target not only because of his off-the-bench activities but also because he was a vulnerable symbol of the Warren Court. The pressure was too much; on May 14, 1969, Fortas resigned. Douglas was no happier knowing that both Hugo Black and Earl Warren fully agreed that Douglas's protégé had to go.

Immediately there were calls to go after other members of the Warren majority, with Douglas as the first target.[10] The hook was that Douglas was president of the Parvin Foundation and heavily involved in the activities of the Center for the Study of Democratic Institutions.

Parvin was involved in a Las Vegas gambling establishment. Although Douglas took no salary from Parvin or the center, he did take travel expenses. All of these connections made tempting targets for reporters and political foes. Douglas wrote to Parvin on his way back from Brazil, just two days before Fortas resigned. "The manufactured case against you and the Foundation is a shocking thing that we must fight to the end and win. But as the issues are formed it may get nastier and nastier. . . . The strategy is to get me off the Court and I do not propose to bend to any such pressure."[11] Douglas resigned from the foundation and other involvements, but the pressure continued.

He knew that his enemies were after him long before the serious impeachment effort was launched. He wrote his attorney, former Defense Secretary Clark Clifford, in October 1969:

> Enclosed is a news item from yesterday's STAR. It is, I think a token that the campaign against me has started all over again. The grossly unfair and malicious character of this particular item is that it relates to episodes that happened before I ever met Mr. Parvin. He did, late in 1961 or early 1962, transfer a fractional interest in a mortgage on the hotel in question to the Parvin Foundation, an interest which the Foundation got rid of because it was on a Las Vegas property that had a gambling casino. But fractional interests in mortgages are always hard to liquidate. . . . There is nothing that this article pertains to with which I had any connection whatsoever.[12]

He also learned from a newsman friend of his that "Clark Mollenhoff of the White House is planting a story that in 1963–64 I was in Santo Domingo trying to get out of Juan Bosch a gambling casino for certain Mafia interests. I was there at the time representing the Parvin Foundation, and preparing a TV adult literacy course." He closed the letter by asking Clifford, "Isn't it time I sued someone?"[13]

The unsuccessful effort to impeach Douglas was spearheaded by Gerald Ford on behalf of an administration that had threatened retribution in the wake of the defeat of Nixon's nominations of Clement Haynsworth and G. Harrold Carswell.[14] The process took its toll on Douglas, but he weathered it, and the charges were ultimately rejected by the House Judiciary Committee.

No sooner had the impeachment process passed than there was a major turnover in the Court. Warren was gone, replaced by Burger. Fortas left, and Black and Harlan resigned just weeks before their deaths in 1971. They were replaced by Blackmun, Powell, and Rehnquist. Douglas became quickly aware that the results of his work of thirty years were now threatened by the Nixon appointees. He immediately clashed with Burger, and it was clear that he was going to be battling the votes of Rehnquist and Powell as well as Blackmun, though he got along well with all three on a personal level. By 1973 it was obvious that Douglas, Marshall, and Brennan would be holding out against the Nixon appointees and White and Stewart, who were leaning to the new conservatives. Douglas was senior on what was increasingly the dissenting bloc, which pitted him directly against Burger on several issues, including most notably the assignment of opinion writing. He found himself producing literally dozens of dissents each year.[15] Douglas battled mightily until a stroke laid him low in January 1974.

He rallied gamely, telling the *New York Times* in July: "There's no chance I'll retire. . . . I'll be there in October, positively."[16] A ramp was constructed so that Douglas could get his wheelchair into the building and up to the bench. Douglas struggled for over a year to stay on the bench and fight the tide of the Burger Court. It was a losing cause, and he resigned in November 1975. Like other justices before and since, Douglas tried as hard as possible not to give in to turmoil within the Court or pressures from without.

INFLUENCE ON DECISIONS

The consequences of internal battles affected not merely the people but also the decisions of the Court. Sometimes, conflict within the Court influenced votes, and on other occasions it shaped important opinions.

Justice Murphy, according to his biographers, was convinced that matters deteriorated so badly in the 1943 term that justices actually cast votes to avoid joining their enemies.

> Although Frankfurter at first "strongly" favored sustaining the state tax involved in the 1943 term case of *Union Brokerage Company v. Jensen,* he reconsidered when he saw that this aligned him with the Axis. Murphy was also convinced that Frankfurter switched his vote for the same reason in another case a few days later. "Even Rutledge remarked about it," Murphy's clerk noted in his diary. Roberts, again according to Murphy, spoke in favor of dismissing a tax case during the same term but voted otherwise when the Axis agreed with him. Murphy, at the same time, was convinced that Black and Douglas were "sometimes blinded in their views by their intense hatred of F.F.!" Recognizing that Jackson was strongly affected by personalities, a former Jackson clerk concluded that how Jackson "felt about . . . Douglas had some effect on some of his votes."[17]

Murphy's biographer, Sydney Fine, notes that the fragmentation in the rulings of the Stone Court clearly resulted from "personal animosities among the justices, not just philosophical differences" and adds that the opinions of the Stone and Vinson years were "tinged with personal rancor."[18] At the same time, Fine observes that it is difficult to know just how much impact any particular disagreement had, though several of the justices reported that they were certain that the battles did move votes.[19]

At times, however, direct evidence does exist of the impact of conflict on rulings. An excellent example is the Court's 1965 ruling in *Griswold v. Connecticut*.[20] Goldberg explains that Warren and Douglas had been engaged in a relatively long-running spat, and for nearly a year they did not speak to one another. In fact, the dispute went at least as far back as 1961. Ironically, Douglas used, of all things, Warren's response to Frankfurter's performance in Court as the basis for some of his criticism. Douglas wrote to retired Justice Sherman Minton:

> You know how enthusiastic we were when Earl Warren came to the Court. But in retrospect it was a bad day. His attitude toward the Court is the attitude of a prosecutor to his staff. We all know how extravagant Felix often is in announcing his opinions. He often embellishes them, as you know. Last Monday was the second time Warren spoke up after Felix had finished, denouncing Felix for "degrading" the Court. Warren had no opinion in the cases. He was purporting to ride herd on Felix.
>
> I've never been a Felix fan, as you know. But I never dreamed I'd be here when a Chief Justice degraded the Court like Earl Warren is doing. It's a nasty spectacle. Perhaps the old boy is off his rocker.[21]

Minton replied that he was sorry to learn that "all is not too well with the finest group of men I ever worked with. I can appreciate the provocation on both Sides."[22]

Douglas was carrying other frustrations, for he had clashed with Warren over a stenographer a few weeks earlier. There had been discussion of the fact that the lady in question was absent without leave. Douglas came to her defense, sending a memorandum to Warren explaining that she had been ill and urging that he not "bear down hard on a lady who was really sick."[23] Warren replied that the woman had not notified anyone and that when his office tracked down a relative to get word to the lady, her sister "advised my office that she was traveling in the South." He also reminded Douglas that the lady had been warned two years earlier about that kind of behavior, which could not be tolerated.[24] Whereupon, Douglas sent a critical memorandum to the conference warning that "an injustice is about to be done."[25] Warren replied that he had no intention of doing anything harsh to her or punishing her for "disloyalty," but to seek her retirement in as gentle a manner as possible, which is what the conference had agreed should be done in the first place.[26]

Warren and Douglas had had this sort of spat before. There were clashes on cases and on process until 1963, when Goldberg reports that the two men hit a parting of the ways. Goldberg explains that he had originally intended to join Douglas's majority opinion in *Griswold,* but Earl Warren came to see him and changed his mind.[27] Because they had been at odds for some time, Warren was uncomfortable with the idea of joining the Douglas opinion. That was a problem because there were only four votes for the Court's opinion, though there was a clear majority to strike down the statute. If Warren joined White's concurrence, which was his original intention, then the Douglas opinion would be only a plurality, leaving serious doubt as to the Court's support for the right to privacy. Goldberg offered to write a concurrence, in which he could join, that would stress the Ninth Amendment argument. Warren agreed. Since Goldberg began by announcing that he joined the opinion of the Court, it was possible to garner a majority to support Douglas without Warren having to join him directly. Ironically, it was Goldberg's Ninth Amendment argument that was most often repeated in future years rather than the rationale used by Douglas.

Not all effects on decisions were of a sort that would cause anxiety, however. Indeed, internal professional clashes have sometimes played exactly the kind of role that they should, driving constructive changes in the final opinion. Thus Justice Hugo Black's opinion for the Court in *Everson v. Board of Education*[28] defined separation of church and state for decades to come. Black, writing for the Court, upheld a New Jersey program that reimbursed parents for the cost of transporting children to private schools against a charge of separation of church and state. It produced a battle royal within the Court, but it was the best kind of fight right from the conference. Of all people, Wiley Rutledge led the charge against Black, warning: "Every religious institution in [the] country will be reaching into [the] hopper for help if you sustain this. We ought to stop this thing right at [the] threshold of [the] public school."[29] Black paid close attention to Rutledge's criticisms.

In particular, Rutledge's opinion moved Black to think carefully about defining what was meant by the establishment clause of the First Amendment. His first draft of *Everson* issued December 6, 1946, said: "Neither a state nor the Federal Government can set up a state church. Neither can pass laws which prefer one religion over another. Neither can force a person to go to or to remain away from a church against his will or force him to profess a belief or disbelief in any religion."[30] Rutledge insisted that Black was still not comprehending the proper scope of the no-establishment clause. In his January draft, Rutledge made the point directly. "Now as then, not simply aid to single sect, but aid to any or all is forbidden."[31] Black marked the point in the margin. A week later, Black's much expanded and significantly modified third draft appeared. At its heart was a new statement of fundamental principles. The January 17, 1947, draft moved away from the no-preference-among-religions language to the language we now know. "Neither a state nor the Federal Government can set up a church. Neither can pass laws which aid one religion, aid all religions, or prefer one religion over another."

In the midst of the fight, Frankfurter had been pressuring Murphy, who held the key vote. Murphy, at the time, had had more than enough of Felix, and he went with Black.

Once Black had arrived at a conclusion on a point of principle, though, he could be unmovable. When the next major religion case, *McCollum,*[32] came to the Court the year after *Everson,* Black knew that Frankfurter was busily organizing the "Anti-Everson lads,"[33] and he was ready for them. It came down to a toe-to-toe battle between Black's forces and Frankfurter's, and Justice Burton's effort to mediate between the two was doomed to failure from the outset.

CREATING THE RELIABLE ANTI-AUTHORITY

At some point battle lines can be drawn so sharply and can exist over such a prolonged period that one justice becomes a reliable anti-authority for another. By the late 1940s, Frankfurter was ready to assume that if Black had anything to do with a position, there was reason to be suspicious. Even if Black was on what Frankfurter regarded as the right side of a case, it might very well be for the wrong reasons or presented in an unacceptable manner. The same was true of Douglas, as far as Frankfurter was concerned. For his part, Douglas, and sometimes Black, was ready to reciprocate. Frankfurter had a similar view of Murphy, another member of "the Axis." To label someone a part of "the Axis" during or just after World War II was as sinister a condemnation as could be made.

Once one assumes that one or more colleagues are reliable anti-authorities, life on the Court becomes in its very nature more rigid and combative, for one assumes that the adversary is beyond redemption. In such a situation, it becomes relatively easy to justify virtually any choice of weapons. The decision to use surrogates may appear acceptable, and, naturally, retaliation seems wholly appropriate. Frankfurter, for example, had no reservations whatever about the use of outside champions, and his colleagues knew it.

> Complimenting an article by one of his most prolific disciples—Alexander Bickel—Frankfurter writes: "I can assure you that explicit analysis and criticism of the way the Court is doing its business really gets under their skin, just as the praise of their constituencies, the so-called liberal journals and well-known liberal approvers only fortifies them in their present result-oriented jurisprudence. . . . You law professors really should sharpen your pens so that there is no mistaking as to what the trouble is an where the blame lies. I can give you proof that if you would speak out, you would get under their skins."[34]

More recent examples include Black's view of Fortas, Rehnquist's response to Brennan, and Douglas's reaction to Warren Burger. Personal antagonism is not a requirement for antiauthority, but there must be an ongoing, more or less consistent dispute over a wide range of subject matter. Thus, Brennan and Rehnquist "agreed in only 273 of 1,815 cases in which one or more justices dissented, just 15 percent of the Court's divided decisions over a span of almost two decades. This was the lowest rate of agreement of any pair of justices over those years. And they disagreed in virtually every case that raised important constitutional issues."[35]

One danger of developing a reliable anti-authority is that it is very easy to assume that such continuous recalcitrant behavior must reflect troublesome motives. Frankfurter was always ready to ascribe evil motives to Black and Douglas.[36] " 'The non-judicial twain of Justices,' he writes of

Black and Douglas, 'are crafty on the job—I'm watching their effort on John [Harlan]. It's hard for a decent man to realize how indecent people operate.' "[37] Douglas was similarly ready to find Warren Burger guilty of skullduggery, as when he accused him of manipulating the assignment of the *Roe v. Wade* opinion by attempting to manage the battle so that it could be kept clear of presidential politics (Burger's benefactor, Richard Nixon, was seeking reelection).

On some occasions, the tension between two justices got so bad that they simply did not communicate with one another beyond what was specifically required for the performance of their duties. Thus Douglas and Frankfurter were not speaking by the start of the 1948 term.[38] Murphy was nearly at that point with Frankfurter by late 1943.[39] Roberts was not speaking to Douglas when he left the Court.[40] "Powell once went through some weeks in which Blackmun did not speak to him, not even to acknowledge a greeting as they passed in the corridor."[41]

THE DRAWING OF THE BATTLE LINE

Even where the situation falls short of the creation of reliable anti-authorities, there are many cases in which justices have drawn a battle line. Clearly Taft drew such a line between himself and Brandeis, and he saw himself in a fight to wrest Holmes from Brandeis's control.[42] Frankfurter drew a hard line around the Axis.

Perhaps to a lesser degree than antiauthority, the drawing of battle lines can create rigidity and exacerbate a sense of distance. It can even have the perverse effect of pushing a colleague away when his or her vote is sorely needed. One possible example is Justice O'Connor's declaration of the war of the footnotes. She chose Blackmun as her target in *FERC v. Mississippi*,[43] which was one of the cases in which the Court was trying to apply the *National League of Cities v. Usery*[44] ruling as implemented by *Hodel v. Virginia Surface Mining*. In her first term on the Court, O'Connor went after Blackmun as if he were the declared enemy of federalism, which was certainly not a well-grounded charge. Blackmun had been the critical vote in both earlier cases, both to support Rehnquist's opinion in *Usery,* which limited the federal government, and to constrain Rehnquist's approach in *Hodel,* the strip mine case, which authorized some authority for the federal government over states and localities. O'Connor's pressure in *FERC* forced Blackmun to defend the other side of the case more vigorously than he might have, given his own ambiguity on the matter. By the time of *Garcia*,[45] Blackmun still was wavering, but he had been pushed hard and, ultimately, he pushed back, providing the critical vote to reverse *Usery*.

It is difficult to know exactly how much such battles influence any given vote. Certainly some justices' willingness or ability to reach consensus in one case can be affected by their conversations with colleagues in another. As discussed in Chapter 4, Harry Blackmun was frustrated by the pressures he was feeling from his colleagues in the *Bakke* case on affirmative action.[46] At the same time, he felt cross-pressured because of work on another opinion that depended upon his interaction with Brennan. Powell went along with Blackmun's draft in a tax case, a draft he thought very weak, because "we don't want to upset Harry in Bakke."[47]

For some justices, a clash in one major case may mark a breaking point in a relationship. For Frankfurter, as we have seen, that case was *West Virginia Board of Education v. Barnette*,[48] when his former allies switched sides and, joined by the Court's new addition, reversed Frankfurter's *Minersville*[49] opinion on mandatory patriotic ceremonies. For Brennan, the break with Frankfurter began with Frankfurter's insistence upon filing a separate concurrence in the Little Rock school case,[50] and became irreparable as a result of Frankfurter's conduct in connection with *Irvin v. Dowd*,[51] when Frankfurter called in a surrogate to go after Brennan.[52]

Even if a breaking point is not reached, a justice will sometimes make such an adamant commitment that it becomes extremely difficult to move and he will not tolerate anyone who asks him to do so. Certainly justices like Black, Frankfurter, and Scalia have taken positions that invite a pitched battle. It is difficult to challenge the position without appearing to criticize the justice who asserted it. Jeffries describes Thurgood Marshall in these terms:

> His style was more confrontational than persuasive. In Conference, he told tales of prejudice in the segregated South, funny stories that invited his colleagues to laugh with him but that also left an aftertaste of rebuke. Sometimes Marshall abandoned humor for caustic sarcasm. What he did not do was to attempt to engage the sympathies of other Justices in one-on-one conversation. Quick to take of-

fense, he was too proud to try to educate his colleagues to his point of view—and too suspicious of their motives to think it worthwhile to try.[53]

THE UNARTICULATED INJURY

Marshall felt what might be called unarticulated injuries, slights that he may never have mentioned but that nonetheless hurt and conditioned his relationships with others. The most common of these seem to be injuries stemming from perceived disrespect, attempts at manipulation, or simple insensitivity.

Two members of the Court who caused such injuries are Burger and Scalia. Scalia's behavior in oral argument led some of his colleagues to regard him as insensitive to their concerns and a bit of a grandstander. Burger's conference behavior, particularly his breach of the long-standing norm that one justice does not interrupt another, was frustrating, as were his perorations in conference that seemed to indicate an assumption that his colleagues were less than intellectually adequate. The suspicion by colleagues that he had, on any number of occasions, attempted to manipulate the voting and opinion assignment left more scars than he knew among his colleagues.

The fact that Burger was sometimes intransigent when he was called on his behavior did not help. In *United States v. United States District Court,*[54] Douglas wrote a positive but insistent letter to Burger that the assignment should have gone to Powell and not White, who was in fact on the opposite side of the crucial issue from the majority of votes.[55] Burger immediately rejected Douglas's assertion and insisted that the assignment remain with White. Douglas promptly wrote Powell and asked him to write, notwithstanding Burger's assignment to White.[56] Powell prepared a deferential note to Douglas with copies to Burger and White, indicating that although he recognized the assignment to White he would nevertheless prepare a memorandum to generate comment. Powell's memorandum eventually obtained enough votes to prevail when Douglas convinced Powell to accommodate Brennan with the modification of an important footnote. Indeed there were several cases in which Burger was told by others that he had erred in assignment but refused to correct the problem, thus fueling suspicions that he was engaged in deliberate manipulation.

Bowsher v. Synar, the case that tested the constitutionality of the Gramm, Rudman, Hollings Budget Deficit Reduction Act, provided another set of concerns. Justice Rehnquist had long wanted to attack the legitimacy of delegations of authority by the Congress to independent regulatory agencies.[57] When Burger prepared his preliminary draft in *Bowsher,* he implied a serious question as to that legitimacy, even though the discussion at conference had rejected that approach. Sandra Day O'Connor, John Paul Stevens, William Brennan, Lewis Powell, and Thurgood Marshall all immediately wrote Burger, calling him on what could hardly have been an oversight.[58] When Burger circulated his second draft, both Brennan and Stevens wrote back to underscore the need to make very clear that the Court was not challenging the agencies. They were not going to allow Burger to get away with even a hint of what the majority clearly did not want him to say.

Many justices have been regarded by their colleagues as insufficiently sensitive. Justice Daniel's biographer notes that he "was sadly subject to the vices of pettiness and arrogance and to an insufferable self-righteousness."[59] Felix Frankfurter never understood that all targets were not fair game. When he bore down on Murphy, attempting to use his Catholicism to manipulate him, he was utterly insensitive. Frankfurter knew that Murphy's vote was critical in *Everson,* and accordingly he wrote:

Dear Frank,

You have some false friends—those who flatter you and play on you for *their* purposes, not for your good. What follows is written by one who cares for your place in history, not in tomorrow's columns, as lasting as yesterday's snow. At least your sister and your brother would acquit me of anything but disinterestedness. I am willing to be judged by them.

The short of it is that you, above all men, should write along the lines—I do not say with the phrasing—of Bob's opinion in Everson. I know what you think of the great American doctrine of Church and State—I also know what the wisest men of the Church, like Cardinal Gibbons thought about it. You have a chance to do for your country and your church such as never come [*sic*] to you before—and may never again. The things we most regret—at least such is my experience—are the opportunities missed. For the sake of history, for the sake of your inner peace, don't miss. No one knows better than you what Everson is about. Tell the world—and shame the devil.[60]

Murphy knew full well that Frankfurter and others insulted him behind his back, precisely because of his religious concerns, referring to him as "St. Frank." He also faced criticism from the Catholic community to which he had been so dedicated for so long. Frankfurter's feigned concern for Murphy's religious sensitivities was so obviously contrived that it was like pouring salt into an open wound.

Douglas, too, was often insensitive to the impact of his behavior on his colleagues, from his law clerks to his brethren. His decisions to leave early in the summer and to be effectively out of touch for large periods grated on other justices, for he missed crucial end of the term conferences. He put the burden on Justice Brennan, leaving him with his conference votes and contacting him for updates. In June 1970 Brennan wrote Douglas, relaying the message that Burger was wondering if he would be in any time that week. Brennan continued; "If you are not coming in, I need some instruction. The Chief Justice held an El Paso conference late Friday afternoon. Seven attended (all but you and Thurgood). Byron and I listened but took no formal part because we're out of El Paso. Without you, there was therefore no quorum."[61] Douglas seemed not to notice that his behavior was placing his two closest friends and allies on the Court, Brennan and Black, in difficult situations.

Warren Burger, a man who was himself quite ready to take offense, was often insensitive, and, like Douglas, his behavior sometimes injured those closest to him on the Court, like Lewis Powell. The case of the stolen footnote discussed in Chapter 4 is only one example. "And if the Chief's high-handedness annoyed Powell, with whom he enjoyed generally good relations, how much more irritating it must have been to the Court's liberals."[62]

THE LOSS OF THE ABILITY TO COMPROMISE

The most obvious immediate impact of conflict in the Court is that it makes compromise difficult or, in some cases, virtually impossible. And, as Justice Blackmun put it, compromise is crucial.

> One thing that the public often does not appreciate is that much of what we do, up here, is done . . . by way of compromise. There are

nine of us. And . . . many times, the prevailing opinion, it might be five to four, or six to three, or even seven to two sometimes, there are paragraphs or sentences or statements in the prevailing opinion that the primary author would prefer not to have there.

But in order to get five votes together we have to get something that those five can agree to. We try to accommodate everyone that we can. But, sometimes, a judgment here is by a vote of five.[63]

It is one thing to find common ground amidst professional differences, particularly when those differences are kept within the walls of the Court. It is quite another thing if the conflicts go public or become personal. Justice Fortas had difficulties with Hugo Black when they differed on issues of constitutional interpretation, but all attempts to work together ceased once Fortas became convinced that the issue was personal and that Black had worked against his confirmation. Once his colleagues found that Felix Frankfurter had little ability to separate the personal and the professional, they almost all found him an extremely difficult person with whom to work.

It should come as no surprise, then, that fragmentation in opinions is high during periods of internal conflict: witness the Stone, Burger, and Rehnquist (before the departures of Brennan and Marshall) Courts. Writing of the Stone period, Sydney Fine observes:

Stone correctly described the 1943 term as "a tough year" for the Court because of the discord among his brethren. Frankfurter told Rutledge during the term that he was "bothered by the too frequent clash of atmosphere, if not in explicit views," in the opinions of the justices. Informing Reed of his approval of a Reed slip opinion, Douglas noted, "I hope someday to be about to reciprocate by writing something to which you will agree." Of the 137 cases decided by full opinions in the term, the justices were unanimous in only fifty-seven, or 42 percent. Not only was this the first time in the history of the Court that the justices had disagreed in a majority of cases in a term, but, as we shall see, they sometimes expressed their differences in personal terms. "Decision day," as Walton Hamilton observed at the close of the term, "has not been the dullest of Washington spectacles."[64]

Sheldon Novick found a similar pattern in 1921. Fewer cases were decided, and more dissenting opinions were issued. Important matters were determined by narrow votes, statutes were struck down by votes of five to four, with bitter dissents, and no single view commanded a majority.[65]

David O'Brien's evaluation of opinion development over history finds significant declines in unanimous opinions and substantial increases in separate opinions that would tend to support the observations made in many biographies of justices who served during periods of high conflict. He also finds, however, that there has been a general increase, particularly since the 1940s, in separate opinions.[66] Not only did the number of opinions increase and unanimity decline, but, particularly during the most conflict-ridden periods of the Burger Court, the number of cases that commanded only a plurality increased sharply. O'Brien suggests that "traditional norms supporting institutional opinions have been eroded."[67]

One may add, however, that the norms have been eroded by an increased willingness of members of the Court to fight their battles in the open. It is interesting, for example, that O'Brien finds a dramatic decline in 5–4 rulings with the retirements of Justices Brennan and Marshall, the last two Warren-era justices on the Court, and with the addition of Reagan and Bush appointees to the Nixon appointees (and the one Ford appointment, John Paul Stevens). Even so, O'Brien finds large numbers of concurrences during the Rehnquist years.[68] Those data fit well with the biographical observations about the nature of conflict on the Court. It is also tempting to hypothesize that one reason for the general increase of separate opinions, the breakdown of the norm O'Brien describes, is that once the informal norms against public fights and restrictions on types of public disputes began to break down, they were not restored. The acceptable level of open conflict was ratcheted upward. The removal of the institutional norm of avoidance of open conflict reduces, to some extent at least, the apparent need for compromise.

Another issue that can exacerbate conflict and reduce the likelihood of compromise is the perception that one is fighting against an established bloc. Frankfurter saw Black, Douglas, and Murphy coming together, and they were joined by Wiley Rutledge when Frankfurter lost his campaign to get Roosevelt to appoint Learned Hand. "Thus instead of an ally, Frankfurter got only another opponent."[69] Things began to look up when Frankfurter saw a bloc of his own likely to form with the arrival of Burton, Minton, and Clark. Vinson was also with him on a number of important cases, but Frankfurter had no use for the chief as a person. That is one reason why, when Vinson died while *Brown v. Board of Education*[70] was pending, Frankfurter was so openly pleased.[71]

Black and Douglas seemed to be facing a conservative bloc in the 1950s, but then came BBD&W (Black, Brennan, Douglas, and Warren), a phalanx against which Frankfurter just could not hope to prevail. With the arrival of John Marshall Harlan, however, Frankfurter thought he had a new ally, but although Harlan was conservative, he was not interested in being a member of a bloc. The fact that the Warren Court was far more fragmented than Frankfurter conceived it did not change his sense that there was a bloc with which to contend and against which to wage a righteous conflict.

Douglas and Thurgood Marshall clearly perceived a bloc forming among the Nixon appointees, not only because that was the announced intention of the administration, but also because the four Nixon appointees were together on so many cases against the positions of Douglas and Marshall. Certainly Marshall had the sense of being closed out in many cases. Brennan, by contrast, saw the ideological bloc but also saw opportunities to split that general affiliation in particular policy areas and specific cases. He exploited the differences among the Nixon and, later, the Reagan justices quite effectively. Because he did not let the view of the bloc control his perspective, he was able to negotiate and compromise.

Another factor that can constrain compromise is the sense that a colleague is not a dependable ally. One of the best-known examples of this problem was Douglas, who drove his friends to distraction. Changing an opinion to get his vote never came with an assurance that he would stay on board. Black, by contrast, was solid.

DECLINE OF COLLEGIALITY

Continual battles, particularly public and personal battles, damage a spirit of collegiality within the Court. Of course, collegiality in the Court does not simply mean conviviality. It is a working spirit and a set of informal understandings about how members of the Court can and should work together. At the most general level, Felix Frankfurter hit the mark when he said that "what is most needed in a Chief Justice is what the

Germans call *ein Tonangeber*—a tonegiver: one who by his example generates in the others complete dedication to the work of the Court."[72] He initially felt that Warren was just that kind of person, although he later changed his assessment. It is somewhat ironic that Frankfurter longed for a Tonangeber, for in fact he was one himself, though the tone he struck was often discordant. Burger fancied himself to be a Tonangeber, but, like Frankfurter, his tone was also often less than soothing.

Specific aspects of collegiality can be affected by various forms of conflict in the Court. One of the most important moments in the Court occurs when the justice who authors a draft opinion begins to receive response memoranda from colleagues. In the vast majority of cases, justices stand ready to accept suggestions for improvements in opinions and even to make meaningful changes if it will lead one or more colleagues to join the opinion. The manner in which a response to a draft is presented, however, can matter considerably. Judge Frank Coffin described this phenomenon quite effectively as "responsive collegiality."[73] Increased tensions can manifest themselves in relatively harsh reactions to drafts. Chief Justice Taft had difficulties with McReynolds in part because of his reactions to draft opinions. Chief Justice Burger's reactions could also be combative, as, for example, in his reaction to Justice Powell's draft in the *Bowers v. Hardwick* case, concerning gay rights claims against the Georgia sodomy statute.[74]

Reactions can be particularly strident if a justice perceives him- or herself as a watchdog that must be ready to react to transgressions by his colleagues. Thurgood Marshall responded harshly in a number of circumstances as he watched the Court taking what he considered large backward steps from civil rights advances of the past. "He stopped short of calling his colleagues racist—but just barely."[75] The situation grew particularly tense after the *Bakke* ruling in 1978.[76] (See Chapter 2.) Marshall was thus especially primed for material written by Powell, who had so angered him in *Bakke*.

For example, in *Batson v. Kentucky,* Powell prepared the opinion for the Court. Marshall shot back with a sharp concurrence asserting that the only way to cure discrimination in jury selection was to eliminate peremptory challenges. Brennan wrote a letter to Thurgood attempting to get him to soften his language since, after all, Powell was moving in a direction preferable to the *Swain* rule that had been controlling for so long.[77] Even though Brennan pointed out to Marshall how unscrupulous prosecutors could get around the *Batson* opinion, Marshall refused to ease his attack despite the fact that he might very well be hurting his own cause.

At some point, the lack of responsive collegiality can even be felt by allies. Douglas's reaction to his friend Bill Brennan in the sit-in cases is a classic example. Douglas wanted to take on the Maryland trespass statute directly and declare it discriminatory in violation of the Fourteenth Amendment because it was being used to enforce segregation. Brennan, in an effort to avoid creating adverse pressure on border state legislators while the Civil Rights Act was pending, urged a less direct strategy that he anticipated would have the same result. Douglas mobilized a coalition that would block Brennan's efforts, but in the end, Brennan succeeded.

Douglas was livid, eventually writing a memorandum to file announcing that "Brennan's opinion which will be filed on Monday, June 22, 1964, was the product of his plan to keep the Court from deciding the basic constitutional issue of the Fourteenth Amendment."[79] He went on to detail the "plan." But a memorandum to the files was not nearly enough for Douglas. He let fly with a blast aimed directly at Brennan in a letter on June 3.

I have your note in No. 110—*Malloy v. Hogan.* My re-examination of this case resulted indirectly from the sit-in cases. I suffered a real shock when I realized you were in dead ernest in vacating *Bell* and remanding it to the State court and thus avoiding the basic constitutional question. I guess I underwent a real trauma when I realized that the spirit of Felix still was the dominant force here.

About that time your opinion in *Garrison* came in and as I read *Garrison* I began to realize I had been reading your opinions with my heart as well as my mind in view of my deep affection for you. So I decided that it was impossible to draw the line between malice in the New York Times case and malice in the *Garrison* case and that I would have to write separately which I did.

At that point I decided perhaps I better look again at *Malloy* to see if I had agreed to anything that might embarrass me in the future. I did so, and as a result realized that I had read it too uncritically the first time when I sent you my return.

This has nothing to do with good intentions or anything else except my basic convictions that I forged rightly or wrongly in the long, bitter years here with Felix. And as I re-read *Malloy,* I began to appreciate that you had not even overruled *Twining*—that it was still there to be used on other occasions and that Felix's highly subjective, personalized interpretations of the Bill of Rights was being perpetuated.

I had trouble enough with *Gideon,* although Hugo steered close enough to the line to make it possible for me to go along. Since receiving your note, I have gone through your opinion and I return it herewith with deletions that would make it palatable to me. . . .

Each of us travels his own path of necessity, and I really see no great urgency in getting a Court opinion. Perhaps the suggestions I have made reach beyond your ability to accommodate.[80]

It was a devastating set of accusations. Moreover, Brennan knew precisely how vicious Douglas meant to be in suggesting that he was behaving like Felix. It was a difficult period for Douglas, who was already embroiled with Warren, among others. That sort of gratuitous antagonism undermines effective collegial relationships.

In a sense, it was Douglas who was acting like Felix, not Brennan. Of course, Douglas had certainly learned the behavior from the master. Frankfurter could annoy his colleagues over the smallest matters. An example was his petulent reaction to a Douglas note after *Mapp v. Ohio.*[81] In January 1962 Douglas wrote to members of the Court that he had visited with Stanley Mosk, then attorney general of California, who thanked Douglas and his colleagues for their ruling in *Mapp.* The California Supreme Court had produced a similar ruling, but by only a 4–3 vote. Two new members were added, but one was disposed toward one side of the case and the other to the opposite side, leaving the state court badly fragmented.

The newspaper campaign, however, against the Cahan decisions, continued unabated. Mosk said that, with the system of elective judges they have in California, pressure on the trial courts was very, very great not to apply the *Cahan* case or to find there were more exceptions to it, or in other words, try to get around it. . . . The result of *Mapp v. Ohio,* according to Mosk, is to take the pressure off the local judges to create exceptions and to follow the exclusionary rule and all its ramifications.[82]

Frankfurter could not resist a reply to the "brethren" in which he "was moved to this word of comment." He was not pleased at Mosk's welcoming of the *Mapp* ruling on the grounds outlined in Douglas's letter. He regretted the fact that "coming from one of the most self-reliant of States, this attitude to look to the federal authority for dealing with a local problem—for such was concern over the *Cahan* doctrine until *Mapp* came along—runs counter to one of my oldest convictions which time has only reinforced."[83] Of course, Douglas could not resist the bait. He wrote a "Memorandum to the Conference," January 30, 1962: "I did not ask Attorney General Mosk. But if I had put the question, I am certain he would have also said, 'Thank God, California is in the Union.' "[84] By this point, the two old adversaries were off and running. Frankfurter shot back the next day: "When next you see Attorney General Mosk please ask him if California was not 'in the Union' before June 19, 1961."[85] Douglas continued the volley. "When I next see Stanley Mosk, I will put your question to him. My guess is he will say that California was not wholly 'in the Union' before *Mapp v. Ohio,* as he thinks, I believe, that the Bill of Rights should be protective of all our constituent members."[86]

TOWARD ALIENATION

After too many battles over too many years, it is easy to slip into a sense of alienation and frustration. Certainly Frankfurter experienced the sense of a long epic battle lost. Ironically, his nemesis, William O. Douglas, had a similar experience. In his latter years, even as he battled to save what he could of his legacy, Douglas felt that it mattered less. He told his wife that he had worked so hard for so long and fought the good fight, but no one seemed to care about reading his work or paying attention to his warnings.[87]

Added to the irony of the Frankfurter and Douglas battles, both felt the impact of doubts about whether they were insiders or outsiders. Frankfurter biographer H. N. Hirsch describes how the sense that he remained an outsider was a continuing issue for Felix.[88] Douglas repeated the idea that he had "but one soul to save" as if it were a mantra.[89] He labeled himself a loner from his earliest days.[90] He loved to poke fun at the establishment, but he also wanted very much to be a part of it. Once on the Court, he wanted his independence, but he also believed passionately in a variety of important principles and wanted the Court to do the right thing. By the end of his career, Douglas was frustrated by the fact that no matter how hard he fought, he could not keep the Court from turning in what he regarded as the wrong way on so many issues.[91]

Black was not afflicted by the insider/outsider tensions felt by Douglas and Frankfurter, but he did face growing frustration as he drew to the end of his career. His battles with Fortas and disputes with long-time allies like Brennan and Douglas were difficult. Like many others, as he neared the end, Black fought all the harder, but, like Douglas, felt his goals slipping away.

One of more obvious recent examples of this phenomenon was Thurgood Marshall.

In race cases particularly, Marshall grew increasingly bitter. He stopped short of calling his colleagues racist—but just barely. At the least, he thought them insensitive. "What do they know about Negroes?" he asked in 1990. "You can't name one member of this Court who [knew] anything about Negroes before he came to this Court."[92]

EXTERNAL VIEWS OF THE COURT CAN BE AFFECTED

The decision by justices like Thurgood Marshall to go public with their battles, not merely in opinions or in courtroom behavior, but in law review articles, speeches, and even televised interviews, can be both cause and effect of conflict in the Court. Whereas the fact of conflict in the Marble Temple has a long history, the ways in which public arguments have been conducted have changed over time.

Chief Justice Taft found McKenna, and particularly McReynolds, guilty of making "grandstand play[s] to the galleries" during the presentation of opinions.[93] There was considerable reaction to the open battles of 1921.

The Court's inability to agree left its decisions weak and unpersuasive, and it came under wide attack. The American Federation of Labor proposed amending the Constitution, to limit the Court's power to decide the constitutionality of statutes. Senator Robert LaFollette proposed an amendment that would have allowed Congress to override Constitutional decisions of the Court. The *New York Times* and the *Wall Street Journal* both endorsed Senator William Borah's relatively mild proposal, which would have required a seven-to-two vote of the Court to overturn any legislation. Still other measures were proposed to strip the Court of part of its jurisdiction and force it to catch up with the growing docket of undecided cases.[94]

Open battles in the Courtroom were far too common during the Stone years, particularly in 1943 and 1944.[95] Melvin Urofsky recalls the public reaction against what appeared to be a judicial loss of composure.

Charles C. Burlingham, one of the pillars of the New York bar, lashed out at the "unhappy state of the Court" in a public letter to the *New York Herald-Tribune.* While one could not expect total agreement on all issues, "there seems to be a growing tendency to disagree, and if this is not checked the effect on the public will be unfortunate, making for doubt and uncertainty and a lack of respect and a loss of confidence in the Court." . . . Burlingham also chastised the Justices for airing their personal differences, which "should be confined within the council chamber and not proclaimed from the bench." . . . On the same page the newspaper editorially reminded the Court of its obligation "to provide a coherent doctrine," and in the interests of the people who must know the law to abide by it, prayed that the Justices would stop their fighting and resume their work in a clear manner.[96]

Of course, the newspapers were also adding fuel to the fire, as articles carried box scores showing that Felix Frankfurter had lost his leadership role in the Court. They also highlighted the apparently growing bloc in the Court, which only exacerbated tensions.

Then there was the explosion that followed Jackson's attack on Black from Nuremburg. The publication of Jackson's open letter to the *New York Times* unleashed a torrent of criticism. Of course, many of the critics forgot that it was in large part the newspaper article by Doris Fleeson concerning the alleged pressure by Black on Truman that had triggered the incident in the first place. Nevertheless, the tone and character of

Jackson's broadside was simply more than anyone was prepared to accept.

The *New York Times* condemned Jackson for "an error of taste" and Black "for the worse offense of lowering judicial standards." The Knoxville (Tennessee) *Journal* called for Black's impeachment, if he did not resign, but the *New York Post* saluted Black's "sterling liberalism" and criticized Jackson's "personal pique." The *Washington Post* demanded the resignations of both Black and Jackson. So did Senator Scott Lucas of Illinois. "There can't be any confidence in the Court as long as the feud goes on," Lucas told reporters. "For the good of themselves, for the good of the Court, and for the good of the country, both Justices should resign."[97]

During the late 1950s and culminating in 1961, the *New York Times* chronicled the courtroom battles and the apparent internal tension in the Court between Chief Justice Earl Warren and Felix Frankfurter.[98] The concern in the media over the public battles did not bother Frankfurter, who told Justice Tom Clark, "I am not a fellow who is for peace by surrendering everything he believes. You remember the Latin poet who said: 'They made a devastation and called it peace.' "[99]

The public clashes brought criticism, but that was not the only forum in which the battles were fought. Douglas was a prolific writer who waged his battle against the Frankfurter view in a variety of law review articles. In his Madison lecture, Douglas had originally made specific reference to Frankfurter by name, but he removed them in the later drafts.[100] In this same vein, Black issued his now famous Carpentier Lectures, which were published as *A Constitutional Faith*.[101] Black used Douglas's opinion in *Griswold,* announcing the right to privacy, and his opinion in the Virginia poll tax case[102] as primary examples of what was wrong with the Court.[103] Frankfurter waged his surrogate battles through Bickel and others even after he had left the Court. Brennan took on the Burger Court, calling upon civil rights and liberties plaintiffs to take their cases to state courts where they might still receive a favorable hearing.[104] Still, these fights remained largely within the legal literature. Things changed.

With the 1980s came increased awareness of the Court and a changing media. The battles of the 1970s over abortion and affirmative action brought a new visibility. Media coverage, though still spotty, increased.

The Reagan administration's strategy of challenging the Court and promising to change it meant careful attention to appointments. The O'Connor nomination was one of the first in which there was broad viewing of the confirmation hearings, as efforts by the left and the right to determine the first woman justice's position on the abortion issue dominated discussions. The Bork battle, too, dramatically raised the visibility of the process.

Increased awareness and visibility, along with technologically more advanced media operations, meant that events like speeches to judicial circuit conferences, which had been relegated to publication in the pages of the little-known volume entitled *Federal Rules Decisions,* were picked up first by the newspapers and then by television, as CNN began a regular process of taping the presentations. In these circuit speeches the media caught the first elements of the battles of Stevens and Marshall over the Court's summary judgment behavior and its tendency to issue rulings far broader than were absolutely required to resolve the cases.

The justices also began to give more interviews, though there had been some earlier, the best known of which was Hugo Black's televised interview with Eric Sevareid in 1970. With the increased coverage of their public disagreements, the justices knew they were in the spotlight. Bill Moyers produced a series on the Court for PBS in which Justices Blackmun and O'Connor gave unusually candid commentaries on conflict in the Court.

Thurgood Marshall dropped his self-imposed gag rule and launched a series of public statements, beginning with his circuit speeches.[105] In 1983, he issued a law review that was a stinging indictment of the Court's use of summary dispositions and later published a critique of the constitutional bicentennial.[106] Ordinarily, the law reviews might have gone relatively unnoticed, but not in the media climate of the mid-1980s and not when Marshall's arguments were matched by those issued by other members of the Court. The 1988 term was particularly hard for Marshall, and he let loose in his circuit address: "Thus it is difficult to characterize last term's decisions as a product of anything other than a deliberate retrenching of the civil rights agenda. In the past 35 years or more we have truly come full circle. We are back where we started."[107] The more pressed he felt, the harder he fought, warning that he was not about to cave in to those who wanted him to retire. In 1990, Marshall gave an interview on the ABC News Primetime Live Program in which he lashed out at Reagan, Bush, and his other adversaries. The media had long since found that battles on the Court sold and it has covered the story ever since.

CONCLUSION

There have been a variety of consequences that have flowed from the battles among the justices over the years, both battles that have remained within the Court and those that have gone public. Ranging from the ultimate decision by some justices to leave the Court, because it just was not worth the fight, to the far more common daily frustrations that can add up over the years, conflict can affect life on the Court and the rulings it issues. It is not so much that the Court disposes of a case differently because of internal controversies, though that can happen, but the nature of the rulings may very well be affected by the ability of members of the Court to compromise.

It is also true that the clashes among the justices have sometimes become petty and personal. These have even sometimes been taken into the public arena where they have done the Court little good as an institution.

It should come as no surprise that an institution like the Court should be subject to the same proclivities that affect every human institution. In fact, what is truly surprising is that the members of the Court have been significantly able to overcome these tensions and have done their jobs so effectively in the face of pressures that might destroy other organizations. Indeed, the next question to consider is why the members of the Court do not fight more than they do.

SIX

WHY DON'T THEY FIGHT
MORE OFTEN?

In the final analysis, what is amazing about the Court is not that there are conflicts, but that there are not more of them and that the clashes that do arise are handled, with some exceptions, so well. After all, these are nine people who cannot take refuge in anonymity. They face the pressure of a significant work load that contains a host of questions other political institutions at all levels of government either will not or cannot resolve. The justices could respond to any of the many potential causes of conflict described in Chapter 2, and they could carry grudges. Some justices have done so, but most have not, at least not in ways that have been disruptive to the institution.

It is important to consider why the justices do not fight more than they do and how the Court as an institution shapes an operating character that allows such strong, independent, trained adversaries to work together closely and well for so many years and with so many different kinds of members in the group. To be sure, it is tempting *not* to explore this question. For reasons discussed in the last few chapters, there is good reason to believe that the Court has not been doing as well recently at managing conflict as in the past. Still, the Court works surprisingly well as a political institution. In an era that often emphasizes what is wrong with governmental bodies, it is important to study which ones work and why.

The Court works because of a combination of relatively obvious institutional concerns and a set of far more subtle patterns of professional behavior among the justices, including the institutional norms and relationships within the Court, its pattern of workways, and the performance of the chief justice.

INTERNALIZING INSTITUTIONAL NORMS

David O'Brien has written very effectively about what he calls the process of institutionalization of the Supreme Court.[1] It is the historical process by which the Court has come to build its institutional character, workways, and norms. Although it is true that the organization has become larger and more complex over its two centuries of work, leading some observers to conclude that it has been bureaucratized, the fact is that the Court remains an organization where informal norms and unwritten rules of conduct are extremely important. One member of the Court can make a significant difference not only in the work product of the body but also in the very character and quality of working life in the institution. Several factors help to constrain conflict and control those disputes that do break out nevertheless. They include (1) a set of basic facts of Supreme Court life, (2) a long-standing effort to separate professional and personal disagreement, (3) group dynamics that encourage limitation on conflict, and (4) the character of the justices themselves.

The Facts of Life

Even the most petulant person who comes to the Court must understand certain realities that govern his or her professional and, to some extent, personal life. First, for most of the things a justice wishes to accomplish, four additional votes are needed. There are some exceptions, like the case of the so-called "rule of four," according to which four justices can vote to add a case to the docket, and the ability of a justice sitting as circuit justice to issue stays of various lower court orders pending Supreme Court review.

Even changes in the operation of the Court require agreement, as Earl Warren found out when he tried to make relatively modest changes in the Court's schedule and physical arrangements. When Warren came to the Court there were still quill pens on the counsel table, the docket entries were done by hand rather than with a typewriter, and the Court pages were still wearing short pants. Warren led the Court to change all of these and went on to modify its conference schedule as well as eliminating the informal restriction that the Court announced its rulings only on "opinion Monday." He even installed a sound system with microphones for the justices and counsel.

Even with these mild changes, however, Warren ran into opposition, particularly from Frankfurter. Felix often saw himself as the defender of the institutional culture. His diaries proudly proclaim how he admonished Chief Justice Vinson, who was attempting to bring changes to Court operations.

The Chief formally proposed a change in the order of procedure on opinion day whereby motions for admission to the bar would be the first order of business and the reading of opinions would follow. . . . When it came my turn I spoke somewhat at length on the importance of not breaking with a tradition that is as old as the Court, that tradition, particularly in this disordered world, which is a fragile fabric, should be adhered to as one of the great social forces of justice unless change is called for in the interest of the administration of justice. . . . I asked the Conference to think twice and thrice before disobeying the injunction, "Remove not the ancient landmarks of thy Fathers."[2]

Even though the conference agreed to the changes over his objections, Frankfurter wrote to Vinson, saying that such departures from past traditions should not be made "by a mere majority vote against the strong feeling of the minority."[3]

The second fact of life is that no member of the Court can force any other justice to do anything within the normal course of business. All were appointed by the president and confirmed by the Senate for life unless they retire or are impeached. Even the chief justice can be rebuffed. Justice Douglas recited the story of what happened when Chief Justice Hughes sent a messenger to Justice McReynolds's chambers because he feared that McReynolds would be late.

The messenger entered, and being brought into the presence of McReynolds, began to tremble and shake. He bowed low and said, "Mr. Justice, the Chief Justice says you should come at once and put on your robe." McReynolds, looking up and calling the messenger by name, said, "Tell the Chief Justice that I do not work for him." McReynolds turned up in Court about thirty minutes later.[4]

The third basic rule is that justices will have to work with their colleagues for years, since a new member comes to the Court only about every two years. A dispute that gets out of hand today may interfere with an attempt to build a majority in a later case or even destroy the ability to work together effectively. Walter Murphy observed that "when a Justice has won a fight over a decision, he may be well advised to offer the olive branch to the loser, knowing that today's opponent will often be tomorrow's ally."[5] That is one reason why the development of battle lines or the designation of reliable anti-authorities, discussed in Chapter 5, can be so problematic. It is also the reason why Justice Scalia's behavior toward Justice O'Connor has raised eyebrows.

Fourth, the Court is basically an antidemocratic body, in the sense that it is a small, elite group of generally nonrepresentative, unelected Americans who make critically important decisions that occasionally overturn the wishes of the majority as enacted by the legislative or executive branches. This elite operates within a nation that celebrates the fact that it is a constitutional republic based upon democratic principles. The task of the Court is therefore difficult, and its political legitimacy is always precarious. Fortunately, the Court has tended to retain that basic support when it needed it, though it has certainly faced serious criticism and opposition in particular policy areas, such as abortion and desegregation cases.

The classic story of the Court's ability to draw on foundation support came during the 1930s, when President Roosevelt attempted to get around a string of adverse rulings by pushing his Court-packing plan. The ostensible purpose of the plan was to help the "nine old men" handle their work load. Chief Justice Hughes managed a masterful response. In a letter to the Senate, Hughes made it quite clear that the Court's docket was current, leaving the question whether the executive branch could say the same of its work. He also handled the matter in such a way as to frame Roosevelt's effort as a blatant attack on the integrity of the Supreme Court as an institution. It was a very effective response.

More recently, Richard Nixon's counsel in the Watergate tapes case let it be known that the president was not certain he would obey a ruling from the Supreme Court to turn over the tapes of White House conversations if it were issued by a divided Court. It became instantly apparent that any such action would in itself be grounds for immediate impeachment, regardless of other charges. To underscore the point, the unanimous Court recited the famous language from John Marshall's *Marbury v. Madison* ruling that "it is the province and duty of this Court 'to say what the law is.' "[6]

Fifth, beyond the need to take care with its public stature, the Court needs help to accomplish most of the things it wishes to do. The justices must always be cognizant of the need to elicit the assistance of others, unless they wish their rulings to remain words on paper. That is not, of course, to suggest that the Court must defer in all things to other branches, which would undermine its institutional integrity. But if the justices are going to make critically important pronouncements, they cannot afford to convey an external image of weakness and fragmentation that would make the Court an easy target for political opposition or simple resistance.

These facts of Supreme Court life are powerful forces that counsel care and control in the relationships among justices, both internal and external. They may not always be strong enough to constrain frustrated people in difficult circumstances, but they are ignored at the justice's (and the Court's) peril.

Separation of Personal and Professional Disagreement

The justices are trained advocates who know how to have a fight on the job and go out for a drink together after work the same day. Justice Powell put it this way:

> News stories sometimes portray a picture of discord among the justices. A strong dissenting opinion is often characterized as "bitter," and a five-four decision is said to reflect deep-seated personal animosities among the justices. These stories are wide of the mark. They result perhaps from failure to understand that judges, like lawyers, may disagree strongly without personal rancor or ill will. The fact is that a genuine cordiality exists among the justices. As Justice Douglas has put it: "We have fierce ideological clashes, but at the same time we are a happy, harmonious group. That is true now, and it has been true all of my days [on the Court]."[7]

Most serious students of the Court would say that Powell overstated the point, but the idea is sound. They would also note that he wrote this comment in 1975 when many of his toughest battles yet lay ahead.

There are numerous examples of justices who rarely ever agreed professionally and were nevertheless able to have a good personal relationship or even a solid friendship. Ironically, the pugnacious William O. Douglas got along well on a personal level with people like Sherman Minton and William Rehnquist whose constitutional positions were anathema to him.

The man who could be so thoughtless and dismissive on the job could be sensitive and caring on a personal level. Thus, Murphy's biographer Sydney Fine, reports that "Douglas and Murphy grew closer during Murphy's last two years on the Court as Douglas joined Rutledge in seeking to ease the pain of their colleague's final illnesses."[8] Douglas wrote Sherman Minton frequently after his retirement. He invited Rehnquist to his mountain cabin at a time when the two men were battling regularly in cases. He was a source of amusement, including a regular stock of jokes, to Byron White, when the two men could not have been further apart on such issues as the First Amendment freedom of expression.

On occasion, this concern with defending the boundary between the personal and the professional takes the form of one justice complimenting another on an opinion, even if he or she decides it is not possible to join that writing. Justice Brennan provides an example: "On *New York Times v. Sullivan,* Hugo called me up to say, 'You know I can't join you. It's an excellent opinion and I congratulate you, but you know damn well I can't join you.' "[9]

Of course, there comes a point at which that kind of separation becomes hard to maintain. Justices like Frankfurter were known for not making that distinction very well. If a justice uses what Walter Murphy refers to as the tactic of "increasing personal regard" (flattery, support, and the like) in order to put together a majority there is always the risk that comes with deliberately blurring the line between personal and professional.[10] Even so, most justices do try very hard to maintain that important distinction.

Group Dynamics Encourage Limitations on Conflict

Quite apart from the "rules," which could be ignored by anyone harsh enough to do so (McReynolds is the classic case), there are specific group dynamics that flow from the size and unique nature of this special work group. The Court is a small, enduring, high-status group of highly trained and experienced men and women in a unique institutional setting. They operate under special pressures and time constraints and enjoy unusual guarantees of independence and career security. The biographical literature highlights three elements that are particularly helpful for preventing conflict from getting out of hand: the formation of enduring friendships, the importance of humor, and a sense of empathy, both personal and professional.

Most Supreme Court biographers point to one or a few special friendships that made the hard times bearable for the justice about whom they write. There was, of course, the relationship between Joseph Story and John Marshall in the early years. Even the irascible Justice Peter V. Daniel found a good friend in Chief Justice Taney. "The one invariably delightful relationship of Daniel's Court experience was with Taney. This friendship, unparalleled in Daniel's life, was marked by affection and respect coupled with reasonable difference of opinion."[11] John Marshall Harlan (the elder) had a number of important friendships during his years at the Court, notwithstanding his disagreements with many of his colleagues on the merits, including the fact that his appointment had been opposed by Chief Justice Waite and Justice Miller.

Waite quickly became John's most intimate friend on the Court, one with whom he enjoyed an easy, informal social as well as business relationship. Asking for advice, for instance, in a difficult municipal bond case (the Court handled many of these), Harlan jokingly remarked, "You may come to the conclusion that my mind has become confused by reading the decisions of our court, or that I have seen Ben Butler on his Yacht & tasted some of his New England rum." He went on to comment about the summer activities of some of their colleagues: "The last I heard from Bro Woods he was at Newark. Bros Matthews and Blatchford will, I fear, get such lofty ideas in the Mountains that there will be no holding them down to mother Earth when they return to Washington. Bro Bradley, I take it, is somewhere studying the philosophy of the Northern Lights, while Gray is, at this time, examining into the Precedents in British Columbia. Field, I suppose has his face towards the setting sun, wondering perhaps, whether the Munn case or the essential principles of right and justice will ultimately prevail."[12]

Harlan was also fond of Justice David Brewer, even though the two were about as far apart ideologically as they could be.[13]

Chief Justice Fuller had a warm friendship with Holmes, among many others. Fuller went out of his way to make his colleagues feel appreciated. One time, for example, Holmes went to Chicago to deliver a speech and was warmly received by large crowds of judges and lawyers who cheered him resoundingly. This reception occurred after Holmes had been elevated from the Supreme Judicial Court of Massachusetts to the United States Supreme Court but before he had taken his seat. What Holmes did not know was that Fuller had written an old friend in Chicago ahead of time to hatch a bit of a publicity campaign for Holmes. Just before Holmes's arrival in town, the Chicago *Legal News* published an article entitled "A Compliment to Chief Justice Holmes." It related that a recent ruling issued by the English Court of Appeals had been based on a quotation from Justice Holmes's book, *The Common Law*. Fuller wrote to his Chicago friend:

> Judge Holmes will be in Chicago as I understand it the latter part of next week on the occasion of the dedication or opening of the Law School and the installation of Pres't. James. It occurred to me that Bradwell would like to print in the *Legal News* the matter I enclose. It might be headed 'compliment to Judge Holmes.' But I do not wish Bradwell to know that I had anything to do with it and I fear that if I send it to him he would get me in his paper somehow.
>
> So I send it yo you. Can't you write on top of page 1—'Compliment to Judge Holmes' & give it to Bradwell, or get Harry to do so. If B. publishes it, send me an extra copy.
>
> All of this is in confidence. I do not wish our honorable friend to know that it comes from me.[14]

Even some members of the group known as the "four horsemen" had good relationships with others. Holmes was pleased at how life in the Court was going in the years after Justice Sutherland was appointed. He wrote: "The meetings are pleasanter than I have ever known them . . . largely [due] to the C.J. but also to the disappearance of men with the habit of our older generation, that regarded a difference of opinion as a cockfight, and often left a good deal to be desired in point of manners."[15] Sutherland had a warm friendship over the years with Pierce Butler.

Of the Roosevelt appointees, Murphy and Rutledge had a strong friendship.[16] Of course, Black and Douglas came to share a very important relationship. So important was it, that even though they had some hard years and many differences in the 1960s, Black was ready to put everything on the line for Douglas. When the effort was made to impeach

Douglas, some of those involved sought the help of Black's son to convince Hugo to persuade Douglas to resign. Black replied:

> I have known Bill Douglas for thirty years. He's never knowingly done any improper, unethical or corrupt thing. Tell his detractors that in spite of my age, I think I have one trial left in me. Tell them that if they move against Bill Douglas, I'll resign from the Court and represent him. It will be the biggest, most important case I ever tried.[17]

Black and Douglas also shared fine friendships with William J. Brennan, Jr. Brennan recalled: "I was close to Justice Douglas from my very first day on the Court. It was October 16, 1956, which also happened to be Douglas's birthday. Every October 16 until his death . . . my wife and I had dinner with the Douglases."[18] Of Black he said: "He was a delightful warm friend. Absolutely warm friend." Recalling many pleasant evenings with the Blacks, Brennan quipped: "He was a great steak and potatoes man. He used to take a special pride in his ability to broil steaks. Actually, he sometimes overdid it. He had a terrible voice, but he used to love to sing."[19]

Brennan remembered how helpful Black was to him in difficult times. He recalled the occasion when he had just circulated his first draft in the *Malloy v. Hogan* case. Black had written criticisms and had called to talk about them. Brennan lost his temper and said something like, "the hell with it." It seemed to Brennan that Black must have virtually run over from his chambers. He told Brennan that the Court was a pressure-filled place and that he should go home and get away from things for the day. He did. It was just the right word from just the right person at the most appropriate moment.[20]

When Justice Powell came to the Court, he struck up a friendship with Potter Stewart. Some time later, he developed a close friendship with Byron White.[21] Indeed, Powell made friends with a variety of people at the Court, including the staff.

> Powell would be missed. Court personnel were sorry to see him go. Typical was the verdict of Justice Marshall's messenger, a wizened old man who usually had little to say. That afternoon, Mr. Gaines was making the rounds of the chambers and happened on a Powell

clerk commiserating with Brennan's secretary. "Yes," he interjected, "it's a terrible day. It's like a funeral around here."[22]

Justice O'Connor was another person who developed a close friendship with Powell, and he had great regard for her as well. When O'Connor first came to the Court, Powell persuaded one of his experienced secretaries to apply for O'Connor's clerical position. From that moment on, O'Connor was in his debt. "Lewis was the only Justice whom I felt absolutely free to visit with about issues in argued cases."[23] For his part, Powell worried about her health and was concerned about whether she was working too hard.

The Crucial Presence of Humor

Good friendships are rare in anyone's life, but a sense of humor, even among co-workers who are not friends, is necessary in virtually every workplace. The Supreme Court is no exception. Fortunately, some of the quick minds who have served in the Marble Temple have had a ready wit as well.

Justice Roberts told the story that Justice Holmes would come into the conference room and go directly over to Justice Sutherland. He would then beg his colleague, "Sutherland, J., tell me a story." Sutherland's biographer adds, "this entreaty was unfailingly honored to the accompaniment of roars of judicial laughter."[24]

Once, Douglas sent Earl Warren a copy of an article by Glendon Schubert entitled "A Psychometric Model of the Supreme Court" and inquired whether they should look into this business of judging by the numbers further. Warren replied:

Why not have a Psychometric Machine for deciding cases on the Supreme Court? Then elect Presidents with a Univac, Congress votes according to Dr. Gallup's computer, and then select presidents of corporations through an IBM machine.

A young fellow was told to report for duty as President of a great corporation. He did so and was congratulated on his rapid progress. He replied that he didn't know how it came to be. He had no experience of any kind, but while he was filling out his questionnaire for employment in the locker room, he dropped it on the floor and two or three fellows in their golf shoes stepped on it. The next thing he was ordered to report as President. Maybe we can all go fishing the year around.[25]

In 1966 Warren and Abe Fortas engaged in a major discussion about the proper color and style of judicial robes. Warren sent Fortas the following note:

Recently an article appeared in a leading Washington newspaper in which the distinguished Mr. Justice Fortas mentioned that "black robes were too awesome for the Members of the Supreme Court of the United States."

After consulting with several designers of considerable note, the enclosed robe is submitted for your consideration.

If the color combination is too subdued and lacking in color, the following suggestions may be helpful.

Of course, this momentous decision may not be unanimous as the Chief Justice might think it would add fervor to the accusations already made, so he would probably favor Blue and Gold (University of California colors.)

Mr. Justice Black would obviously object because the present color of the robe, and his name, are synonymous.

Mr. Justice Douglas might prefer a "robe of many colors" as worn by Joseph in the Bible, to match the vivid neckties he formerly wore. However, he may have an open mind as he has recently been wearing more subdued and somber neckties.

Mr. Justice Clark would no doubt take offense as he is so loyal to the color of the "yellow rose of Texas."

Mr. Justice Harlan will dissent regardless of the color.

Mr. Justice Brennan naturally, being of Irish heritage, would insist most emphatically on Kelly green.

Mr. Justice Stewart might object to the crimson red as it might detract from his bronzed sun-tan. Royal purple might be a substitute, but might raise the question of a number of "reigning monarchs."

Mr. Justice White would surely agree that the color white should be ruled out—because of the obscenity cases.

Perhaps your next alternative, Abe, would be to consider the furs of the animal kingdom, such as zebra, mink, silver fox, moleskin, kangaroo, beaver, raccoon, and Persian lamb. On second thought, this leaves the road open to those (opponents) who might shout "dirty skunk," and, Abe, that would be difficult to "weasel" out of.

If I can be of any further help, PLEASE don't hesitate to command me.

Servicefully yours,

P.S. For your information, appropriate and becoming wigs have been forwarded to you for your approval.[26]

Fortas could not possibly let the opportunity pass for a reply.

There is a great clothes designer named Pucci. He might have some interesting ideas. We should also ask Chanel and Schiapanelli and Elizabeth Arden to enter the competition (or do they make only perfume—if so, that won't quite cover the situation, or the situations). But I do think we should have an international competition. We could give one Writ of Certiorari as the prize. The rules of the competition should be carefully drawn. Some Californians might submit a proposal for a topless robe. We should avoid temptation by excluding this at the outset.

Of course, my vote is predetermined. I'm for the crimson robe, with leopard trim and corol—I think corol is correct—but maybe it's part of an automobile, like the exhaust pipe. I don't think I said anything as silly as the statement quoted in the papers—but maybe I did. If the robes are too awesome, maybe bathing suits would do. But the Court has always guarded its secrets, and this is no time for initiating disclosure.[27]

Even the most staid of the Justices have sometimes been tempted to wisecrack. The great Chief Justice Charles Evans Hughes, who is said to have looked "like God," had a good sense of humor. With all of his dignity, Hughes loved a good joke. He recalled the story of how a woman in a New York hotel walked out of an elevator and, seeing the Chief Justice, said in hushed tones, " 'Oh, I thought you were dead.' Hughes smiled and bowed, saying, 'Sorry to disappoint you, madam.' "[28]

As the Hughes story suggests, the jokes were not always kept within the Court. There was a long-running discussion between Franklin Roosevelt and Douglas about initiating some kind of friendly competition between the "nine old men" and the cabinet.

Douglas wrote to his friend Franklin Roosevelt:

My Dear Mr. President:

I have just received the original of a cartoon drawn by Herbert Block and published a month or so ago. It is entitled "Nine Young Men." It shows members of this Court in a huddle in the corridors of the Supreme Court building. One of the more spirited, whose identity is not disclosed is saying, "Let's phone the cabinet members and see if we can get up a ball game."

I did not want to take this matter up officially without first sounding you out informally on the proposition.

Of course, all "ringers" should be excluded. I refer especially to General Watson, Admiral McIntyre and Steve Early.

Yours Faithfully[29]

The president picked up the challenge and answered:

Dear Bill,

The thought behind the ball game between the Nine Young Men and the Cabinet is an excellent one, even though you may eliminate General Watson, Admiral McIntyre, and Colonel Early.

I come back with a counter proposal, however. The Cabinet insists that the Chief Justice pitch and Mr. Justice McReynolds catch. Our battery will be the Secretary of State, pitcher, and the Secretary of the Interior, catcher. Except for the Secretary of the Navy, who is away, these are our oldest members—and, incidentally, it gives some advantage to the Supreme Court because an experienced battery counts and yours will be about ten years older than ours.

We also suggest no substitutes be put in—and we suggest further that the Umpires be the President and the Speaker of the House. This seems fair. Finally, we insist that your "Nine" waive in advance any judicial authority over umpires' decisions, and that in publicity after the game no minority opinions will be filed. So far, so good![30]

A discussion followed about just how some kind of competition might take place. The baseball season ended and Douglas and Roosevelt had to look for an alternative sport. The idea of a football game was out, but there was the possibility of a poker game. Since Douglas and Roosevelt participated in a more or less regular poker game at the White House, it seemed a natural. Of course, there immediately arose a question of propriety. Would some of the justices' personal or religious convictions preclude such a contest? To answer this question, Douglas had prepared a legal memorandum on the question "whether Baptists could play poker."

Justice Blackmun tells the story of how he discovered how to tweak Justice O'Connor. Blackmun wears a hearing aid, and he discovered that the device would squeal if he brushed his hand through his hair past the ear. He noticed that when this happened in conference, Justice O'Connor would look around the room, he thought because she wondered whether the room was bugged. Thereafter, Blackmun would make it a point to get off a squeal every now and again in conference just to get his colleague going.[31]

Sometimes the humor even spills over into opinions. Justice Scalia simply could not resist a parody of Dracula in a recent opinion, leading one wag to enjoy a double-entendre in his newspaper story. He observed that if there's blood on an opinion, it must have been written by Scalia!

Seriously, the more intense the setting, the more important humor seems to be. Few work settings offer greater intensity than the Supreme Court. There is no disrespect in noting that the institution is terribly human and that the justices are as capable of the kind of laughter that we all need as any other group of bright, articulate men and women.

The Importance of Empathy

Precisely because of the tradition of secrecy and privacy, and the tendency not to display justices' personal lives in public, there is a need within the Court for mutual support, particularly in periods of personal stress. Fortunately, that support has often been forthcoming, even from justices who are otherwise adversaries.

Empathy begins with a simple recognition of crises or emergencies in the lives of one's colleagues. Justices often serve on the Court at an age when they face some of life's greatest challenges: illnesses that come with advancing age as well as the sheer effects of aging. At an age when most people are about to begin retirement, Justice Powell came to the court only to undertake the heaviest work load he had ever experienced. Many members of the Court have done great work at over eighty.

As members of the Court age, they encounter other experiences in addition to their own physical infirmity. They face illness and deaths of spouses, other family members, and life-long friends. Justice Brennan experienced the death of his first wife and then helped Justice Rehnquist when his wife was facing a terminal illness. Justice Black lost his first wife and, at the end of his life, lay in a hospital bed next door to the room occupied by Justice John Marshall Harlan. Brennan watched his long-time friend Bill Douglas deteriorate in a most painful way.

Beyond health and age, Justice Blackmun pointed out that the society moves away from one's own experience. Justice Powell had difficulty with changing gender roles and with the whole question of homosexuality simply because these things were so far outside his own personal and life experience.

The justices feel the sheer weight of the job before them, not only the work load but the character of the questions they are asked to resolve. Colleagues had to watch Justice Blackmun vilified for his opinion in *Roe v. Wade*. Whether one agrees with a colleague or not, it is difficult simply in human terms to watch a person endure such pain. Justices Douglas and Black consoled each other regularly, often laughing off harsh criticisms as they tried to protect individual rights in an era of pressure for social, political, and religious conformity. But those digs hurt. The widow of one of Hugo's closest friends wrote a hateful letter that said that she was pleased that her husband had not lived to see Black's opinion in the school prayer case because "the shock of that decision would have hastened his demise."[32] Black replied:

Courts, of course, do not write opinions on the basis of public approval or disapproval, but on the basis of the belief of the judges about the controlling law whether it is statutory or constitutional. I have mentioned what I did to you about a very few of the multitudinous expressions of approval of the Court's opinion by leading church men throughout the country merely because you seem to think that everyone felt the other way.

It may be true that you are correct in thinking that Dave would have disagreed with the Court's holding on the momentous constitutional question that was presented, but I am not so sure as you are.

Dave was a lawyer, and a good one, with a familiarity with constitutional problems needed in order to express the most informed views. He was, as I said, also a religious man. It was this kind of man that I recall in our old University days. I am not so sure, however, that Dave would ever have wanted political office-holders to write the prayers that I am sure came spontaneously from his heart during all the days that I knew him. Unless I did not know him as well as I thought I did, I am confident that had I received a communication from him about this particular decision, he, like many others who have written, would most likely have referred to verses 1 to 18 of the sixth Chapter of Matthew.

You know, of course, that I have not written this letter for publication, but to you alone, as the widow of a dear friend whose friendship I cherished and whose good life I have felt worthy of emulation.[33]

Even the most ardent adversaries on the Court often recognize human needs. When Justice Douglas experienced his stroke while in Nassau for a speaking engagement on New Year's Eve 1974, Chief Justice Burger, upon learning of the tragedy, immediately telephoned President Ford in Colorado and asked for a presidential aircraft to fly Douglas's doctor to him and return Douglas to Walter Reed Army Hospital the next day.

The pressure, pain, and life experiences faced by members of the Court elicit from colleagues the support anyone in such a situation needs. In that spirit the other wives of the Court welcomed Justice Rehnquist's wife to what was then called "the sisterhood," the women of the Court, with a poem when Rehnquist was confirmed. When one has shared the pain of personal and professional stress with colleagues and received their support in return, it is difficult to let mere disputes over small matters, or even sometimes significant arguments, to erase the sense of extended family.

The Question of Character

There is a tendency to focus on the characters of the Court, the justices whose quirks and foibles make good targets for derision, but it is well to recall that the vast majority of the members of the Court have, as Henry Abraham observes, been people of high character and qualifications,[34] notwithstanding the political process by which they were selected and the variation in their technical skills.[35]

Potter Stewart said of Justice Harlan (the younger): "To remember him simply as a fine legal scholar is to miss the full measure of the man. What truly set him apart was his character, not his scholarship. His generous and gallant spirit, his selfless courage, his freedom from all guile, his total decency. . . . He was a human being of great worth."[36] Powell was looked to as a peacemaker and conciliator. He was missed after his retirement. He was concerned by the conflict he saw after he left and spoke out in a speech to the Association of the Bar of the City of New York entitled "Stare Decisis and Judicial Restraint." The story was reported in the *New York Times* under the title, "The Loving but Concerned Voice of a Noncombatant."[37]

SUPREME COURT WORK PATTERNS

The ways the justices do their work provide safeguards and releases for pressure that may build up. These work patterns include debate by written opinion, the presence of clerks and staff, the availability of alternative dispute resolution techniques, and the ability to vent frustration.

Justice Brennan explained that there is often a mistaken impression about just what constitutes collegiality in the Supreme Court. It most assuredly is not a situation in which justices wander in and out of each other's chambers in a kind of legislative corridor lobbying effort. Most justices would not think of barging into another's chambers unannounced. Neither is it a kind of conviviality, though that atmosphere may exist among some members of the Court. Brennan observed: "It may have been that way at one time, but it hasn't been since I've been here. The way you attract votes is through circulations [of memoranda and draft opinions]. We do have one to one conferences on occasion, but rarely."[38] Since the debate is carried out in writing, each participant must take time and care with what he or she says. The distance and time involved in generating a reply allows for a sober second thought.

Another potential screen for responses that might create conflict is the presence of law clerks and staff. The ability to work through drafts and discuss possible approaches allows an airing of ideas in a setting where they are not going to trigger conflict with another justice. Indeed, justices often hire at least one clerk whose ideological presdispositions do not match their own to promote the likelihood that a clerk will spot an ominous approach or use of language immediately.

On some occasions, justices will use their colleagues to help screen potential concerns. Thus, Justice Blackmun called upon Justice Brennan to read his draft *Roe v. Wade* opinion from the perspective of a Catholic to help him to eliminate needlessly provocative or potentially offensive language.

If a conflict does arise, the Court's workways provide most of the tools of alternative dispute resolution (ADR) already in place to help iron out the tensions before they get out of hand. Negotiation is a continuous process—indeed coin of the realm—at the Court for reducing opposition and perhaps even attracting additional support. Mediation is sometimes used, and justices like Brennan have been effective at bringing together disparate positions. There is a kind of arbitration in the sense that disputes among two justices are submitted to resolution by the nine, with the decision carrying the force of precedent for the future. There are even equivalents to what are termed in ADR literature minitrials, in the sense that justices use oral arguments to present hypothetical situations whose possible consequences must be explored. The decision process is anything but binary. There is room to avoid collisions.

If an impasse is reached, however, there is the safety valve of the ability to write separate opinions, either concurring or dissenting. As Justice Powell explained to one of his clerks, "Sometimes, Jay [Wilkinson], there are things one has to do. I suppose that, to be worthy to sit on this Court, you have to be willing to go it alone."[39]

Even in issues of collegial governance on matters of process within the Court, the justice can circulate memoranda that can be used in the future to remind colleagues about the mistakes of the past.

It is not necessary to swallow frustration and internalize anger. Certainly some of the dissenting opinions of Justices Douglas, Marshall, Brennan, and Blackmun were, among other things, a way to get the tension out in their later years as the majority moved further away from them on important issues. Nevertheless, reason is not a requirement to publish a separate opinion. It is possible to vent, though it is still wise to do so in a reasonable way.

THE ROLE AND TALENTS OF A CHIEF JUSTICE

There is one more historically important mechanism for the management of conflict within the Court: an effective chief justice. A number of chiefs have had both the personal qualities and professional talents to be able to play a critical role in leading headstrong colleagues in a way that avoided destructive conflict. Justice Samuel Miller said that when he came to Washington he knew that Taney had gone after the Bank of the United States, had been rewarded for it with a seat on the Court, and had authored the infamous Dred Scott opinion, and, he added, "I hated him for" all of those things. However, "from my first acquaintance with him, I realized that these feelings toward him were but the suggestions of the worst elements of our nature, for before the first Term of my service in the Court had passed, I more than liked him; I loved him."[40] Chief Justice Hughes quoted Justice Benjamin Curtis speaking about the skills of his colleague Chief Justice Taney:

> For it is certainly true and I am happy to be able to bear direct testimony to it that the surpassing ability of the chief justice, and all his great qualities of character and mind, were more fully and constantly exhibited in the consultation room, while presiding over and assisting the deliberation of his brethren, than the public knew, or can ever justly appreciate. There, his dignity, his love of order, his gentleness, his caution, his accuracy, his discrimination were of incalculable importance. The real intrinsic character of the tribunal was greatly influenced by them, and always for the better. . . . He was as absolutely free from the slightest trace of vanity and self-conceit as any man I ever knew. . . . The preservation of the harmony of the members of the court and of their good will to himself, was always in his mind.[41]

As to Hughes himself, colleagues of very different political persuasions were lavish in their praise of his abilities. The combative Robert Jackson said of Hughes: "The majestic presence of Chief Justice Hughes as a presiding officer shed a native and simple dignity upon all of the Court's proceedings. A keen and experienced advocate of the bar, he knew the problems and the arts of the working lawyer. No one ran away with his Court."[42] He added: "Even when passions were running high and his own associates were in sharp division, he never lost his poise. He was an ideal presiding judge."

Hughes understood that the job gave its occupants "a special opportunity for leadership."[43] And by all accounts, he used that opportunity extremely effectively. Felix Frankfurter, hardly one to give undeserved praise to the leadership qualities of others, labeled him " 'Toscanini Hughes,' the maestro, the man with the remarkable gift of bringing things out of people."[44]

Hughes used all of the elements of his office effectively and sensitively. Merlo Pusey, Hughes's biographer, tells the story of his assignment policy. The chief justice would do his assignments after the Saturday conference and send out the notifications to the justices' homes (at the time the new Court building had not yet been built). He withheld the notifications to Justice Cardozo, however, because he had suffered a heart attack but was so diligent that he would plunge right into his assigned opinions without taking even one day of the weekend for rest. Since he did not want Cardozo to know that he was trying to protect his health, Hughes also delayed the distribution of assignments to Justice Van Devanter who lived in the same apartment building as Cardozo.[45]

Hughes also exercised skills in conference that not only voided needless conflict but also served as an example to his colleagues to do the same. Justice Roberts described him as follows:

Strong views were often expressed around the conference table, but never in eleven years did I see the Chief Justice lose his temper. Never did I hear him pass a personal remark. Never did I know him to raise his voice. Never did I witness his interrupting a Justice or getting into a controversy with him, and practically never did any one of his associates overstep the bounds of courtesy and propriety in opposing the views advanced by the Chief.[46]

Among the often forgotten chiefs with great skill is Melville Weston Fuller. When he came to the Court, Fuller determined to conquer each of the other justices with friendship, and by most accounts he succeeded.[47] He was most admired by his colleagues for his "skill in avoiding acrimony in the conference room."[48] Fuller was a gifted mediator. Holmes explained that Fuller liked to "tinker a compromise."[49]

Fuller knew how to mix business and pleasure both inside and outside the Court. When Justice David Brewer took his oath of office, Fuller hosted a banquet for him with the other members of the Court. Of course, Fuller also invited the the Senate Judiciary Committee. Not only was it a good time and a warm welcome for his new colleague, but the dinner also gave Fuller the opportunity to wage his successful lobbying effort to get passage of the Circuit Court of Appeals Act.[50]

Chief Justice Warren was also a gifted leader, even though he could not match the intellectual power of Frankfurter, Black, or Douglas. The story of his leadership of the Court to a unanimous ruling in *Brown v. Board of Education* is a classic example of his skills.[51] Chief Justice Rehnquist has also received high marks from his colleagues, even those with whom he had major ideological differences, because of his conference performance and his personal warmth.

The lesson to be learned from the great chiefs is that the members of the Court appreciate a strong leader who can keep the business of the Court moving while maintaining a sensitive and supportive attitude toward everyone regardless of personality or politics. Weak chiefs like White and Stone were uniformly criticized and overbearing ones like Burger were not appreciated. Strength and courtesy clearly are highly valued on the Court as elsewhere.

CONCLUSION

A number of features explain how it is that a Court that can so easily devolve into a continuing clash among powerful individuals with great independence does not do so. The combination of institutional qualities, work patterns, and leadership have been extremely important over the years in limiting conflict on the Court.

In the end, however, it is the character and sensitivity of the justices, their respect for the Court as an institution, and their willingness to subordinate their own personal frustrations to the interest of that institution that makes all the difference. It would seem, then, that the qualities that make for a good colleague on the Court should perhaps play a significant role in the selection of candidates for the office. The institution matters, and, fortunately, most of the justices who have been members of it have understood its importance, and its vulnerabilities, and have responded to its traditions and to their colleagues accordingly.

SEVEN

NINE SCORPIONS IN A BOTTLE OR THE MOST COLLEGIAL INSTITUTION IN TOWN?

This study began with a reference to the tradition of the handshake, a ceremony that has been a reminder of the importance of collegiality and professional courtesy among the justices for over a century. What becomes clear after a detailed consideration of the biographies of the justices is that Justice Byrnes may have been onto something when he "likened the handshake formality to 'the usual instruction of the referee in the ring. Shake hands, go to your corner and come out fighting.' "[1] Although the handshake before oral arguments or conference sessions has sometimes marked the beginning of the next round of conflict, it is also a reminder that professional conflict is one thing and conduct damaging to one's colleagues or the institution quite another.

CONFLICT IS NORMAL

At the end of this study, it is clear that the primary concern is not whether there are battles among the justices. Conflict is a normal part of organizational life. Given the unique characteristics of the United States Supreme Court as an institution, there is every reason to expect conflict, even intense disputes, at times. It is not helpful to treat such confrontations as shocking if we wish to really understand the Court as a critically important American political institution. Neither is it particularly useful for justices, active or retired, to suggest that somehow the members of the Court are able to avoid what all serious students of the Court know is a fact of life. Given the number of potential causes of conflict in the Court, though, it is rather surprising how controlled the justices have been over all the years of the institution.

THE LOCUS AND FOCUS OF CONFLICT

The question, then, is not whether there is conflict, even intense disputes, but where and how the disagreements are contested. If they are professional and internal, they pose no particular difficulty. Within limits, even some strong external professional debates have not damaged the Court and may indeed have provided it with a certain kind of strength. When the sense of limits is lost, however, even professional disputes can be troublesome when fought out in public. Danger threatens if the boundary between the professional and the personal is breached. When personal disputes go public serious issues arise, including what the clash does to the stature of the Court and, perhaps more important, what the implications may be for effective working relationships within the Court.

What If All of Washington Used Supreme Court Rules of Engagement?

Internal professional disputes are part of the work life of any multimember deliberative body. In the Supreme Court, disputes can help to focus and refine opinions. The fact that disputes are most often conducted on paper and generally circulated to all members of the Court and that drafts of all opinions, including dissents and concurrences, are circulated so that there are no surprises, no tricks or ambushes, helps to make the process less a contest and more a deliberation.

How might life in Washington change if there were a rule that required legislators and important executive branch officials to circulate their statements to all other officials of both parties prior to release, allowing time for the others to prepare responses? What a tantalizing picture particularly if there were a corollary obligation to make all such pronouncements in writing, with public presentation limited to a few minutes of commentary issued in the presence of all other members of the decision process. Add to that the constraint that once the policy declaration was made, the decision makers could issue no reply to criticism. To that set of restrictions, add the requirement that the decisions on disputes of the past are expected, absent clear justification to the contrary, to bind behavior in the future. What would happen if, as Justice Jackson so boldly put it, participants in political wars in the nation's capitol had "to wage it with the weapons of the open warrior, not those of the stealthy assassin?"[2]

If these rules of engagement were followed within the Court all the time, then Justice Powell's observation that conflicts could be serious but not personal or destructive to the institution would be absolutely correct. "Judges, like lawyers, may disagree strongly without personal rancor or ill will."[3] If and when members of the Court decide not observe the tradi-tional strictures or simply permit emotions to get the better of them, then the Court may indeed resemble "nine scorpions in a bottle."

What If the Court Ignores Its Own Rules and Traditions?

Chapters 3 and 4 described a range of ways that members of the Court have taken professional disputes beyond the limits, crossed the line be-tween professional and personal, and even brought personal battles into the public eye. Danger signs exist, however, that suggest when and how the justices may be approaching trouble.

When the Court is in the process of significant shifts in membership, and particularly when there is a deliberate effort to change course, the danger of excessive conflict is present. Certainly a study of the transition to the Taney Court and more recently of the transition from the Warren to the Burger Court is instructive. When long-time veterans of the Court are suddenly confronted by younger men and women with what are intended to be sharply different views, the potential for conflict is high. In examin-ing such shifts, it is important to realize that they do not occur immedi-ately. In the case of the transition from Warren to Burger, given confir-mation delays and the like, the Court was in flux from 1969 until about 1974, when the new justices had fully settled in.

A shift in the chief justice may be an important influence as well, as in the replacement of Hughes by Stone. Hughes credited his success as chief to the fact that he had served under Chief Justice White.

> Whatever little success I may have achieved when I became Chief Justice, I think was largely due to the lessons I learning [sic] in watching [Chief Justice] White during the years when I was an Asso-ciate Justice and seeing how it ought not to be done. . . . And so if I had any virtues as Chief Justice they were due to my determination to avoid White's faults. . . . White did not take hold the way a Chief Justice should in guiding the discussion and taking a position in ex-pounding the matters before the Court.[4]

Burger, by contrast, was not willing to learn from his predecessors. Fortu-nately, Rehnquist seems to have learned from the Burger years and from his own study of the Court's history.[5] One of the things he has not done, and perhaps could not do given the times and recent history, is to address the problem of fragmentation.

The excessive fragmentation of the Court noted by O'Brien, particularly during the 1980s and 1990s, flashes a warning. The expansion of separate opinions, among other uses, provides a means to vent disagreement, and these opinions have clearly been used for that purpose. But the character of separate opinions has changed. Furthermore, the rise in the number of pluralities and opinions for the Court joined only in discrete parts by members of the Court is particularly troublesome. It is as though the members of the Court are avoiding the task of compromise and are moving back toward the tradition of seriatim opinions that John Marshall worked so hard to eliminate. Granted, too much concern with consensus may paper over in public what are serious differences within the institution. Conversely, however, too little concern with the coherence of institutional decisions in order to purchase tranquility and avoid hard negotiations within the Court is conflict by another means, and it is far less helpful than a careful compromise hammered out through intense negotiations. The current spate of opinions in which one justice concurs in parts A, C, E, and F, and two other justices concur only in parts A and E is reminiscent of Alexander Hamilton's complaint about the plethora of state court rulings with no coherent synthesis in a national body.[6] His observation that so many opinions "are a hydra in government from which nothing but confusion and chaos can proceed" is worth remembering for those who prefer apparent peace to effective institutional judgment.[7]

There is also a growing tendency toward counter-concurrences and concurrences filed as counter-opinions against dissents from denial of certiorari or denials of stay petitions. This tactic is not a mechanism to vent frustration for the losers. The concurring justice has won in the denial of certiorari or stay. This device has simply become another battleground, which seems to offer no useful outcome except the tallying of debating points among the justices.

The proliferation of opinions offers a certain irony. On the one hand, it would seem to be a way to avoid confrontation and pitched battles over compromises where the fifth vote for the full opinion is needed. Everyone can express his or her views, join together at certain more or less mechanical points, but avoid finding a common ground for the Court. On the other hand, however, the proliferation of concurring opinions exacerbates the battle of the footnotes. When there are four concurrences, three of which criticize the plurality in strong terms, the author of the plurality has virtually no way to answer the challenges to the opinion for the Court without attacking the authors of the concurrences by name. It is impossible in these circumstances simply to respond to "the concurring opinion." Any challenge by name, in turn, is likely to precipitate a similarly direct response from the justice whose concurrence was just critiqued. When there are counter-concurrences among the group of justices who are presumably in agreement on the case, the potential for direct attacks also increases. One is reminded of Justice Brennan's note to Justice Powell in which he criticized himself for doing too much separate writing and determined to try to join more opinions.[8] The difficult challenge of forging a unified opinion is worth the effort, both internally and externally.

Another tradition that has largely been rejected may be worthy of reconsideration, the so-called freshman phenomenon. Robert Jackson and William O. Douglas both suggested at various times that it takes as much as three to five years to settle in as a justice at the Court. There have been exceptions, including most prominently Hugo Black, who plunged right in, launching dissents and dissents from denials of certiorari in his first term. Black caused more than a little controversy in the Court because of his aggressive style, which in turn encouraged Stone's determination to put pressure on Black to cool down. His decision to use Marquis Childs and the *St. Louis Post Dispatch* to do the job, however, only made matters worse.

In the past decade or so the tradition of the calm and relatively quiet first year has declined considerably. Among the most notable examples of those who chose not to adopt it were Sandra Day O'Connor and Antonin Scalia. In O'Connor's case, there was considerable pressure on her during confirmation to demonstrate her strength and independence, qualities that should have been readily apparent to anyone who knew her background. She went right into the fray, taking on Blackmun without perhaps fully understanding the dynamics within the Court of the decision process from the *Usery* ruling on in the area of federalism. She also locked horns with White. There was also the matter of the misstep of protocol in involving herself in an issue of reargument when she was on the dissenting side, which got her into a tiff with Powell. Scalia's plea that it is the academic "devil in me" that caused him to take such an aggressive approach in oral argument and in some of his opinions was no more helpful than similar explanations offered by Professor Frankfurter. Justice Souter, by contrast, took the more traditional approach and it has seemingly served him well.

Several explanations exist for the demise of the freshman phenomenon. If pressure is brought to bear to be the swing vote on a critical issue, it is difficult for a justice to take a low profile, even in the first year. Obviously, when a president has deliberately chosen a justice, or a number of them, to be dramatic change agents, a clash is to be expected. Moreover, if a justice is on record, perhaps well before the confirmation process, as having a dramatically different perspective from the Court's center of gravity, there is every reason to anticipate increased conflict unless that justice determines to observe a version of the freshman restraint. Scalia is the most obvious recent example of someone who chose to press arguments on the Court he had been making for years before he got there.

Finally, most appointees now come from the U.S. Circuit Court of Appeals rather than from other backgrounds. As Justice Goldberg explained, it is a very different matter for people to come into the Supreme Court from a governor's office, like Warren, a regulatory agency, like Douglas, private practice, like Fortas, Goldberg, or Powell, or the legislature, like Black, than it is to have a group that is overwhelmingly elevated from an appeals court. Much of the job looks the same as the Court of Appeals, but the institution and its role in American government is very different. Goldberg was of the view that Supreme Court justices do not spring full blown from the Court of Appeals. Although there is no way to be certain, it appears that the shift may have changed not only the dynamics of internal operation but the way that separate opinions are viewed as well.

The Assault on the Barrier Between the Personal and the Professional

If there is one area that seems to pose particular danger for the Court as an institution, it is the perception that conflicts have become more personal and that the barrier that formerly existed between the personal and professional is frequently breached. The fact that several justices have denied that personal relationships are a problem seems not to have improved matters at all. The issue here is, in important respects, both a matter of fact and of perception.

On the facts, it is difficult for those who have followed the Court's opinions and coverage of speeches and publications during the 1980s and 1990s to accept the contention that there is no more conflict than at any other time in the Court's history. Members of the Court must be presumed to know that such matters as speeches to circuit conferences will receive much wider coverage than in a former day. When those speeches are strongly critical of particular actions by the Court, it is clear to observers just where the criticisms are directed. When, for example, Justice Scalia issues a scathing indictment that directly attacks another justice by name in paragraph after paragraph of the opinion in what is clearly an attack on the courage and forthrightness of that colleague, the contention that readers simply do not understand the Court will not do.

In addition to these very direct behaviors, there are indeed other issues of perception. The contention that these are just lawyers doing what lawyers do is not convincing. Justices of the "one Supreme Court" provided for in Article III of the Constitution do not represent individual clients or themselves. They have an obligation to the institution. If there is one goal of conflict management within the Court it should be to avoid external personal conflicts and to ensure that external professional conflicts are waged in the best interest of the institution. From time to time there will be violations of that goal, as there have been throughout the history of the Court. Exceptions are, however, different from an apparent abandonment of the informal controls and a concomitant ratcheting up of conflict. The barrier between the personal and professional serves a real and useful purpose.

In the end, though, to paint the Court as "nine scorpions in a bottle" is to go too far. Compared with other political institutions, it has, with some exceptions, handled conflict well under difficult circumstances and high expectations. It can certainly make a credible claim to being the most collegial of the three major governmental bodies in Washington.

APPENDIX
JUSTICES OF THE UNITED STATES
SUPREME COURT

John Jay	1789–1795
John Rutledge	1789–1791
William Cushing	1789–1810
James Wilson	1789–1798
John Blair, Jr.	1789–1796
James Iredell	1790–1799
Thomas Johnson	1791–1793
William Paterson	1793–1806
Samuel Chase	1796–1811
Oliver Ellsworth	1796–1800
Bushrod Washington	1798–1829
Alfred Moore	1799–1804
John Marshall	1801–1835
William Johnson	1804–1834
Henry Brockholst Livingston	1806–1823
Thomas Todd	1807–1826
Joseph Story	1811–1845
Gabriel Duvall	1811–1835
Smith Thompson	1823–1843
Robert Trimble	1826–1828
John McLean	1829–1861
Henry Baldwin	1830–1844
James Moore Wayne	1835–1867
Roger Brooke Taney	1836–1864
Philip Pendleton Barbour	1836–1841
John Catron	1837–1865
John McKinley	1837–1852
Peter Vivian Daniel	1841–1860
Samuel Nelson	1845–1872
Levi Woodbury	1846–1851
Robert Cooper Grier	1846–1870
Benjamin Robbins Curtis	1851–1857
John Archibald Campbell	1853–1861

Nathan Clifford	1858–1881
Noah Haynes Swayne	1862–1881
Samuel Freeman Miller	1862–1890
David Davis	1862–1877
Stephen Johnson Field	1863–1879
Salmon Portland Chase	1864–1873
William Strong	1870–1880
Joseph P. Bradley	1870–1892
Ward Hunt	1873–1882
Morrison Remick Waite	1874–1888
John Marshall Harlan	1877–1911
William Burnham Woods	1880–1887
Stanley Matthews	1881–1889
Horace Gray	1881–1902
Samuel Blatchford	1881–1893
Lucius Quintus Cincinnatus Lamar	1888–1893
Melville Weston Fuller	1888–1910
David Josiah Brewer	1889–1910
Henry Billings Brown	1890–1906
George Shiras, Jr.	1892–1903
Howell Edmunds Jackson	1893–1895
Edward Douglass White	1894–1921
Rufus Wheeler Peckham	1895–1909
Joseph McKenna	1898–1925
Oliver Wendell Holmes, Jr.	1902–1932
William Rufus Day	1903–1922
William Henry Moody	1906–1910
Horace Harmon Lurton	1909–1914
Charles Evans Hughes	1910–1916, 1930–1941
Willis Van Devanter	1910–1937
Joseph Rucker Lamar	1910–1916
Mahlon Pitney	1912–1922
James Clark McReynolds	1914–1941
Louis Dembitz Brandeis	1916–1939
John Hessin Clarke	1916–1922
William Howard Taft	1921–1930
George Sutherland	1922–1938
Pierce Butler	1922–1939

Edward Terry Sanford	1923–1930
Harlan Fiske Stone	1925–1946
Owen Josephus Roberts	1930–1945
Benjamin Nathan Cardozo	1932–1938
Hugo Lafayette Black	1937–1971
Stanley Forman Reed	1938–1957
Felix Frankfurter	1939–1962
William Orville Douglas	1939–1975
Frances William Murphy	1940–1949
James Francis Byrnes	1941–1942
Robert Houghwout Jackson	1941–1954
Wiley Blount Rutledge	1943–1949
Harold Hitz Burton	1945–1958
Frederick Moore Vinson	1946–1953
Tom Campbell Clark	1949–1967
Sherman Minton	1949–1956
Earl Warren	1953–1969
John Marshall Harlan	1955–1971
William Joseph Brennan, Jr.	1956–1990
Charles Evans Whittaker	1957–1962
Potter Stewart	1958–1981
Byron Raymond White	1962–1993
Arthur Joseph Goldberg	1962–1965
Abe Fortas	1965–1969
Thurgood Marshall	1967–1991
Warren Earl Burger	1969–1986
Harry Andrew Blackmun	1970–1994
Lewis Franklin Powell, Jr.	1971–1987
William Hubbs Rehnquist	1971–
John Paul Stevens	1975–
Sandra Day O'Connor	1981–
Antonin Scalia	1986–
Anthony McLeod Kennedy	1988–
David Hackett Souter	1990–
Clarence Thomas	1991–
Ruth Bader Ginsburg	1993–
Stephen Breyer	1994–

NOTES

PREFACE

1. *A Supreme Court Justice Is Appointed* (New York: Random House, 1964).
2. *The Elements of Judicial Strategy* (Chicago: University of Chicago Press, 1964).
3. *Storm Center,* 3d ed. (New York: Norton, 1993).

CHAPTER 1. THE SYMBOLIC HANDSHAKE

1. Willard L. King, *Melville Weston Fuller* (New York: Macmillan, 1950), p. 134. Elder Witt, *Congressional Quarterly Guide to the U.S. Supreme Court,* 2d ed. (Washington, D.C., 1990), p. 748. See also Mary Ann Harrell, *Equal Justice Under Law: The Supreme Court in American Life* (Washington, D.C.: Foundation of the American Bar Association, 1975), p. 127, and David O'Brien, *Storm Center,* 3d ed. (New York: Norton, 1993), p. 152.
2. Quoted in Joseph P. Lash, *From the Diaries of Felix Frankfurter* (New York: Norton, 1975), p. 313.
3. Stephen Wermeil, "Low Roading on the High Court," *Wall Street Journal,* September 13, 1982, p. 30
4. Bill Moyers, *In Search of the Constitution* (Public Affairs Television, 1987).
5. Actually, the comparison between the politics of the Court and those of the curia are not new. See Walter F. Murphy, *The Vicar of Christ* (New York: Ballantine Books, 1980).
6. Walter F. Murphy, *Elements of Judicial Strategy* (Chicago: University of Chicago Press, 1964), p. 2. See also Alexander Meiklejohn, *Political Freedom* (New York: Oxford University Press, 1965), pp. 32–33 (first published in 1948).
7. This concept is discussed at greater length in Phillip J. Cooper and Howard Ball, *The United States Supreme Court: From the Inside Out* (Englewood Cliffs, N.J.: Prentice-Hall, 1995), chap. 10.
8. John P. Frank, "Hugo Black: He Has Joined the Giants," in Jesse H. Choper, ed., *The Supreme Court and Its Justices* (Chicago: American Bar Association, 1987), p. 115.
9. E. E. Schattschneider, *The Semi-Sovereign People* (New York: Holt, Rinehart and Winston, 1960).
10. See Sheldon Goldman and Charles M. Lamb, eds., *Judicial Conflict and Consensus* (Lexington: University Press of Kentucky, 1986).
11. Bernard Schwartz, *Super Chief: Earl Warren and His Supreme Court* (New York: New York University Press, 1983), pp. 29–31.

12. Charles Evans Hughes, *The Supreme Court of the United States* (New York: Columbia University Press, 1928), p. 68.

13. John R. Schmidhauser, *Judges and Justices: The Federal Appellate Judiciary* (Boston: Little, Brown, 1979); Henry J. Abraham, *Justices and Presidents: A Political History of Appointments to the Supreme Court.* (New York: Oxford University Press, 1974).

14. *Roe v. Wade,* 410 U.S. 113 (1973).

15. *Cruzan v. Director, Missouri Department of Health,* 497 U.S. 261 (1990).

16. See Bradley C. Canon, "Courts and Policy: Compliance, Implementation, and Impact," in John B. Gates and Charles A. Johnson, *The American Courts: A Critical Assessment* (Washington, D.C.: Congressional Quarterly, 1991), pp. 441–42.

17. Hugo L. Black and Elizabeth Black, *Mr. Justice and Mrs. Black,* (New York: Random House, 1986), p. 85.

18. Ibid., p. 86

19. The battle over Roberts's retirement letter and Earl Warren's courtroom clashes with Felix Frankfurter are examples of incomplete and festering conflicts that affected working relationships.

20. Interview with author (name withheld on request).

21. Examples include Justice Jackson's threat directed at Justice Murphy to publish an opinion exposing Murphy's involvement as U.S. attorney general in approving wiretaps when Murphy was later preparing vehement dissents on the evils of wiretapping. *Goldman v. United States,* 316 U.S. 129 (1942). Justice Douglas used the threat of exposure on a number of occasions, one of the most serious of which was his warning that he would expose what he saw as opinion assignment abuses by Chief Justice Burger in *Roe v. Wade.*

CHAPTER 2. WHY DO THEY FIGHT?

1. Leonard Baker, *Brandeis and Frankfurter* (New York: New York University Press, 1986), pp. 335, 418.

2. William O. Douglas, Memorandum to the Conference, November 21, 1960, Douglas Papers, Box 1258. Douglas told his secretary to type the memo but not to circulate it until he had an opportunity to show it to Earl Warren and discuss it with him. Douglas never made good on his threat.

3. Robert H. Jackson to Chairmen, House and Senate Judiciary Committees, June 7, 1946, with a copy to Harry Truman, Jackson Papers, Library of Congress, Box 26.

4. Autobiography Manuscript, Jackson Papers, Library of Congress, Box 188, pp. 223–25.

5. J. Woodford Howard, *Mr. Justice Murphy* (Princeton: Princeton University Press, 1968), pp. 282–83.

6. Ibid., pp. 283–85.

7. R. Kent Newmyer, *Supreme Court Justice Joseph Story: Statesman of the Old Republic* (Chapel Hill: University of North Carolina Press, 1985), p. 93.

8. Ibid., p. 204.

9. Donald G. Morgan, *Justice William Johnson: The First Dissenter* (Columbia: University of South Carolina Press, 1954).

10. Alpheus T. Mason, *William Howard Taft Chief Justice* (New York: Simon and Schuster, 1965), p. 217.

11. Ibid.

12. Ibid.

13. 347 U.S. 483 (1954).

14. See Richard Kluger, *Simple Justice* (New York: Vintage Books, 1975).

15. John C. Jeffries, Jr., *Justice Lewis F. Powell, Jr.* (New York: Charles Scribner's Sons, 1994), p. 261.

16. Ibid.

17. 411 U.S. 1 (1973).

18. Ibid., p. 35.

19. Ibid., p. 71.

20. Ibid., p. 126.

21. Ibid., p. 130.

22. Docket sheets in *Bradley v. State Board of Education of Virginia,* No. 72-550 and *School Board of the City of Richmond v. State Board of Education,* No. 72-549, Brennan Papers, Box 419.

23. Warren Burger, Memorandum to the Conference, April 26, 1973, Brennan Papers, Box 301.

24. Memorandum to the Conference, April 30, 1973, Brennan Papers, Box 301, p. 7.

25. Memorandum to the Conference, May 3, 1973, Brennan Papers, Box 301.

26. Thurgood Marshall to Byron White, May 10, 1973, Brennan Papers, Box 301.

27. *Milliken v. Bradley,* 418 U.S. 717 (1974).

28. Ibid., p. 789.

29. Ibid., p. 808.

30. Ibid., pp. 814–15.

31. 438 U.S. 265 (1978).

32. Jeffries, *Justice Powell,* pp. 487–88.

33. Ibid., p. 488.

34. 438 U.S. 265 (1978), at 388.

35. Thurgood Marshall, Memorandum to the Conference, April 13, 1978, Brennan Papers, Box 465, pp. 1–2.

36. Ibid., pp. 2–3.

37. 476 U.S. 79 (1986).

38. Thurgood Marshall to William J. Brennan, February 28, 1986, Marshall Papers, Box 396.

39. David O'Brien, *Storm Center,* 3d ed. (New York: Norton, 1993), p. 180.

40. Ibid., p. 525.

41. William J. Brennan, Jr., "Constitutional Adjudication and the Death Penalty: A View From the Court," *Harvard Law Review* 100 (1986): 313, 330.

42. See Jeffries, *Justice Powell,* pp. 451–54. See Blackmun's dissents from denials of stay in *Campbell v. Wood,* 128 L.Ed.2d 682 (1994), and *Collins v. Collins,*127 L.Ed.2d 435 (1994).

43. 410 U.S. 113 (1973). See Blackmun's opinions in *Webster v. Reproductive Health Services,* 492 U.S. 490 (1989) and *Ohio v. Akron Center for Reproductive Health,* 497 U.S. 524 (1990).

44. Harry Blackmun to Warren Burger, January 18, 1972, Douglas Papers, Box 1523, and Blackmun Memorandum to the Conference, May 18, 1972, Brennan Papers, Box 282.

45. *Webster v. Reproductive Health Services,* 492 U.S. 490 (1989), p. 449.

46. *Planned Parenthood v. Casey,* 120 L.Ed.2d 674, 744–45 (1992).

47. 330 U.S. 1 (1947).

48. *Illinois ex rel McCollum v. Board of Education,* 333 U.S. 203 (1948).

49. See Felix Frankfurter to Wiley Rutledge, January 6, 1948, Rutledge Papers, Box 166, and Felix Frankfurter to Robert Jackson, January 6, 1948, Jackson Papers, Box 143.

50. Black Papers, Box 295.

51. Tinsley E. Yarbrough, *John Marshall Harlan: Great Dissenter of the Warren Court* (New York: Oxford University Press, 1992), pp. 129–30.

52. 358 U.S. 1 (1958).

53. Interview with Associate Justice William J. Brennan, Jr., Washington, D.C., October 29, 1986.

54. Kim Isaac Eisler, *A Justice For All* (New York: Simon and Schuster, 1993), pp. 155–56.

55. Ibid., p. 156.

56. Ibid.

57. H. N. Hirsch, *The Enigma of Felix Frankfurter* (New York: Basic Books, 1981), p. 5.

58. Ibid., p. 128.

59. Ibid., pp. 5–6.

60. Arthur Sears Henning, "Frankfurter's Hold on Court Losing Force," *Chicago Tribune,* June 21, 1943, Douglas Papers, Box 329.

61. 310 U.S. 586 (1940).

62. 316 U.S. 584 (1942).

63. 319 U.S. 624 (1943).

64. William O. Douglas, *The Court Years* (New York: Random House, 1980), p. 44.

65. Ibid.

66. Interview of William O. Douglas by Elizabeth Black, quoted in Hugo L. Black and Elizabeth Black, *Mr. Justice and Mrs. Black* (New York: Random House, 1986), p. 72

67. Hirsch, *Enigma,* p. 176.

68. Melvin I. Urofsky, "Conflict Among the Brethren: Felix Frankfurter, William O. Douglas and the Clash of Personalities and Philosophies on the United States Supreme Court," *Duke Law Journal* (1988): 71, 91.

69. Hirsch, *Enigma,* p. 182.

70. Ibid., p. 190.

71. Bernard Schwartz, "Felix Frankfurter and Earl Warren: A Study of a Deteriorating Relationship," *Supreme Court Review* (1980): 115.

72. William O. Douglas to Hugo L. Black, June 22, 1941, Douglas Papers, Library of Congress, Box 308.

73. William O. Douglas to Hugo L. Black, September 8, 1941, Black Papers, Box 59.

74. Bernard Schwartz, *Super Chief: Earl Warren and His Supreme Court* (New York: New York University Press, 1983), p. 53.

75. Joseph P. Lash, ed., *From the Diaries of Felix Frankfurter* (New York: Norton, 1975), p. 155.

76. William O. Douglas, *The Court Years* (New York: Random House, 1980), p. 22.

77. Copy of the interview tape provided during an interview with Mrs. Elizabeth Black, Arlington, Virginia, August 28, 1986.

78. The discussion of the assignment controversy later indicates the difficulties that arose in connection with *Swann v. Charlotte-Mechlenburg Bd. of Ed.,* 402 U.S. 1 (1970), and *United States v. Nixon,* 418 U.S. 683 (1974) because of Burger's insistence on claiming a right to lead.

79. Newmyer, *Supreme Court Justice Joseph Story,* p. 220.

80. Merlo J. Pusey, *Charles Evans Hughes,* 2 vols. (New York: Macmillan, 1951), 1:278.

81. Ibid.

82. Lash, *From the Diaries of Felix Frankfurter,* p. 75.

83. William O. Douglas to Hugo Black, June 22, 1941, Douglas Papers, Box 308.

84. J. Woodford Howard, *Mr. Justice Murphy: A Political Biography.* (Princeton: Princeton University Press, 1968), p. 398.

85. Ibid., pp. 396–97.

86. Oral History File, Harry S. Truman Papers, Truman Library, Independence, Missouri.

87. Bruce Allen Murphy, *Fortas* (New York: Morrow, 1988), p. 539.

88. John P. Frank, *Justice Daniel Dissenting* (Cambridge, Mass.: Harvard University Press, 1964), p. 170.

89. Quoted in ibid., p. 170.

90. Quoted in ibid., pp. 170–72.

91. See David McCulloch, *Truman* (New York: Simon and Schuster, 1992).

92. Quoted in Schwartz, "Felix Frankfurter and Earl Warren," p. 72.

93. Quoted in ibid., p. 73.

94. Lash, *From the Diaries of Felix Frankfurter,* p. 270.

95. Ibid., p. 303.

96. See *United Steelworkers of America v. Weber,* 443 U.S. 193 (1979), Rehnquist, J., dissenting.

97. Bruce Murphy, *The Brandeis/Frankfurter Connection* (New York: Oxford University Press, 1982) p. 9.

98. Interview with author.

99. William O. Douglas to Franklin Roosevelt, January 3, 1941, Roosevelt Papers, Roosevelt Library, PSF 186 File.

100. A. O. Sarkissian, "Speeches and Statements of U.S. Supreme Court Judges on the Issues of the Day," Government Division, Library of Congress, March 22, 1956, p. 6.

101. Ibid., p. 1.

102. Leon Friedman and Fred L. Israel, eds., *The Justices of the United States Supreme Court 1789–1969: Their Lives and Major Opinions* (New York: Bowker, 1969), pp. 233–34.

103. Chief Justice Harlan Fiske Stone to President Franklin D. Roosevelt on July 20, 1942, quoted in Elder Witt, *Congressional Quarterly Guide to the Supreme Court,* 2d ed. (Washington, D.C.: Congressional Quarterly, 1990), p. 752.

104. Susan E. Grogan, "The Extrajudicial Writings of William O. Douglas," Unpublished paper presented at the Annual Meeting of the Law and Society Association, Washington, D.C., 1987, p. 3, n.6.

105. Laura Kalman, *Abe Fortas* (New Haven: Yale University Press, 1990), p. 310.

106. Ibid., p. 312.

107. See Howard Ball and Phillip Cooper, *Of Power and Right* (New York: Oxford University Press, 1992), chap. 13.

108. Alpheus T. Mason, *William Howard Taft Chief Justice* (New York: Simon and Schuster, 1965), pp. 215–19.

109. Emanuel Celler to Harlan Fiske Stone, August 13, 1942, Douglas Papers, Box 357. He responded, Harlan Fiske Stone to Emanuel Celler, August 15, 1942, Douglas Papers, Box 357.

110. Lash, *From the Diaries of Felix Frankfurter,* p. 155.

111. William O. Douglas to Chief Justice Earl Warren, June 27, 1957, Warren Papers, Box 350.

112. William O. Douglas to Warren Burger, May 26, 1971, Douglas Papers, Box 1485.

113. Phil Cogswell, "Lawyers Hike 6 Miles in Woods to Find Justice Douglas," *Portland Oregonian,* in Douglas Papers, Box 1499.

114. See Schwartz, *Super Chief,* pp. 495–501.

115. Ibid., p. 761.

116. Ibid.

117. Hugo Black, *A Constitutional Faith* (New York: Alfred A. Knopf, 1968) p. 11.

118. *Griswold v. Connecticut,* 381 U.S., at 510, Black, J., dissenting.

119. *A Constitutional Faith,* p. 30.

120. See his dissents in *National RR Passenger Corp. v. National Assn of RR Passengers* (1974), Douglas, J., dissenting; *O'Shea v. Littleton* (1974), Douglas, J., dissenting; *United States v. Richardson* (1974), Douglas, J., dissenting; *Schlesinger v. Reservists Against the War* (1974), Douglas, J., dissenting; and *Warth v. Seldin* (1975).

121. *Warth v. Seldin,* 422 U.S. 490, 519 (1975), Douglas, J., dissenting.
122. *SEC v. Medical Committee for Human Rights* (1972) 404 U.S. at 411.
123. William O. Douglas, Memorandum to the Conference, October 23, 1961.
124. Ibid., p. 3.
125. Ibid.
126. Felix Frankfurter, Memorandum to the Conference, October 22, 1942, Douglas Papers, Box 77.
127. See Sidney Fine, *Frank Murphy: The Washington Years* (Ann Arbor: University of Michigan Press, 1984), p. 245.
128. Pusey, *Charles Evans Hughes,* 1:275
129. 437 U.S. 153 (1978).
130. Jeffries, *Justice Powell,* p. 249.
131. Ibid.
132. Ibid.
133. Ibid., p. 507.
134. Thurgood Marshall, Memorandum to the Conference, April 12, 1972, Douglas Papers, Box 1523.
135. In *Gooding v. Wilson,* Burger indicated that the conference vote had been inconclusive and he intended to put the case down for another conference. Douglas, who had decided to assign the opinion to Brennan, wrote Burger objecting that the vote had been a clear 5–2 to affirm. William O. Douglas to Warren Burger, December 17, 1971, Douglas Papers, Box 1524. Burger's purpose became more clear when he replied: "Here again there is no harm in writing, but if your position is now firmed up, I see no point in reviewing a Conference discussion. Indeed, I think it very likely this case will be rearmed. I, for one, will not take part in overruling Chaplaincy, directly or indirectly, with a seven-member Court" (Warren Burger to William O. Douglas, December 20, 1971, Douglas Papers, Box 1524). Brennan also wrote a memorandum indicating his disagreement with Burger's handling of assignments. "Douglas had a similar problem with Burger in *United States v. United States District Court,* where Burger assigned the opinion to White even though Douglas was convinced that there were five votes in support of a more expansive ruling on constitutional grounds. He assigned the opinion to Lewis Powell, though Burger continued to support the idea that White should write" (William O. Douglas to Warren Burger, March 6, 1972, Douglas Papers, Box 1523; Warren Burger to William O. Douglas, March 7, 1972, Douglas Papers, Box 1523; William O. Douglas to Lewis Powell, March 8, 1972, Douglas Papers, Box 1523).
136. Potter Stewart to Warren Burger, December 29, 1970, Douglas Papers, Box 1485.
137. William O. Douglas to Warren Burger, May 1, 1972, Douglas Papers, Box 1523.
138. 410 U.S. 113 (1973).
139. 410 U.S. 179 (1973).
140. William O. Douglas to Warren Burger, December 18, 1971, Douglas Papers, Box 1523.

141. Warren Burger to William O. Douglas, December 20, 1971, Brennan Papers, Box 281.

142. Harry A. Blackmun to Warren Burger, January 18, 1972, Douglas Papers, Box 1523.

143. Memorandum to the Conference, May 18, 1972, Brennan Papers, Box 282.

144. William O. Douglas to Warren Burger, June 1, 1972, Brennan Papers, Box 281.

145. Memorandum from Mr. Justice Douglas, June 2, 1972, Douglas Papers, Box 1588.

146. Ibid., p. 2.

147. Ibid., p. 3.

148. William O. Douglas to Warren Burger, July 4, 1972, Douglas Papers, Box 1588.

149. Warren Burger, July 27, 1972, Douglas Papers, Box 1588, p. 4.

150. William O. Douglas to Warren Burger, August 7, 1989, Douglas Papers, Box 1588.

151. 413 U.S. 189 (1973).

152. Jeffries, *Justice Powell,* p. 305.

153. See Memorandum to the Conference, June 13, 1974, Brennan Papers, Box 325.

154. David Margolick, "Marshall Assails High Court On Its Summary Procedures," *New York Times,* September 11, 1982.

155. Jeffries, *Justice Powell,* 265.

156. Ibid.

157. Ibid., p. 534.

158. Ibid.

CHAPTER 3. HOW DO THEY FIGHT? THE
PROFESSIONAL FIGHTS

1. *Webster v. Reproductive Health Services,* 106 L.Ed.2d 410 (1989).

2. 410 U.S. 113 (1973).

3. 102 L.Ed.2d 854 (1989).

4. 106 L.Ed.2d, at p. 445.

5. Ibid., p. 445.

6. Ibid.

7. Ibid.

8. Ibid., p. 441.

9. Ibid., p. 447.

10. Ibid.

11. Ibid.

12. Ibid., p. 448.

13. Ibid.

14. Ibid.

15. Ibid.

16. R. Kent Newmyer, *Supreme Court Justice Joseph Story: Statesman of the Old Republic* (Chapel Hill: University of North Carolina Press, 1985), p. 204.

17. Ibid., pp. 204–5.

18. Ibid., p. 219.

19. John P. Frank, *Justice Daniel Dissenting* (Cambridge, Mass.: Harvard University Press, 1964).

20. Ibid., p. 161.

21. Ibid., p. 236.

22. Ibid., p. 166.

23. Sheldon M. Novick, *Honorable Justice: The Life of Oliver Wendell Holmes* (Boston: Little, Brown, 1989), pp. 343, 476 n.31.

24. 323 U.S. 214 (1944).

25. 319 U.S. 624 (1943).

26. 341 U.S. 494 (1951).

27. See *Adderley v. Florida,* 385 U.S. 48 (1966).

28. Bruce Allen Murphy, *Fortas* (New York: Morrow, 1988), pp. 223–24.

29. Ibid., pp. 537–38.

30. Vincent Blasi, ed., *The Burger Court: The Counter-Revolution that Wasn't* (New Haven: Yale University Press, 1982). Richard Funston, *Constitutional Counterrevolution?* (Cambridge, Mass.: Schenkman Publishing, 1977).

31. See his dissents in *Board of Regents v. Roth,* 408 U.S. 564 (1972); *Mathews v. Eldridge,* 424 U.S. 319 (1976); *Cleveland v. Loudermill,* 470 U.S. 532 (1985); *Weinberger v. Salfi,* 422 U.S. 749 (1975); *Bishop v. Wood,* 426 U.S. 341 (1976); *Paul v. Davis,* 424 U.S. 693 (1976); *O'Bannon v. Town Court Nursing Center,* 447 U.S. 773 (1980). On Court access, see *Warth v. Seldin,* 422 U.S. 490 (1975), dissent.

32. *Gertz v. Welch,* 418 U.S. 323 (1974), dissent; *Miller v. California,* 413 U.S. 15 (1973), dissent; *Paris Adult Theatre v. Slaton,* 413 U.S. 49 (1973), dissent; *Herbert v. Lando,* 441 U.S. 153 (1979), dissent; *Time v. Firestone,* 424 U.S. 448 (1976), dissent; *Hazelwood School Dist. v. Kuhlmeier,* 484 U.S. 260 (1988); *Perry v. Sindermann,* 408 U.S. 593 (1972); *Connick v. Myers,* 461 U.S. 138 (1983), dissent; *Perry Education Assoc. v. Perry Local Educators' Assoc.* 460 U.S. 37 (1983).

33. See his dissents in *Beal v. Doe,* 432 U.S. 438 (1977); *Maher v. Roe,* 432 U.S. 464 (1977); *Poelker v. Doe,* 432 U.S. 519 (1977); *Harris v. McRae,* 448 U.S. 297 (1980); *Webster v. Reproductive Health Services,* 492 U.S. 490 (1989).

34. See his dissents in *Profitt v. Florida,* 428 U.S. 242 (1976); *Gregg v. Georgia,* 428 U.S. 153 (1976).

35. See Marshall's dissents in *San Antonio Independent School District v. Rodriguez,* 411 U.S. 1 (1973); *Washington v. Davis,* 426 U.S. 229 (1976); *Personnel Administrator v. Feeney,* 442 U.S. 256 (1979); *Memphis v. Greene,* 451 U.S. 100 (1981).

36. See Marshall's opinions in *Milliken v. Bradley,* 418 U.S. 717 (1974); *Univer-*

sity of California Regents v. Bakke, 438 U.S. 265 (1978); and *Richmond v. Croson,* 488 U.S. 469 (1989).

37. *Industrial Union Dept., AFL-CIO v. American Petroleum Institute,* 488 U.S. 607 (1980).

38. 435 U.S. 519 (1978).

39. 198 U.S. 45 (1905).

40. Ibid., p. 75.

41. Tinsley E. Yarbrough, *John Marshall Harlan: Great Dissenter of the Warren Court* (New York: Oxford University Press, 1992).

42. Peter Irons, *Brennan vs. Rehnquist* (New York: Alfred A. Knopf, 1994), p. 49.

43. *Brewer v. Williams,* 430 U.S. 387 (1977).

44. John C. Jeffries, Jr., *Justice Lewis F. Powell, Jr.* (New York: Charles Scribner's Sons, 1994), pp. 401–2.

45. Irons, *Brennan vs. Rehnquist,* p. 261.

46. Quoted in ibid.

47. Quoted in ibid., p. 17. The case was *Moreno v. U.S. Department of Agriculture,* 413 U.S. 528, 545–47 (1973), Rehnquist, J., dissenting.

48. *Columbus Bd. of Ed. v. Penick,* 443 U.S. 449 (1979).

49. Irons, *Brennan vs. Rehnquist,* p. 252.

50. Ibid.

51. 460 U.S. 491 (1983). See also Irons, *Brennan vs. Rehnquist,* p. 193.

52. 460 U.S. 491 (1983), cited in Irons, *Brennan vs. Rehnquist,* p. 52.

53. Ibid.

54. Ibid.

55. Ibid., p. 528.

56. Ibid., pp. 529–30.

57. *Texas v. Johnson,* 491 U.S. 391 (1989).

58. Irons, *Brennan vs. Rehnquist,* p. 163.

59. See *FBI v. Abramson,* 456 U.S. 615 (1982).

60. Ibid., p. 643.

61. Ibid., pp. 385–86 n.7.

62. 456 U.S. 742 (1982).

63. Indeed, Blackmun's colleagues should have been well aware that he had reached a point in his career where he was willing to come out swinging. See his dissent in *Cabell v. Chavez-Salido,* 454 U.S. 432 (1982), in which he wrote: "Today's decision rewrites the Court's precedents, ignores history, defies common sense, and reinstates the deadening mantle of state parochialism in public employment." (ibid., p. 449). Blackmun accused the majority of 'misstating the standard of review it has long applied' in alien cases and of 'thoroughly eviscerating' his Dougall opinion. "I can only conclude, that the California's exclusion of these appellees from the position of deputy probation officer stems solely from state parochialism and hostility toward foreigners who have come to this country lawfully." (ibid., p. 463). See also Irons, *Brennan vs. Rehnquist,* pp. 278–79.

64. *FERC v. Mississippi,* 456 U.S., p. 761, n.25.

65. Ibid., p. 762 n.27.

66. Ibid., p. 767 n.30.

67. Ibid., p. 769 n.32.

68. See e.g., *Bowen v. Roy,* 476 U.S. 693 (1986).

69. Bill Moyers, "In Search of the Constitution," (Public Affairs Television, Inc., 1987).

70. 457 U.S. 853 (1982).

71. 73 L.Ed.2d at 470.

72. Ibid., p. 474.

73. H. N. Hirsch, *The Enigma of Felix Frankfurter* (New York: Basic Books, 1981), p. 140.

74. William O. Douglas, *Go East Young Man* (New York: Dell, 1974), p. 452.

75. David O'Brien, *Storm Center,* 3d ed. (New York: Norton, 1993), p. 252.

76. Ibid., p. 253.

77. See Brennan's dissents in *Glass v. Louisiana,* 85 L.Ed.2d 514, 520–21 (1985). See also William J. Brennan, Jr., "Constitutional Adjudication and the Death Penalty: A View From the Court," *Harvard Law Review* 100 (1986): 313.

78. See his dissent in *Campbell v. Wood,* 128 L.Ed.2d 682 (1994) (Washington hanging case).

79. Bernard Schwartz, *Super Chief: Earl Warren and His Supreme Court* (New York: New York University Press, 1980), pp. 160–61.

80. *Callins v. Collins,* 127 L.Ed.2d 435, 437 (1994), Blackmun, J., dissenting from denial of cert.

81. 481 U.S. 279 (1987).

82. 127 L.Ed.2d, p. 438 n.1.

83. Ibid., p. 438.

84. Ibid., p. 449.

85. Ibid., p. 436.

86. Alpheus T. Mason, *William Howard Taft Chief Justice* (New York: Simon and Schuster, 1965), p. 216.

87. Novick, *Honorable Justice,* p. 370.

88. Sidney Fine, *Frank Murphy: The Washington Years* (Ann Arbor: University of Michigan Press, 1984), p. 262.

89. Ibid., p. 261.

90. Ibid., pp. 263–64.

91. Schwartz, *Super Chief,* pp. 122–23. The case was *Milanovich v. United States,* 365 U.S. 551 (1961). See *New York Times,* March 21, 1961, p. 18.

92. Schwartz, *Super Chief,* p. 123.

93. William O. Douglas to Hugo L. Black, December 17, 1957, Douglas Papers, Box 308.

94. Murphy, *Fortas,* p. 224.

95. Transcript, Bill Moyers, "In Search of the Constitution: Mr. Justice Blackmun," (Washington, D.C.: Public Affairs Television, 1987), p. 24.

96. PBS video, *This Honorable Court.*

97. William O. Douglas, *The Court Years* (New York: Random House, 1980), p. 181.

98. Fine, *Frank Murphy,* p. 254.

99. Schwartz, *Super Chief,* p. 306. See *New York Times,* June 11, 1961, Section 6, p. 31.

100. Douglas, *Court Years,* p. 181.

101. Ibid., p. 178.

102. Bernard Schwartz, "Felix Frankfurter and Earl Warren: A Study of a Deteriorating Relationship," *Supreme Court Review* 1980: 115, 122.

103. Joseph P. Lash, ed., *From the Diaries of Felix Frankfurter* (New York: Norton, 1975), p. 209.

104. At least this was true until the 1990s, when the Court chopped the number of cases to be accorded full dress treatment nearly in half.

105. Christopher E. Smith, *Justice Antonin Scalia and the Supreme Court's Conservative Moment* (Westport, Conn.: Praeger, 1993), pp. 61, 71.

106. See generally, Hugo Black and Elizabeth Black, *Mr. Justice and Mrs. Black* (New York: Random House, 1986).

107. See Douglas, *Court Years,* p. 173.

108. Fine, *Frank Murphy,* pp. 256–57.

109. James F. Simon, *The Antagonists: Hugo Black, Felix Frankfurter, and Civil Liberties in Modern America* (New York: Simon and Schuster, 1989), p. 117.

110. Schwartz, *Super Chief,* p. 71.

111. Meiklejohn prepared a collection consisting of his monograph, some articles, and a few of his other public statements and published them as *Political Freedom: The Constitutional Powers of the People* (New York: Oxford University Press, 1965).

112. *American Communications Association v. Douds,* 339 U.S. 382 (1950), Black, J., dissenting.

113. Ibid., p. 451.

114. 341 U.S. 494 (1951).

115. 341 U.S., p. 524, Frankfurter, J., concurring.

116. 341 U.S., p. 524.

117. *Harvard Law Review* 62 (1949): 891.

118. (New York: Atheneum, 1969).

119. 249 U.S. 47 (1919).

120. Alexander Meiklejohn, "What Does the First Amendment Mean?" *University of Chicago Law Review* 20 (1953): 461.

121. *McCollum v. Board of Education,* 333 U.S. 203, 231 (1947). See Meiklejohn, "What Does the First Amendment Mean?" p. 475.

122. Meiklejohn, "What Does the First Amendment Mean?" p. 479.

123. *Yates v. United States,* 354 U.S. 298, 340 (1957), Black, J., dissenting in part.

124. Alexander Meiklejohn to Hugo Black, July 28, 1957, Black Papers, Box 42.

125. *Barenblatt v. United States,* 360 U.S. 109 (1958), Black, J., dissenting.

126. Hugo Black, "The Bill of Rights," *New York University Law Review* 35 (1960): 865.

127. Ibid., p. 874.

128. Alexander Meiklejohn to Hugo Black, March 13, 1960, Black Papers, Box 42.

129. Alexander Bickel, "Mr. Justice Black: The Unobvious Meaning of Plain Words," *New Republic,* March 14, 1960, pp. 13–15.

130. Ibid., p. 15.

131. Alexander Meiklejohn to Hugo Black, April 15, 1960, Black Papers, Box 42.

132. Hugo Black to Alexander Meiklejohn, April 22, 1960, Black Papers, Box 42.

133. John P. Frank, "Letter to the Editor," *New Republic,* April 4, 1960, p. 30.

134. Douglas, *Court Years,* p. 205.

135. Quoted in Simon, *The Antagonists,* p. 194.

136. Ibid.

137. His concern about surrogate warriors prompted Frankfurter to recruit biographers for various justices, including himself (Hirsch, *Enigma,* p. 198).

138. Simon, *The Antagonists,* p. 238.

139. Quoted in ibid., p. 238.

140. 356 U.S. 86 (1958).

141. Quoted in Schwartz, "Felix Frankfurter and Earl Warren," p. 129.

142. Ibid.

143. Ibid.

144. 366 U.S. 717 (1961).

145. Kim Isaac Eisler, *A Justice for All* (New York: Simon and Schuster, 1993), p. 162.

146. Ibid., p. 163.

147. Ibid.

148. It appeared as "Does the Fourteenth Amendment Incorporate the Bill of Rights: The Original Understanding," *Stanford Law Review* 2 (1949): 5.

149. Robert H. Jackson to Charles Fairman, October 18, 1949, Jackson Papers, Box 12.

150. Robert H. Jackson to Charles Fairman, February 28, 1950, RHJ to CF, April 5, 1950, CF to RHJ April 25, 1950, Jackson Papers, Box 12.

151. The most extensive treatment of the relationship with Hand is presented in Gerald Gunther, *Learned Hand: The Man and the Judge* (New York: Alfred A. Knopf, 1994).

152. Fine, *Frank Murphy,* p. 138.

153. Quoted in J. Woodford Howard, *Mr. Justice Murphy: A Political Biography.* (Princeton: Princeton University, 1968), p. 399.

154. Simon, *The Antagonists,* p. 169.

155. Melvin I. Urofsky, "Conflict Among the Brethren: Felix Frankfurter, William O. Douglas and the Clash of Personalities and Philosophies on the United States Supreme Court," *Duke Law Journal* (1988): 71, 94.

156. Alpheus T. Mason, *Harlan Fiske Stone: Pillar of the Law* (New York: Viking, 1956), p. 470.

157. Simon, *The Antagonists,* p. 102. The case was *McCart v. Indianapolis Water Co., 302 U.S. 419 (1938).

158. Mason, *Harlan Fiske Stone,* p. 472.

159. Quoted in Simon, *The Antagonists,* p. 104.

160. 481 U.S. 279 (1987).

161. Jeffries, *Justice Powell,* pp. 446–49.

162. Ibid., p. 449.

163. Ibid., p. 451.

164. *Walz v. Tax Commission,* 397 U.S. 664, 703 (1970), Douglas, J., dissenting.

165. 463 U.S. 783 (1983).

166. Irons, *Brennan vs. Rehnquist,* p. 122.

167. See his dissent in *Paris Adult Theatre v. Slaton,* 413 U.S. 49 (1973) and *Miller v. California,* 413 U.S. 15 (1973).

168. *Columbia Law Review* 64 (1964): 1.

169. William O. Douglas, "The Supreme Court and Its Case Load," *Cornell Law Quarterly* 45 (1960): 401.

170. See William Brennan, "Some Thoughts on the Supreme Court's Caseload," *Judicature* 66 (1983): 230; "The National Court of Appeals: Another Dissent," *University of Chicago Law Review* 40 (1973): 479.

171. *Doe v. Commonwealth's Attorney,* 425 U.S. 901 (1976).

172. *Snepp v. United States,* 444 U.S. 507 (1980).

173. See *Hutto v. Davis,* 454 U.S. 370 (1982), Brennan, J., dissenting; *Pennsylvania v. Mimms,* 434 U.S. 106 (1977), Stevens, J., dissenting; and *Rose v. Locke,* 423 U.S. 48 (1975), Brennan, J., dissenting.

174. *Rose v. Locke,* 423 U.S. 48, 59 (1975), Brennan, J., dissenting.

175. *Hutto v. Davis,* 454 U.S. 370, 382 (1982), Brennan, J. dissenting.

176. Ibid.

177. Ibid, pp. 387–88.

178. *Harris v. Rivera,* 454 U.S. 339, 349 (1981), Marshall, J., dissenting.

179. "A Court Reflecting Its Country," *New York Times,* June 20, 1986.

CHAPTER 4. HOW DO THEY FIGHT? INTERNAL AND PERSONAL BATTLES

1. William O. Douglas, Conference Notes, *Dennis v. United States,* December 9, 1950, Douglas Papers, Box 206.

2. Interview with the author.

3. Loren Beth, *John Marshall Harlan: The Last Whig* (Lexington: University of Kentucky Press, 1992), p. 174.

4. Merlo J. Pusey, *Charles Evans Hughes* 2 vols. (New York: Macmillan, 1951), 1:277.

5. Beth, *John Marshall Harlan,* p. 174.

6. Sheldon M. Novick, *Honorable Justice: The Life of Oliver Wendell Holmes* (Boston: Little, Brown, 1989), p. 254.

7. Ibid.

8. Pusey, *Charles Evans Hughes,* 1:277.

9. Novick, *Honorable Justice,* p. 345.

10. Ibid., pp. 342–43.

11. Pusey, *Charles Evans Hughes,* 1:670.

12. Sidney Fine, *Frank Murphy: The Washington Years* (Ann Arbor: University of Michigan Press, 1984), pp. 242–43.

13. Ibid., p. 250.

14. Address of William O. Douglas to the Association of Trial Lawyers of the City of New York, April 11, 1957, p. 3.

15. Fine, *Frank Murphy,* p. 243.

16. Ibid., p. 251.

17. H. N. Hirsch, *The Enigma of Felix Frankfurter* (New York: Basic Books, 1981), p. 165.

18. William O. Douglas, *The Court Years* (New York: Random House, 1980), p. 226.

19. Bernard Schwartz, *Super Chief: Earl Warren and His Supreme Court* (New York: New York University Press, 1980), p. 261.

20. John C. Jeffries, Jr., *Justice Lewis F. Powell, Jr.* (New York: Charles Scribner's Sons, 1994), pp. 532–33.

21. Ibid., pp. 247–48.

22. Ibid., p. 379. Douglas faced off against Burger in the assignment of *United States v. United States District Court,* when Burger assigned the opinion to White even though Douglas was convinced that there were five votes in support of a more expansive ruling on constitutional grounds. He assigned the opinion to Lewis Powell, though Burger continued to support the idea that White should write. William O. Douglas to Warren Burger, March 6, 1972, Douglas Papers, Box 1523; Warren Burger to William O. Douglas, March 7, 1972, Douglas Papers, Box 1523; William O. Douglas to Lewis Powell, March 8, 1972, Douglas Papers, Box 1523.

23. *Gregg v. Georgia,* 428 U.S. 153 (1976).

24. Jeffries, *Justice Powell,* p. 429.

25. Ibid., pp. 445–46.

26. 469 U.S. 528 (1985).

27. 426 U.S. 833 (1976).

28. Howard Ball, *Judicial Craftsmanship of Fiat* (Westport, Conn.: Greenwood, 1978).

29. Harry Blackmun, Memorandum to the Conference, June 11, 1984, Brennan Papers, Box 656.

30. Warren Burger to Harry Blackmun, June 11, 1984, Brennan Papers, Box 656.

31. John Paul Stevens to Warren Burger, June 12, 1984, Brennan Papers, Box 656.

32. Thurgood Marshall, Memorandum to the Conference, April 12, 1972, Douglas Papers, Box 1523.

33. See Memorandum to the Conference, June 13, 1974, Brennan Papers, Box 325.

34. William Brennan, Memorandum to the Conference, May 22, 1972, Brennan Papers, Box 283.

35. Warren Burger, Memorandum to the Conference, November 13, 1972, and November 20, 1972, Brennan Papers, Box 283.

36. *Miller v. California,* 413 U.S. 15 (1973). See also *Paris Adult Theatre v. Slaton,* 413 U.S. 49 (1973).

37. Walter Murphy has argued that there are times when a justice may wish to employ direct confrontation as a strategy, but that it should be done with care. *Elements of Judicial Strategy* (Chicago: University of Chicago, 1964), pp. 204–6.

38. Hirsch, *Enigma,* p. 145

39. Douglas, *Court Years,* p. 222.

40. *Illinois ex rel McCollum v. Board of Education,* 333 U.S. 203 (1948).

41. See Felix Frankfurter to Wiley Rutledge, January 6, 1948, Rutledge Papers, Box 166, and Felix Frankfurter to Robert Jackson, January 6, 1948, Jackson Papers, Box 143.

42. Howard Ball, *We Have a Duty* (Westport, Conn.: Greenwood, 1987).

43. 408 U.S. 238 (1972).

44. Jeffries, *Justice Powell,* pp. 426–27.

45. Murphy, *Elements of Judicial Strategy,* p. 55.

46. Philippa Strum, *Louis D. Brandeis: Justice for the People* (Cambridge, Mass: Harvard University Press, 1984), p. 369.

47. Jeffries, *Justice Powell,* p. 489.

48. Ibid., p. 490.

49. Ibid., p. 558.

50. Memorandum, Hugo Black to the Conference, re *Malinski v. New York,* March 23, 1945, Black Papers, Box 118.

51. Bill Moyers, "In Search of the Constitution: Mr. Justice Blackmun," (Washington, D.C.: Public Affairs Television, 1987), Transcript, p. 8.

52. Remarks by Justice O'Connor in Bill Moyers, "In Search of the Constitution" (Washington, D.C.: Public Affairs Television, Inc., 1987).

53. James F. Simon, *The Antagonists: Hugo Black, Felix Frankfurter, and Civil Liberties in Modern America* (New York: Simon and Schuster, 1989), p. 170.

54. Schwartz, *Super Chief,* p. 35.

55. Ibid.

56. Alpheus T. Mason, *William Howard Taft Chief Justice* (New York: Simon and Schuster, 1965), p. 217.

57. John Clarke to Wilson, September 9, 1922, cited in ibid., pp. 165–67.

58. Cited in ibid., pp. 215–16.

59. Cited in ibid., p. 219.

60. Ibid., p. 220.

61. Novick, *Honorable Justice,* p. 316.

62. Ibid., pp. 316–17.

63. Ibid.

64. Strum, *Louis D. Brandeis,* p. 371.

65. See Hirsch, *Enigma.*

66. J. Woodford Howard, *Mr. Justice Murphy* (Princeton: Princeton University Press, 1968), pp. 268–69.

67. Ibid., p. 398.

68. Ibid., pp. 396–97.

69. Murphy, *Elements of Judicial Strategy,* p. 56.

70. Fine, *Frank Murphy,* p. 262.

71. Quoted in ibid., p. 249.

72. William O. Douglas to Felix Frankfurter, December 8, 1933, Douglas Papers, Box 6, p. 1.

73. Felix Frankfurter to William O. Douglas, February 5, 1934, Douglas Papers, Box 6.

74. William O. Douglas to Hugo L. Black, June 22, 1941, Douglas Papers, Library of Congress, Box 308.

75. Douglas to Black, September 8, 1941, Black Papers, Box 59.

76. Schwartz, *Super Chief,* p. 53.

77. Joseph P. Lash, ed., *From the Diaries of Felix Frankfurter* (New York: Norton, 1975), p. 155.

78. Interview with Justice Arthur Goldberg, August 27, 1986.

79. Interview with Justice Harry Blackmun, for Howard Ball and Phillip J. Cooper, *Of Power and Right* (New York: Oxford University Press, 1992), November 19, 1986.

80. Jeffries, *Justice Powell,* p. 256.

81. Schwartz, *Super Chief,* p. 53.

82. Ibid., p. 54.

83. There is a clash over the conference debate on *Lambert v. California,* 355 U.S. 225 (1957), ultimately written by Douglas. See Melvin Urofsky, "Conflict Among the Brethren: Felix Frankfurter, William O. Douglas and the Clash of Personalities and Philosophies on the United States Supreme Court," *Duke Law Journal* (1988): 71, 106.

84. See Urofsky, "Conflict Among the Brethren," p. 109.

85. Memorandum to the Conference, November 23, 1960, Douglas Papers, Box 1258.

86. See Hirsch, *Enigma.*

87. See Carl Rowan, *Dream Makers, Dream Breakers* (Boston: Little, Brown, 1993), and Michael D. Davis and Hunter R. Clark, *Thurgood Marshall: Warrior at the Bar* (New York: Citadel Press, 1992).

88. Simon, *The Antagonists,* p. 240.

89. Elizabeth Black, interview with author, Arlington, Va. August 28, 1987.

90. Jeffries, *Justice Powell,* p. 249.

91. Ibid., 250.

92. Ibid., 534.

93. Ibid.

94. Charles Evans Hughes, *The Supreme Court of the United States* (New York: Columbia University Press, 1928), p. 76. See also William H. Rehnquist, *The Supreme Court: How It Was, How It Is* (New York: Morrow, 1987), pp. 183–84.

95. Mason, *William Howard Taft,* p. 214.

96. Ibid.

97. Ibid., p. 215.

98. Thurgood Marshall, "Remarks to the Annual Judicial Conference of the Second Judicial Circuit of the United States," October 17, 1987, 120 F.R.D. 141, 204 (1987).

99. This issue is discussed in greater detail in Howard Ball and Phillip Cooper, *Of Power and Right* (New York: Oxford University Press, 1992).

100. Cathleen Douglas-Stone to the authors, October 16, 1989, p. 2.

101. Hugo L. Black to Harlan F. Stone, August 14, 1945, Douglas Papers, Box 308.

102. Hugo L. Black to William O. Douglas, August 11, 1945, Douglas Papers, Box 308, p. 2.

103. Felix Frankfurter to Harlan F. Stone, September 7, 1945, Frankfurter Papers, Box 64.

104. William O. Douglas to Hugo L. Black, September 13, 1945, Douglas Papers, Box 308.

105. *Jewell Ridge Coal Corp. v. Local 6167, UMW,* 325 U.S. 161 (1945).

106. Doris Fleeson, "Supreme Court Feud," *Washington Star,* May 16, 1946.

107. Ibid.

108. Lash, *From the Diaries of Felix Frankfurter,* p. 75.

109. Robert H. Jackson to Harry Truman, June 7, 1946, Jackson Papers, Box 26.

110. Harry Truman to Robert Jackson, June 8, 1946, Jackson Papers, Box 26.

111. Robert H. Jackson to Chairmen House and Senate Judiciary Committees, June 10, 1946, p. 5.

112. Ibid.

113. 36 U.S. (11 Pet.) 257 (1837).

114. *Craig v. Missouri,* 29 U.S. (4 Pet.) 410 (1830).

115. Carl Brent Swisher, *Roger B. Taney* (New York: Macmillan, 1935), p. 375.

116. There were tensions because Hughes resented the pressure by Roosevelt to hold the ceremony at the White House rather than the Court, but the message sent by the refusal to attend was troublesome.

117. Urofsky, "Conflict Among the Brethren," p. 99.

118. Fine, *Frank Murphy,* p. 244.

119. See Joan Biskupic, "Lifting the Veil On Life Inside the High Court," *Washington Post National Weekly Edition,* August 29–September 4, 1994, p. 33.

120. *New York Times,* June 20, 1986, p. A30.

121. Quoted in Biskupic, "Lifting the Veil."

CHAPTER 5. WHAT DIFFERENCE DOES IT MAKE?

1. Bernard Schwartz, "Felix Frankfurter and Earl Warren: A Study of a Deteriorating Relationship, *Supreme Court Review* (1980): 115, 142.

2. John P. Frank, *Justice Daniel Dissenting* (Cambridge, Mass.: Harvard University Press, 1964), p. 257.

3. R. Kent Newmyer, *Supreme Court Justice Joseph Story: Statesman of the Old Republic* (Chapel Hill: University of North Carolina Press, 1985), p. 380.

4. Alpheus T. Mason, *William Howard Taft Chief Justice* (New York: Simon and Schuster, 1965), pp. 165–67.

5. J. Woodford Howard, *Mr. Justice Murphy: A Political Biography* (Princeton: Princeton University Press, 1968), p. 396.

6. Ibid., pp. 458–59.

7. William O. Douglas to Sherman Minton, April 27, 1961, Douglas Papers, Box 355.

8. William O. Douglas, "The Bill of Rights Is Not Enough," *New York University Law Review* 38 (1963): 207.

9. William O. Douglas, *The Court Years* (New York: Random House, 1980), p. 376.

10. *Congressional Record,* vol. 115, 91st Cong., 1st Sess. (1969), p. 12949.

11. William O. Douglas to Albert Parvin, May 12, 1969, Final Report.

12. William O. Douglas to Clark Clifford, October 23, 1969, Douglas Papers, Box 315.

13. William O. Douglas to Clark Clifford, November 17, 1969, Douglas Papers, Box 315.

14. Discussed in more detail in Howard Ball and Phillip J. Cooper, *Of Power and Right* (New York: Oxford University Press, 1992), pp. 302–8.

15. Ibid., p. 309.

16. "Douglas Not Planning to Retire," *New York Times,* July 16, 1975, p. 47.

17. Sidney Fine, *Frank Murphy: The Washington Years* (Ann Arbor: University of Michigan Press, 1984), p. 248.

18. Ibid.

19. Ibid.

20. 381 U.S. 479 (1965).

21. William O. Douglas to Sherman Minton, April 27, 1961, Douglas Papers, Box 355.

22. Sherman Minton to William O. Douglas, May 4, 1961, Douglas Papers, Box 355.

23. William O. Douglas, Memorandum to the Chief Justice," February 20, 1961, Burger Papers, Box 43.

24. Earl Warren to William O. Douglas, February 21, 1961, Burger Papers, Box 43.

25. William O. Douglas, Memorandum to the Conference, February 21, 1961, Burger Papers, Box 43.

26. Earl Warren, Memorandum to the Conference, February 21, 1961, Burger Papers, Box 43.

27. Justice Arthur Goldberg, Washington, D.C., August 27, 1986, interview with author.

28. 330 U.S. 1 (1947).

29. Howard, *Mr. Justice Murphy*, p. 449.

30. Draft page 6, Box 285, Black Papers.

31. Rutledge 2d draft, p. 26. Rutledge removed this important language while he was editing his January 16 version of what was to be a February 6 printing of the dissent. By then, of course, Black had made the critical change to his language about the scope of nonestablishment.

32. *Illinois ex rel McCollum v. Board of Education,* 333 U.S. 203 (1948).

33. See Felix Frankfurter to Wiley Rutledge, January 6, 1948, Rutledge Papers, Box 166 and Felix Frankfurter to Robert Jackson, January 6, 1948, Jackson Papers, Box 143.

34. H. N. Hirsch, *The Enigma of Felix Frankfurter* (New York: Basic Books, 1981), p. 183.

35. Peter Irons, *Brennan vs. Rehnquist* (New York: Alfred A. Knopf, 1994), p. xii.

36. Hirsch, *Enigma,* p. 153.

37. Ibid., p. 182.

38. Fine, *Frank Murphy,* pp. 253–54.

39. Ibid., pp. 256–57.

40. Ibid., p. 261.

41. John C. Jeffries, Jr., *Justice Lewis F. Powell, Jr.* (New York: Charles Scribner's Sons, 1994), p. 370.

42. Sheldon M. Novick, *Honorable Justice: The Life of Oliver Wendell Holmes* (Boston: Little, Brown, 1989), p. 361.

43. 456 U.S. 742 (1982).

44. 426 U.S. 833 (1976).

45. *Garcia v. San Antonio Metropolitan Transit Authority,* 469 U.S. 528 (1985).

46. Jeffries, *Justice Powell,* pp. 489–90.

47. Ibid.

48. 319 U.S. 624 (1943).

49. *Minersville v. Gobitis,* 310 U.S. 586 (1940).

50. *Cooper v. Aaron,* 358 U.S. 1 (1958).

51. 366 U.S. 717 (1961).

52. See Kim Isaac Eisler, *A Justice For All* (New York: Simon and Schuster, 1993), pp. 162–63.

53. Jeffries, *Justice Powell,* p. 261.

54. 407 U.S. 297 (1972).

55. William O. Douglas to Warren Burger, March 6, 1972, Douglas Papers, Box 1523.

56. William O. Douglas to Lewis Powell, May 4, 1972, Douglas Papers, Box 1523.

57. *Industrial Union Dept., AFL-CIO v. American Petroleum Institute,* 488 U.S. 607 (1980).

58. See *Bowsher v. Synar* file, Marshall Papers, Box 396.

59. Frank, *Justice Daniel Dissenting,* p. 234.

60. Howard, *Mr. Justice Murphy,* pp. 449–50.

61. William J. Brennan to William O. Douglas, June 15, 1970, Douglas Papers, Box 1453.

62. Jeffries, *Justice Powell,* pp. 249–50.

63. Bill Moyers, "In Search of the Constitution: Mr. Justice Blackmun," (Washington, D.C.: Public Affairs Television, 1987), Transcript, p. 9.

64. Fine, *Frank Murphy,* p. 244.

65. Novick, *Honorable Justices,* p. 343.

66. David M. O'Brien, *Storm Center,* 3d ed. (New York: Norton, 1993), pp. 329–33.

67. Ibid., p. 332.

68. Ibid., pp. 332–33.

69. Hirsch, *Enigma,* p. 166.

70. 347 U.S. 483 (1954).

71. Schwartz, "Felix Frankfurter and Earl Warren," p. 72.

72. Ibid., pp. 115, 120.

73. Frank M. Coffin, *The Ways of a Judge* (Boston: Houghton Mifflin, 1980).

74. Jeffries, *Justice Powell,* p. 523.

75. Ibid., p. 261.

76. *Board of Regents v. Bakke,* 438 U.S. 265 (1978).

77. William J. Brennan to Thurgood Marshall, February 24, 1986, Marshall Papers, Box 396.

78. Thurgood Marshall to William J. Brennan, February 28, 1986, Marshall Papers, Box 396.

79. William O. Douglas, Memorandum for the Files, June 20, 1964, Douglas Papers, Box 1314.

80. William O. Douglas to William J. Brennan, June 3, 1964, Douglas Papers, Box 1314.

81. 367 U.S. 643 (1961).

82. William O. Douglas to Tom C. Clark, January 25, 1962, Warren Papers, Box 351.

83. Frankfurter to The Brethren, January 30, 1962, Warren Papers, Box 351.

84. Memorandum to the Conference, January 30, 1962, Warren Papers, Box 349.

85. Felix Frankfurter to William O. Douglas, January 31, 1962, Black Papers, Box 349.

86. William O. Douglas to Felix Frankfurter, January 31, 1962, Black Papers, Box 349.

87. Interview with Cathleen Douglas-Stone, Boston, October 16, 1989.

88. Hirsch, *Enigma*, p. 23. See also Robert Burt, *Two Jewish Justices* (Berkeley: University of California Press, 1988).

89. Cathleen Douglas-Stone interview.

90. See William O. Douglas, *Go East Young Man* (New York: Dell, 1974).

91. Ball and Cooper, *Of Power and Right*, chap. 13.

92. Jeffries, *Justice Powell*, p. 261.

93. Mason, *William Howard Taft*, p. 261.

94. Novick, *Honorable Justice*, p. 343.

95. Fine, *Frank Murphy*, pp. 263–64.

96. Melvin I. Urofsky, "Conflict Among the Brethren: Felix Frankfurter, William O. Douglas, and the Clash of Personalities and Philosophies on the United States Supreme Court," *Duke Law Journal* (1988): 71, 97–98.

97. James F. Simon, *The Antagonists: Hugo Black, Felix Frankfurter, and Civil Liberties in Modern America* (New York: Simon and Schuster, 1989), pp. 167–68.

98. See Schwartz, "Felix Frankfurter and Earl Warren," pp. 122–30.

99. Ibid., p. 129–30.

100. Douglas, "The Bill of Rights Is Not Enough," p. 207.

101. (New York: Alfred A. Knopf, 1968).

102. *Harper v. Virginia Bd. of Elections,* 383 U.S. 663 (1966).

103. Hugo Black, *A Constitutional Faith* (New York: Alfred A. Knopf, 1968), p. 30.

104. See, e.g., William J. Brennan, Jr., "State Constitutions and the Protection of Individual Rights," *Harvard Law Review* 90 (1977): 489.

105. Justice Thurgood Marshall, Remarks to the Annual Judicial Conference of the Second Judicial Circuit of the United States, July 1991, 136 F.R.D. 236; Justice Thurgood Marshall, Remarks to the Annual Judicial Conference of the Second Judicial Circuit of the United States, September 8, 1989, 130 F.R.D. 161; Justice Thurgood Marshall, Remarks to the Annual Judicial Conference of the Second Judicial Circuit of the United States, October 17, 1987, 120 F.R.D. 141; Justice Thurgood Marshall, Remarks to the Annual Judicial Conference of the Second Judicial Circuit of the United States, Hartford, Connecticut, September 13, 1984, 106 F.R.D. 118; Justice Thurgood Marshall, Remarks to the Annual Judicial Conference of the Second Judicial Circuit of the United States, September 30–October 1, 1983, 101 F.R.D. 161.

106. Thurgood Marshall, "Supreme Court Summary Dispositions: Either Change the Rules or Stop Giving Short Shrift to Important Rules," *Willamette Law Review* 19 (1983): 313; Thurgood Marshall, "The Constitution: A Living Document," *Howard Law Journal* 30 (1987): 915.

107. Justice Thurgood Marshall, Remarks to the Annual Judicial Conference of the Second Judicial Circuit of the United States, September 8, 1989, 130 F.R.D. 161, 166–68.

CHAPTER 6. WHY DON'T THEY FIGHT MORE OFTEN?

1. See David O'Brien, *Storm Center,* 3d ed. (New York: Norton, 1993), p. 142 et. seq.

2. Joseph P. Lash, ed., *From the Diaries of Felix Frankfurter* (New York: Norton, 1975), p. 316.

3. Bernard Schwartz, *Super Chief: Earl Warren and His Supreme Court* (New York: New York University Press, 1980), p. 130.

4. William O. Douglas, *The Court Years* (New York: Random House, 1980), p. 219.

5. Walter F. Murphy, *Elements of Judicial Strategy* (Chicago: University of Chicago Press, 1964), p. 52.

6. *United States v. Nixon,* 418 U.S. 683, 705 (1974).

7. Lewis Powell, "Myths and Misconceptions About the Supreme Court," in Jesse H. Choper, ed., *The Supreme Court and Its Justices* (Chicago: American Bar Association, 1987), p. 207.

8. Sydney Fine, *Frank Murphy: The Washington Years* (Ann Arbor: University of Michigan Press, 1984), p. 255.

9. Interview with Justice William J. Brennan, Jr., Washington, D.C., October 29, 1986.

10. Murphy, *Elements of Judicial Strategy,* pp. 49–54.

11. John P. Frank, *Justice Daniel Dissenting.* (Cambridge, Mass.: Harvard University Press, 1964), p. 234.

12. Loren Beth, *John Marshall Harlan: The Last Whig* (Lexington: University of Kentucky Press, 1992), p. 135.

13. Ibid., p. 160.

14. Williard L. King, *Mellville Weston Fuller* (New York: Macmillan, 1950), pp. 282–83.

15. Joel Francis Paschal, *Mr. Justice Sutherland* (Princeton: Princeton University Press, 1951), p. 115.

16. Fine, *Frank Murphy,* p. 255.

17. Douglas, *Court Years,* p. 377.

18. Brennan interview.

19. Ibid.

20. Ibid.

21. John C. Jeffries, *Justice Lewis F. Powell, Jr.* (New York: Charles Scribner's Sons, 1994), p. 265.

22. Ibid., p. 545.

23. Ibid., p. 507.

24. Paschal, *Mr. Justice Sutherland,* p. 116.

25. Earl Warren to William O. Douglas, November 28, 1961, Douglas Papers, Box 380.

26. Earl Warren to Abe Fortas, Warren Papers, Box 352.

27. Abe Fortas to Earl Warren, Warren Papers, Box 352.

28. Douglas, *Court Years,* p. 220.

29. William O. Douglas to Franklin Delano Roosevelt, June 23, 1939, PSF William O. Douglas, FDR Papers, FDR Library.

30. FDR to William O. Douglas, June 27, 1939, FDR Papers, FDR Library.

31. PBS video, *This Honorable Court.*

32. Cornelia Edington to Hugo Black, undated, Black Papers, Box 363.

33. Hugo Black to Cornelia Edington, July 26, 1962, pp. 1-2, Black Papers, Box 363.

34. Henry J. Abraham, *Justice and Presidents,* 2d ed. (New York: Oxford University Press, 1985), pp. 27-28.

35. O'Brien, *Storm Center.*

36. Quoted in Nathan Lewin, "Justice Harlan: The Full Measure of the Man," in Choper, *The Supreme Court and Its Justices,* p. 135.

37. *New York Times,* October 18, 1989, p. A14. Cited in Jeffries, *Justice Powell,* p. 558.

38. Brennan interview.

39. Jeffries, *Justice Powell,* p. 305.

40. Quoted in William H. Rehnquist, *The Supreme Court* (New York: Morrow, 1987), pp. 150-51.

41. Quoted in Charles Evans Hughes, "Roger Brooke Taney: A Great Chief Justice," in Choper, *The Supreme Court and Its Justices,* p. 63.

42. Robert H. Jackson, "The Judicial Career of Chief Justice Charles Evans Hughes," in Choper, *The Supreme Court and Its Justices,* p. 103.

43. Charles Evans Hughes, *The Supreme Court of the United States* (New York: Columbia University Press, 1928), p. 68.

44. Quoted in Robert J. Steamer, *Chief Justice* (Columbia: University of South Carolina Press, 1986), p. 54.

45. Merlo J. Pusey, *Charles Evans Hughes,* 2 vols. (New York: Macmillan, 1951), 1:678.

46. Ibid., p. 676.

47. King, *Melville Weston Fuller,* chap. 10.

48. Ibid., p. 134.

49. Ibid., p. 139.

50. Michael J. Brodhead, *David J. Brewer* (Carbondale: Southern Illinois University Press, 1994), pp. 76-77.

51. See Schwartz, *Super Chief,* chap. 3.

CHAPTER 7. NINE SCORPIONS IN A BOTTLE

1. Peter Irons, *Brennan vs. Rehnquist* (New York: Alfred A. Knopf, 1994), p. 3.

2. Robert H. Jackson to Chairmen, House and Senate Judiciary Committees, June 7, 1946, with a copy to Harry Truman, Jackson Papers, Box 26.

3. Lewis Powell, "Myths and Misconceptions About the Supreme Court," in Jesse H. Choper, *The Supreme Court and Its Justices* (Chicago: American Bar Association, 1987), p. 207.

4. Quoted in Joseph P. Lash, *From the Diaries of Felix Frankfurter* (New York: Norton, 1975), pp. 313-14.

5. William Rehnquist, *The Supreme Court: How It Was, How It Is* (New York: Morrow, 1987).

6. *Industrial Union Dept., AFL-CIO v. American Petroleum Institute,* 488 U.S. 607 (1980).

7. Alexander Hamilton, James Madison, and John Jay, *The Federalist Papers* (New York: Mentor, 1961), No. 78.

8. William J. Brennan to Lewis Powell, January 28, 1976, Brennan Papers, Box 368.

SELECTED BIBLIOGRAPHY

Abraham, Henry J. *Justices and Presidents: A Political History of Appointments to the Supreme Court.* New York: Oxford University Press, 1974.

Abraham, Henry J., and Bruce Allen Murphy. "The Influence of Sitting and Retired Justices on Presidential Supreme Court Nominations." *Hastings Constitutional Law Quarterly* 3 (1976): 37.

Alsop, Joseph, and Turner Catledge. *The 168 Days.* New York: Doubleday, Doran, 1938.

Atkins, Burton, and Terry Sloope. "The 'New' Hugo Black and the Warren Court." *Polity* 18 (1986): 621.

Baker, Leonard. *Brandeis and Frankfurter.* New York: New York University Press, 1986.

_____. *John Marshall: A Life in Law.* New York: Macmillan, 1974.

Ball, Howard. "Hugo L. Black: Twentieth-Century Jeffersonian." *Southwestern Law Review* 9 (1977): 1049.

_____. *Judicial Craftsmanship or Fiat?* Westport, Conn.: Greenwood Press, 1978.

_____. *We Have a Duty.* Westport, Conn.: Greenwood Press, 1987.

Ball, Howard, and Phillip J. Cooper. *Of Power and Right.* New York: Oxford University Press, 1992.

Beth, Loren. *John Marshall Harlan: The Last Whig.* Lexington: University of Kentucky Press, 1992.

Beveridge, Albert J. *The Life of John Marshall.* Boston: Houghton-Mifflin, 1916–1919.

Bickel, Alexander M. *The Unpublished Opinions of Mr. Justice Brandeis.* Chicago: University of Chicago Press, 1957.

Black, Hugo L. "The Bill of Rights." *New York University Law Review* 35 (1960): 865.

_____. *A Constitutional Faith.* New York: Alfred A. Knopf, 1968.

_____. "William Orville Douglas." *Yale Law Journal* 73 (1964): 915.

Black, Hugo L., and Elizabeth Black. *Mr. Justice and Mrs. Black.* New York: Random House, 1986.

Black, Hugo L., Jr. *My Father: A Remembrance.* New York: Random House, 1975.

Blasi, Vincent, ed. *The Burger Court: The Counter-Revolution that Wasn't.* New Haven: Yale University Press, 1982.

Brandeis, Louis D. *Other People's Money.* New York: Harper and Row, 1967.

Brennan, William J., Jr. "Constitutional Adjudication and the Death Penalty: A View from the Court." *Harvard Law Review* 100 (1986): 313.

_____. "The National Court of Appeals: Another Dissent." *University of Chicago Law Review* 40 (1973): 479.

_____. "Some Thoughts on the Supreme Court's Caseload." *Judicature* 66 (1983): 230.

Brodhead, Michael J. *David J. Brewer.* Carbondale: Southern Illinois University Press, 1994.

Bullock, Charles S., III, and Charles M. Lamb, eds. *Implementation of Civil Rights Policy.* Monterey, Calif.: Brooks/Cole, 1984.

Casper, Gerhard, and Richard A. Posner. *The Workload of the Supreme Court.* Chicago: American Bar Foundation, 1976.

Casper, Jonathan D. *Lawyers Before the Warren Court: Civil Liberties and Civil Rights, 1957–66.* Urbana: University of Illinois Press, 1972.

Chafee, Zechariah. *Free Speech in America.* New York: Atheneum, 1969.

Choper, Jesse H., ed. *The Supreme Court and Its Justices.* Chicago: American Bar Association, 1987.

Clark, Tom C. "Internal Operation of the United States Supreme Court." *Judicature* 51 (1959): 43.

Cohen, William. "Justice Douglas and the Rosenberg Case: Setting the Record Straight." *Cornell Law Review* 70 (1985): 211.

Cooper, Phillip J., and Howard Ball. *The United States Supreme Court: From the Inside Out.* Englewood Cliffs, N.J.: Prentice-Hall, 1995.

Countryman, Vern. *The Judicial Record of Justice William O. Douglas.* Cambridge, Mass.: Harvard University Press, 1974.

Danelski, David. *A Supreme Court Justice Is Appointed.* New York: Random House, 1964.

Davis, Michael D., and Hunter R. Clark. "Conflict and Its Resolution in the Supreme Court." *Journal of Conflict Resolution* 11 (1967): 73.

_____. *Thurgood Marshall: Warrior at the Bar.* New York: Citadel Press, 1992.

Dolbeare, Kenneth M., and Philip E. Hammond. *The School Prayer Decisions: From Court Policy to Local Practice.* Chicago: University of Chicago Press, 1971.

Douglas, William O. "The Bill of Rights Is Not Enough." *New York University Law Review* 38 (1963): 207.

_____. *The Court Years.* New York: Random House, 1980.

_____. "The Dissenting Opinion." *Lawyers Guild Review* 8 (1948): 467.

_____. *Go East Young Man.* New York: Dell, 1974.

Douglas-Stone, Cathleen. "William O. Douglas: The Man." In *Supreme Court Historical Society Yearbook, 1981.* Washington, D.C.: Supreme Court Historical Society, 1981.

Dunham, Allison, and Philip B. Kurland. *Mr. Justice.* Chicago: University of Chicago Press, 1956.

Dunne, Gerald T. *Hugo Black and the Judicial Revolution.* New York: Simon and Schuster, 1977.

_____. *Justice Joseph Story and the Rise of the Supreme Court.* New York: Simon and Schuster, 1970.

_____. "Justices Hugo Black and Robert Jackson: The Great Feud." *St. Louis University Law Journal* (1975): 465.

Eisler, Kim Isaac. *A Justice for All.* New York: Simon and Schuster, 1993.

Elsmere, Jane Shaffer. *Justice Samuel Chase.* Muncie, Ind.: Janevar Publishing Company, 1980.

Fairman, Charles. "Does the Fourteenth Amendment Incorporate the Bill of Rights: The Original Understanding." *Stanford Law Review* 2 (1949): 5.

Fine, Sidney. *Frank Murphy: The Washington Years.* Ann Arbor: University of Michigan Press, 1984.

Fortas, Abe. "Mr. Justice Douglas," *Yale Law Journal* 73 (1964): 913.

Frank, John P. *Justice Daniel Dissenting.* Cambridge, Mass.: Harvard University Press, 1964.

Friedman, Leon, and Fred L. Israel, eds., *The Justices of the United States Supreme Court 1789–1969: Their Lives and Major Opinions.* New York: Bowker, 1969.

Funston, Richard. *Constitutional Counterrevolution?* Cambridge, Mass.: Schenkman Publishing, 1977.

Gates, John B., and Charles A. Johnson. *The American Courts: A Critical Assessment.* Washington, D.C.: Congressional Quarterly, 1991.

Goebel, Julius, Jr. *History of the Supreme Court of the United States.* New York: Macmillan, 1971.

Goldman, Sheldon, and Charles M. Lamb. *Judicial Conflict and Consensus.* Lexington: University Press of Kentucky, 1986.

Gunther, Gerald. *Learned Hand: The Man and the Judge* (New York: Alfred A. Knopf, 1994.

Hamilton, Alexander, James Madison, and John Jay. *The Federalist Papers.* New York: Mentor, 1961.

Harrell, Mary Ann. *Equal Justice Under Law: The Supreme Court in American Life.* Washington, D.C.: Foundation of the American Bar Association, 1975.

Highsaw, Robert B. *Edward Douglas White: Defender of the Conservative Faith.* Baton Rouge: Louisiana State University Press, 1981.

Hirsch, H. N. *The Enigma of Felix Frankfurter.* New York: Basic Books, 1981.

Howard, J. Woodford. *Mr. Justice Murphy: A Political Biography.* Princeton: Princeton University Press, 1968.

_____. "The Fluidity of Judicial Choice." *American Political Science Review* 62 (1968): 43.

Hughes, Charles Evans. *The Supreme Court of the United States.* New York: Columbia University Press, 1928.

Hutchinson, Dennis J. "The Black-Jackson Feud." *Supreme Court Review* (1988): 203.

Irons, Peter. *Brennan vs. Rehnquist.* New York: Alfred A. Knopf, 1994.

Jackson, Robert H. *The Supreme Court in the American System of Government.* Cambridge, Mass.: Harvard University Press, 1955.

Jeffries, John C., Jr. *Justice Lewis F. Powell, Jr.* New York: Charles Scribner's Sons, 1994.

Johnson, Charles, and Bradley C. Canon. *Judicial Policies: Implementation and Impact.* Washington, D.C.: Congressional Quarterly, 1984.

Kalman, Laura. *Abe Fortas.* New Haven: Yale University Press, 1990.

_____. *Legal Realism at Yale, 1927–1960.* Chapel Hill: University of North Carolina Press, 1986.

King, Willard L. *Melville Weston Fuller: Chief Justice of the United States.* New York: Macmillan, 1950.

Kluger, Richard. *Simple Justice.* New York: Vintage Books, 1975.

Lash, Joseph P., ed. *From the Diaries of Felix Frankfurter.* New York: Norton, 1975.

Leonard, Charles A. *A Search for a Judicial Philosophy: Mr. Justice Roberts and the Constitutional Revolution of 1937.* Port Washington, N.Y.: Kennikat Press, 1971.

Lewis, Walker. *Without Fear or Favor: A Biography of Chief Justice Roger Brooke Taney.* Boston: Houghton Mifflin, 1965.

Lytle, Clifford M. *The Warren Court and Its Critics.* Tucson: University of Arizona Press, 1968.

McCloskey, Robert G. *The Modern Supreme Court.* Cambridge, Mass.: Harvard University Press, 1972.

McCullough, David. *Truman.* New York: Simon and Schuster, 1992.

Magee, James J. *Mr. Justice Black: Absolutism on the Court.* Charlottesville: University Press of Virginia, 1980.

Marshall, Thurgood. "The Constitution: A Living Document." *Howard Law Journal* 30 (1987): 915.

_____. "Supreme Court Summary Dispositions: Either Change the Rules or Stop Giving Short Shrift to Important Rules." *Willamette Law Review* 19 (1983): 313.

Mason, Alpheus T. *Brandeis: A Free Man's Life.* New York: Viking, 1946.

_____. *Harlan Fiske Stone: Pillar of the Law.* New York: Viking, 1956.

_____. *The Supreme Court from Taft to Burger.* 3d ed. Baton Rouge: Louisiana State University Press, 1979.

_____. *William Howard Taft Chief Justice.* New York: Simon and Schuster, 1965.

Meador, Daniel J. "Mr. Justice Black: A Tribute." *University of Virginia Law Review* 57 (1971): 1109.

_____. "Mr. Justice Black and His Law Clerks." *Alabama Law Review* 16 (1963): 57.

Meiklejohn, Alexander. *Political Freedom: The Constitutional Powers of the People.* New York: Oxford University Press, 1965.

_____. "What Does the First Amendment Mean?" *University of Chicago Law Review* 20 (1953): 461.

Mendelson, Wallace. *Justices Black and Frankfurter: Conflict on the Court.* 2d ed. Chicago: University of Chicago Press, 1966.

Morgan, Donald G. *Justice William Johnson: The First Dissenter.* Columbia: University of South Carolina Press, 1954.

Murphy, Bruce Allen. *The Brandeis/Frankfurter Connection*. New York: Oxford University Press, 1982.

———. *Fortas*. New York: Morrow, 1988.

Murphy, Paul L. *The Constitution in Crisis Times 1918–1969*. New York: Harper and Row, 1972.

Murphy, Walter F. *Elements of Judicial Strategy*. Chicago: University of Chicago Press, 1964.

———. "In His Own Image: Mr. Chief Justice Taft and Supreme Court Appointments." *Supreme Court Review* (1961): 159.

———. *The Vicar of Christ*. New York: Ballantine Books, 1980.

Murphy, Walter F., and Joseph Tanenhaus. *The Study of Public Law*. New York: Random House, 1971.

Newmyer, R. Kent. *Supreme Court Justice Joseph Story: Statesman of the Old Republic*. Chapel Hill: University of North Carolina Press, 1985.

Novick, Sheldon M. *Honorable Justice: The Life of Oliver Wendell Holmes*. Boston: Little, Brown, 1989.

O'Brien, David. *Storm Center*. 3d ed. New York: Norton, 1993.

Paper, Lewis J. *Brandeis*. Secaucus, N.Y.: Citadel Press, 1983.

Parrish, Michael E. "Justice Douglas and the Rosenberg Case: A Rejoinder." *Cornell Law Review* 70 (1985): 1048.

Paschal, Joel Francis. *Mr. Justice Sutherland*. Princeton: Princeton University Press, 1951.

Peltason, Jack W. *Federal Courts in the Political Process*. Garden City, N.Y.: Doubleday, 1955.

Powell, Thomas Reed. "Public Rides to Private Schools." *Harvard Educational Review* 17 (1947): 73.

Pusey, Merlo J. *Charles Evans Hughes*. 2 vols. New York: Macmillan, 1951.

Rehnquist, William H. *The Supreme Court: How It Was, How It Is*. New York: Morrow, 1987.

———. "The Supreme Court: Past and Present." *American Bar Association Journal* 59 (1973): 363.

Rodell, Fred. *Nine Men: A Political History of the Supreme Court of the United States from 1790 to 1955*. New York: Random House, 1955.

Rowan, Carl. *Dream Makers, Dream Breakers*. Boston: Little, Brown, 1993.

Rumble, Wilfred E., Jr. *American Legal Realism*. Ithaca, N.Y.: Cornell University Press, 1968.

Schattschneider, E. E. *The Semi-Sovereign People*. New York: Holt, Rinehart and Winston, 1960.

Schmidhauser, John R. *Judges and Justices: The Federal Appellate Judiciary*. Boston: Little, Brown, 1979.

Schwartz, Bernard. "Felix Frankfurter and Earl Warren: A Study of a Deteriorating Relationship." *Supreme Court Review* (1980): 115.

———. *Super Chief: Earl Warren and His Supreme Court*. New York: New York University Press, 1983.

Sevareid, Eric. *Conversations With Notable Americans.* Washington, D.C.: Public Affairs Press, 1976.

Shogan, Robert. *A Question of Judgment: The Fortas Case and the Struggle for the Supreme Court.* Indianapolis: Bobbs-Merrill, 1972.

Silverstein, Mark. *Constitutional Faiths: Felix Frankfurter, Hugo Black and the Process of Judicial Decision Making.* Ithaca, N.Y.: Cornell University Press, 1984.

Simon, James F. *The Antagonists: Hugo Black, Felix Frankfurter, and Civil Liberties in Modern America.* New York: Simon and Schuster, 1989.

———. *In His Own Image: The Supreme Court in Richard Nixon's America.* New York: David McKay, 1973.

———. *Independent Journey: The Life of William O. Douglas.* New York: Harper and Row, 1980.

Steamer, Robert J. *Chief Justice: Leadership and the Supreme Court.* Columbia: University of South Carolina Press, 1986.

Strum, Philippa. *Louis D. Brandeis: Justice for the People.* Cambridge, Mass: Harvard University Press, 1984.

Swisher, Carl Brent. *Roger B. Taney.* New York: Macmillan, 1935.

———. *Stephen J. Field: Craftsman of the Law.* Washington, D.C.: Brookings Institution, 1930.

Trimble, Bruce R. *Chief Justice Waite: Defender of the Public Interest.* Princeton: Princeton University Press, 1938.

Urofsky, Melvin I. "Conflict Among the Brethren: Felix Frankfurter, William O. Douglas and the Clash of Personalities and Philosophies on the United States Supreme Court." *Duke Law Journal* (1988): 71.

———. *The Douglas Letters.* Bethesda, Md.: Adler and Adler, 1987.

U.S. House of Representatives, Final Report by the Special Subcommittee on H.Res. 920 of the Committee on the Judiciary. *Associate Justice William O. Douglas.* 91st Cong., 2d sess., 1970.

Warner, Hoyt Landon. *The Life of Mr. Justice Clarke.* Cleveland, Ohio: Western Reserve University Press, 1959.

Westin, Alan F. *The Supreme Court: Views from the Inside.* Westport, Conn.: Greenwood Press, 1983.

White, Edward. *Earl Warren: A Public Life.* New York: Oxford University Press, 1982.

Witt, Elder. *Congressional Quarterly Guide to the U.S. Supreme Court.* 2d ed. Washington, D.C.: Congressional Quarterly, 1990.

Yarbrough, Tinsley E. *John Marshall Harlan: Great Dissenter of the Warren Court.* New York: Oxford University Press, 1992.

———. *Mr. Justice Black and His Critics.* Durham, N.C.: Duke University Press, 1988.

OPINIONS CITED

INDEX